With: Sean Casteel,
Wm. Michael Mott,
Olav Phillips

TIM R. SWARTZ

AMERICA'S STRANGE AND SUPERNATURAL HISTORY

INCLUDES: Prophecies Of The Presidents
By Arthur Crockett & Timothy Green Beckley

AMERICA'S STRANGE AND SUPERNATURAL HISTORY

Inner Light/Global Communications

Illustration by Carol Ann Rodriguez, Mt. Rushmore Insert by Tim R. Swartz

America's Strange and Supernatural History
By Tim R. Swartz
With Additional Material By: Sean Casteel, Wm. Michael Mott, Olav Phillips
Special Introduction by Timothy Green Beckley

Includes **Prophecies of the Presidents**
By Arthur Crockett & Timothy Green Beckley

Copyright © 2014 Timothy Green Beckley, Inner Light/Global Communications
All rights reserved.

No part of these manuscripts may be copied or reproduced by any mechanical or digital methods and no excerpts or quotes may be used in any other book or manuscript without permission in writing by the Publisher, Timothy Green Beckley, except by a reviewer who may quote brief passages in a review.

Published in the United States of America By Timothy Green Beckley dba Inner Light/Global Communications, Box 753 • New Brunswick, NJ 08903

Cover By Tim R. Swartz - Includes © Cloki | Dreamstime.com - USA On Planet Earth Photo

- Staff Members -
Timothy G. Beckley, Publisher
Carol Ann Rodriguez, Assistant to the Publisher
Sean Casteel, Editorial Consultant
William Kern, Editorial Consultant
Tim R. Swartz, Editorial Consultant

Sign Up Online For Our Free Weekly Newsletter and Mail Order Version of Conspiracy Journal and Bizarre Bazaar

www.conspiracyjournal.com

Order Hot Line: 1-732-602-3407

PayPal: MrUFO8@hotmail.com

America's Strange and Supernatural History

CONTENTS

America The Beautiful...And The Strange 4

Bones, Bodies and Strange Predecessors 7

East Bay Walls, Enigmatic Feature or Remnants of a Lost Civilization in Northern California? 27

Weird Stuff From the Sky 35

Mysterious Fumes! Poisonous Gas Warfare From Outer Space? 53

Who Was The Mad Gasser of Mattoon? 69

Return to Sleepy Hollow 80

An Unnatural History of Indiana 88

Cannibalism and Ghosts in American History 116

Rural Mysteries and the Bigger Picture 130

Are There Still Monsters? 150

Prophecies of the Presidents 169

America's Strange and Supernatural History

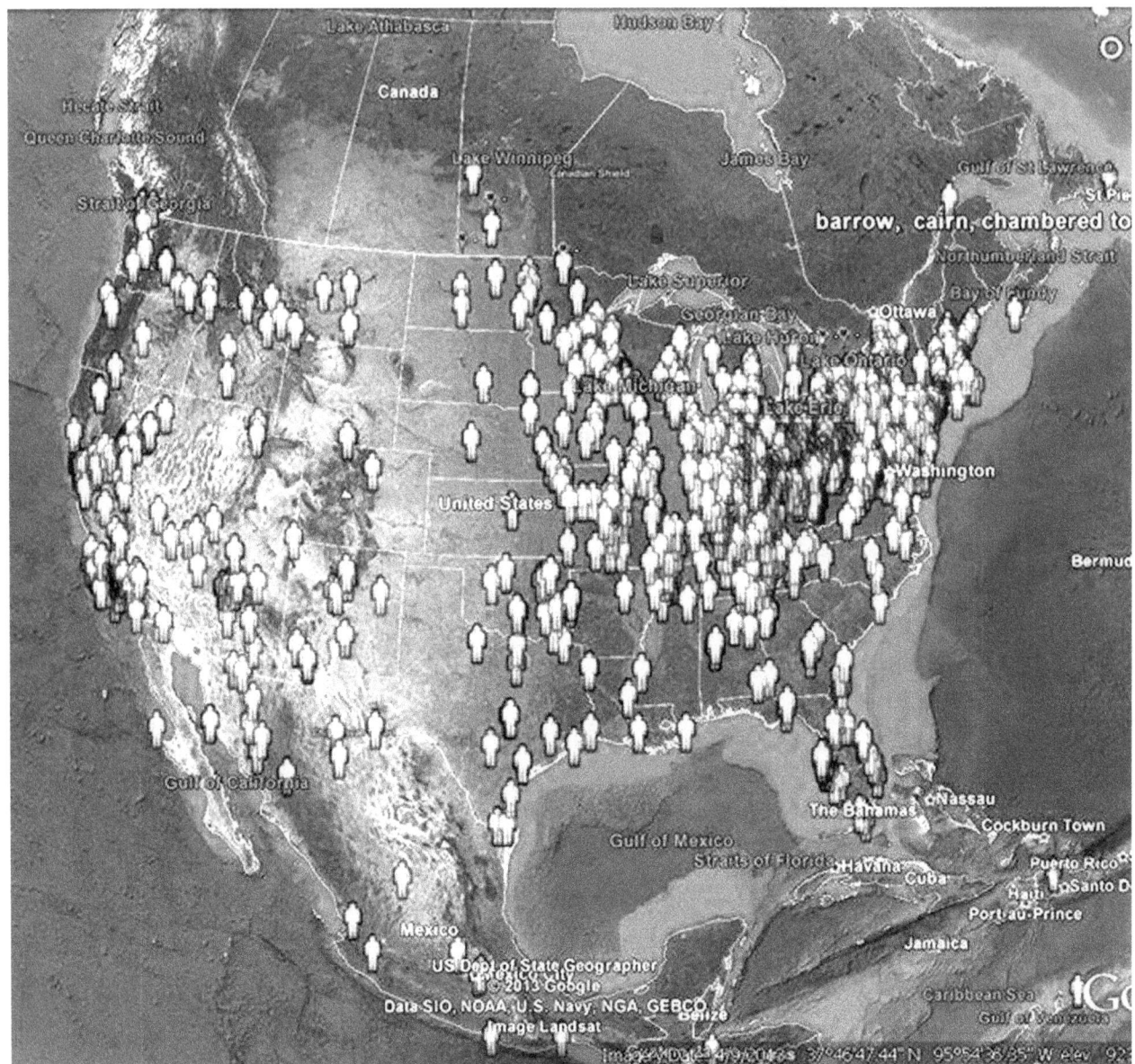

This map is a Google earth map created by researcher Cecelia Hall, who has mapped all the giant skeleton reports of "Stone Builders, Mound Builders and the Giants of Ancient America" – a giant skeleton research organization. Worldwide there are over 1,400 and counting and over 1,000 in the U.S. alone.

AMERICA THE BEAUTIFUL...AND THE STRANGE

By Timothy Green Beckley

You don't have to go far from home to encounter the strange, the bizarre and the unknown. I found that early on when I visited a mysterious site in North Carolina known for its strange phenomena. The Brown Mountain Lights appear just above the mountain crest, dance around and circle hikers as if they are under intelligent control. Jim Moseley, Allen Greenfield and I spoke with a number of the witnesses who told us that when they approached these spheres, the odd orbs would disappear and then reappear directly behind them as if playing a cat and mouse game.

Sightings of these enigmatic "fireballs" go back to the times of the pioneers, and even the Native-Americans tell tales of these ghostly globes that bob and weave about as if signaling to them.

I have visited many other areas in the good ole USA that are connected with the supernatural.

There is the vast Mojave Desert in California where UFOs have landed and space visitors have supposedly spoken to just normal, everyday people. There is even a haunted opera house – yes, I said opera house – in Death Valley where giants may be buried as well as enormous seafaring vessels!

And don't forget Edwards Air Force Base, where President Eisenhower is said to have had an official meeting with extraterrestrials and an albino Bigfoot has been observed roaming the perimeter of the military instillation.

No one would likely dispute the fact that times are stranger in America than ever before, and indications are that things are getting weirder with each passing day.

America's Strange and Supernatural History

But a look at our hidden – SECRET – history alerts us to the startling fact that our country has been steeped in "high strangeness" since its founding fathers signed the Declaration of Independence and, provocatively, even before. Christopher Columbus – as verified by an entry in his ship's log – witnessed the crashing of a glowing, amber-colored orb into the sea while he was passing through the treacherous waters of what has become widely known as the Bermuda Triangle, thus making the famed explorer the first UFO observer in the New World.

And while historians and scholars tend to ignore or shrug off anything that falls outside the realm of the conventional, it is nevertheless apparent that our proud nation owes a great "debt of ingratitude" to the mysterious, the macabre, the downright bizarre and the unseen realm of the occult.

The acclaimed researchers in this volume dare to make many inquiries . . .

Did the ancient Lemurians, a Pacific Ocean race similar to the fabled Atlanteans to the east, erect the mysterious walls found in the eastern part of the San Francisco Bay area? Writer Olav Phillips explores the enigma first hand.

And did the gators get your grannie? America has been the location of many bizarre "sky falls," including alligators that have rocketed themselves out of the clouds along with the more familiar frogs and chunks of metal that seem to defy analysis.

I, along with my friend Circe, returned to Sleepy Hollow, New York – of "Headless Horseman" fame – and discovered that paranormal activity is still rampant there, while author Tim Swartz would like suitable explanations for all the supernatural mysteries of his native Indiana.

Sean Casteel provides an overview of historical incidents of cannibalism, stories that go back as far as "The Starving Time" of the Jamestown colony in 1609, and Wm. Michael Mott offers up some of the UFO and creature sightings he has collected from the state of Mississippi.

Also included are tales of uniquely American monsters like "The Jersey Devil" and "The Killer Kangaroo" of Tennessee.

And then there are the presidents of the United States – from their eerie ghostly appearances to their personal psychic experiences and encounters with the denizens of the "other side." Not even our most highly placed executives are immune when the hand of the paranormal reaches out to touch them, whether they remain among the living or not.

America's Strange and Supernatural History

In a bonus section – "The Spiritual Destiny of America" – the future of America as seen through the eyes of prophecy and the occult is revealed, along with: * The origin of the Great Seal of the United States.

* Our psychic presidents (including Lincoln, Washington, and Kennedy).

* The coming Polar Shift and America's fate.

* The reincarnation of Atlantis.

* America's great curses.

* The Secret Government – who's really in control?

* Space visitors watch over America. All the presidents since Eisenhower are said to have met with extraterrestrials on American soil.

You can feel the chills already, eh? Read "America's Strange and Supernatural History" and get ready to kick those chills up a notch or two.

mrufo8@hotmail.com

On YouTube at: Mr UFO's Secret Files

On the Internet: www.TheOuterEdgeRadio.com

www.conspiracyjournal.com

Chapter One

Bones, Bodies and Strange Predecessors

EVEN a casual glance through a history book will uncover stuff that is out of the ordinary and can only be described as just plain weird. Scholars tend to ignore or shrug off anything that falls outside of the conventional...yet the records remain, open for anyone who dares to delve deeper in search of weird history.

Compared to the age of other countries, the United States is barely a teenager. Yet, the history of the United States already has a rich collection of tales from the world of the weird. Even before the U.S. was created, North America had been host to numerous strange occurrences, the likes that would probably give Charles Fort shivers of ecstasy up and down his spine.

One of the greatest historical mysteries has to do with who were the first people to discover and inhabit North America. Conventional theory explains that the first inhabitants came across the Bering Strait around 16,000 - 13,000 years before present. However, recent discoveries indicate that there were humans in North America possibly as far back as 50,000 years ago – maybe even longer.

In 2003, unusual stone tools were unearthed along the Savannah River in South Carolina. Radiocarbon tests of carbonized plant remains where artifacts were unearthed indicate that the sediments containing these artifacts are at least 50,000 years old, meaning that humans inhabited North American long before the last ice age.

The findings are significant because they suggest that humans inhabited North America well before the last ice age more than 20,000 years ago, a potentially explosive revelation in American archaeology.

University of South Carolina archaeologist, Dr. Albert Goodyear, said that the dates could actually be older. "Fifty-thousand should be a minimum age since there may be little detectable activity left."

Dr. Goodyear first recovered stone tool artifacts in soils around the Savannah River that were later dated by an outside team of geologists to be 16,000 years old. In 1998, Dr. Goodyear, nationally known for his research on the ice age Paleo-Indian cultures, dug below the 16,000-year Clovis level at the site and found unusual stone tools up to a meter deeper.

"This site is the oldest radiocarbon dated site in North America," Goodyear says. "However, other early sites in Brazil and Chile, as well as a site in Oklahoma also suggest that humans were in the Western Hemisphere as early as 30,000 years ago to perhaps 60,000."

Dr. Goodyear's discoveries are certainly controversial. However, he is not the only one to suggest that the original occupants of the Americas may not have arrived via the Bering Strait. Brazilian archeologist Niede Guidon contends that artifacts discovered in the Serra da Capivara national park show that ancient inhabitants of South America may have arrived as far back as 100,000 years ago by boat from Africa, or even Australia.

A 1999 BBC documentary, Ancient Voices, suggests that the dimensions of prehistoric skulls found in Brazil match those of the aboriginal peoples of Australia and Melanesia. Other evidence suggests that these first Americans were later massacred by invaders who came from Asia across the Bering Strait.

Walter Neves, an archaeologist from the University of Sao Paolo, has taken extensive skull measurements from dozens of skulls dug from a depth equivalent to 9,000 to 12,000 years ago, including the oldest, a young woman who has been named Lucia.

"The measurements show that Lucia was anything but Asian," he says.

The next step was to reconstruct a face from Lucia's skull. First, a CAT scan of the skull was done, to allow an accurate working model to be made. Then a forensic artist, Richard Neave from the University of Manchester, UK, created a face for Lucia. The result was surprising: "It has all the features of a negroid face," says Dr Neave.

The skull dimensions and facial features match most closely the native people of Australia and Melanesia. These people date back to about 60,000 years, and were themselves descended from the first humans, who left Africa about 100,000 years ago.

Is there any evidence that early Australians had the capability to travel more than 8,450 miles at that time? The answer comes from cave paintings in a region at the northern tip of Western Australia. Here, the oldest painting of a boat anywhere in the world was discovered. The style of the art means it is at least 17,000 years old, but it could be up to 50,000 years old. The crucial detail is the high prow of the boat. This would have been unnecessary for boats used in calm, inland waters. The design suggests it was used on the open ocean.

Archaeologists speculate that such an incredible sea voyage, from Australia to Brazil, would not have been undertaken knowingly but by accident.

However, if the first Americans had drifted from Australia, where are their descendants now? Again, the skulls suggest an answer. The shape of the skulls changes between 9,000 and 7,000 years ago from being exclusively negroid to exclusively mongoloid, or Asian. Combined with rock art evidence of increasing violence at this time, it appears that the Asian people from the north invaded and wiped out the original Americans.

The only evidence of any survivors comes from Terra del Fuego, the islands at the remotest southern tip of South America. The pre-European Fuegans, who lived stone age-style lives until recently, show hybrid skull features which could have resulted from intermarrying between mongoloid and negroid peoples. Their rituals and traditions also bear some resemblance to the ancient rock art in Brazil.

At the same time, discoveries elsewhere in Brazil are adding to the mystery of how the Americas were settled. In what may be another blow to the Clovis model of humans' coming from northeast Asia, molecular geneticists showed in 2013 that the Botocudo indigenous people living in southeastern Brazil in the late 1800s shared gene sequences commonly found among Pacific Islanders from Polynesia.

The Botocudo people, who lived in inland regions of southeastern Brazil, stands out, having skull shapes that were intermediate between those of other

America's Strange and Supernatural History

Palaeoamericans and a presumed ancestral population in eastern Asia. A genetic analysis taken from 14 Botocudo skulls kept in a museum collection in Rio de Janeiro showed that the mitochondrial DNA from two of the skulls included a haplogroup commonly found in Polynesia, Easter Island and other Pacific island archipelagos.

The researchers say that it is possible that the DNA could have come from Polynesians who voyaged from remote islands to the western coast of South America. Those traders or their progeny would then have made their way to southeastern Brazil and settled or interbred with natives. The problem with this theory, according to scientists, is that the Andes are a formidable barrier that west coast residents typically did not climb or cross. Although researchers have suggested that ancestors of some species of chickens made their way to Chile through trade with pre-Columbian seafarers from Polynesia.

The fact remains that evidence is growing that groups of people, other than Asians from Siberia, contributed to the gene pool of humans in North and South America.

Other sites, including Valsequillo in Mexico and Monte Verde in Chile, also indicate the presence of communities tens of thousands of years ago. These sites have led archeologists to speculate that peoples traveled various routes, such as across oceans, to reach the Americas and at different stages.

There is also the fact that a team of Uruguayan researchers working at the Arroyo del Vizcaíno site in Uruguay has found evidence in ancient sloth bones that suggests humans were in the area as far back as 30,000 years ago. The researchers found over a thousand bones from approximately 27 different animals at the site, most of which once belonged to the now extinct giant sloth.

What was most remarkable however, were the deep slash markings on some of the bones, indicative of human stone tools. Also interesting was that the bones were all from the remains of large, full grown sloths, animals that would have been up to 15 feet tall and weighed approximately two to four tons, all in a single place where they wouldn't have died in other ways such as from falling off a cliff.

Taken together, it appears the sloths were killed individually, as needed, and eaten, most likely, by humans as no other known animal could have pulled off such a feat. The team also found a stone that appears to have been fashioned to serve as a scraping tool.

Giants In North America

It is not unreasonable to expect that ancient humans were perfectly capable of finding ways of discovering and traveling to the America's. We are, and always have been, an extremely resourceful species. What is actually going on is the inability for a majority of scientists to venture outside of their comfort zone to even remotely consider evidence that flies against what they were originally taught.

So, if scientists are hard-pressed to consider that ancient humans were considerably more active and mobile than once thought, what is the probability that any of them would open their minds enough to examine artifacts that have been discovered in strata millions of years old? Or, to seriously look at bones discovered in North America that bear a close resemblance to other, ancient species of humans such as Cro-Magnon or Neanderthals?

Not very likely.

Yet, all across North America, ancient mounds, attributed to Native American tribes such as the Adena and Hopewell, were excavated and were found to contain skeletons that appear to be from other members of the human family tree. These ancient bones were puzzling because often they were people of great stature. Reports of bodies seven to nine feet tall were not uncommon. Many of these discoveries occurred in the 19th century and were chronicled in magazines as well as local and national newspapers.

Even more puzzling is the fact that these skeletons have somehow managed to vanish over the years despite their apparent value to history. Writers such as Micah Hanks have addressed the theory that the Smithsonian Institute may have deliberately been involved in disposing of any evidence that may disprove the Bering Strait theory of early North America migration.

In his article *Big Buried Secrets: Giant Skeletons and the Smithsonian*, Hanks notes that there are no easy answers to this mystery as newspaper hoaxes were common in the 19th century and that journalists may have taken greater liberties with the facts when reporting on alleged discoveries of giant skeletons.

12th Annual Report of the Bureau of Ethnology to the Secretary of the Smithsonian Institution, 1890-1891
Dunleith Illinois

No. 5, the largest of the group, was carefully examined. Two feet below the surface, near the apex, was a skeleton, doubtless an intrusive Indian burial...Near the original surface, 10 or 12 feet from the center, on the lower side, lying at full length on its back, was one of the largest skeletons discovered by the Bureau agents, the length as proved by actual measurement being between 7 and 8 feet. It was clearly traceable, but crumbled to pieces immediately after removal from the hard earth in which it was encased.

However, local and state historic registries also duly recorded these unusual archeological discoveries in their regions. So newspaper hoaxes cannot explain away every incident of uncovering giant human skeletons.

American Antiquarian, April 1878
Lake County Illinois

Mr. W.B. Gray, of Highland Park, also mentions the discovery of a skull in a mound near Fox Lake, in Lake County, Illinois. This skull is certainly very remarkable; the frontal lobe or arch seems to be entirely wanting; the large projecting eye-brows, deep set eye sockets, the low, receding forehead, and the long, narrow and flat shape of the crown rendered it a very animal-looking skull. If it was not a posthumous deformation it certainly is a remarkable skull and might well pass for the "missing link."

History of Jefferson County, N.Y., 1878

"One of the most conclusive evidences of ancient military occupation and conflict, occurs in Rutland, near the residence of Abner Tamblin, one mile from the western line of the town, and two miles from the river. It is on the summit of the Trenton limestone terrace, which forms a bold escarpment, extending down the river, and passing across the southern part of Watertown. There here occurs a slight embankment, and ditch irregularly oval, with several gateways; and along the ditch, in several places, have been found great numbers of skeletons, almost entirely of males and lying in great confusion, as if they had been slain in defending it. Among these bones were those of a man of colossal size, and like nine-tenths of the others, furnished with a row of double teeth in each jaw. This singular peculiarity, with that of broad flat jaws, retreating forehead, and great prominence of the occiput, which was common to most of these skulls, may hereafter afford some clue to their history."

Greenville Advance Argus, Greenville, Pennsylvania June 11, 1885
Giant Human Skeletons Found

"J. H. Porter has a farm near Northeast Erie county, Pa., not many miles from where the Lake Shore Railroad crosses the New York State boundary line.

This week some workmen in Mr. Porters employ came upon the entrance to a cave, and on entering it, found heaps of bones within. Many skeletons were complete, and exhibited to the naturalists and archaeologists of the neighborhood.

"They informed the wondering bystanders that the remains were unmistakably those of giants. The entire village of Northeast was aroused by the discovery, and Sunday, hundreds of people from Erie took advantage of their holiday visit to the scene.

"It was at first conjectured that the remains were those of soldiers killed in battle with Indians that abounded in the vicinity during the last century but the size of the skulls and the length of the leg bones dispelled the theory. So far about a hundred and fifty giant skeletons of powerful proportions have been exhumed and indications point to a second cave eastward, which may probably contain as many more.

"Scientists who have exhausted skeletons and made careful measurements of the bones say they are a race of gigantic creatures, compared with which our tallest men would appear as pigmies. There are now arrow heads, stone hatchets or other implements of war with the bodies. Some of the bones are on exhibition at various stores. One is as thick as a good-sized bucket."

The McIvor Times, September 5, 1884
Gigantic Skeletons

"The bones of a gigantic human were discovered in a rock near the Sauk Rapids. The head is massive 31 1/2 in. in circumference, is low in the front and very flat on the top. The femur measures 26 1/4 in., and the fibula 26 1/2 in., while the body is equally long in proportion. From the crown of the head to the sole of the foot, the length is 10 feet 9 1/2 inches. The measure around the chest is 59 1/2 In.

"This giant must have weighed at least 900 lbs, when covered with a reasonable amount of flesh. The petrified remains, and there is nothing left but the naked bones, now weigh 304 lbs. The thumb and fingers of the left hand and the left foot from the ankle to the toes are gone, but all of the other parts are perfect."

SAN ANTONIO EXPRESS

Beach Giant's Skull Unearthed By WPA Workers Near Victoria

Believed to Be Largest Ever Found in World; Normal Head Also Found

That Texas "had a giant on the beach" in the long ago appears probable from the large skull recently unearthed in a mound in Victoria County, believed to be the largest human skull ever found in the United States and possibly in the world.

Twice the size of the skull of normal man, the fragments were dug up by W. Duffen, archaeologist, who is excavating the mound in Victoria County under a WPA project sponsored by the University of Texas. In the same mound and at the same level, a normal sized skull was found. The pieces taken from the mound were reconstructed in the WPA laboratory under supervision of physical anthropologists.

A study is being made to determine whether the huge skull was that of a man belonging to a tribe of extraordinary large men or whether the skull was that of an abnormal member of a tribe, a case of giantism. Several large human body bones also have been unearned at the site.

Marcus B. Goldstein, physical anthropologist employed on the WPA project, formerly was an aide of Ales Hdrlicken, curator of the National Museum of Physical Anthropolgy.

Finds made through excavations in Texas are beginning to give weight to the theory that man lived in Texas 40,000 to 45,000 years ago, it is said.

STAMP SOCIETY MEETS

San Antonio Philatelic Society will hold its first meeting of 1940 at the Y. M. C. A. at 8:30 p. m.

GIANT SKULL—Believed to be possibly the largest found in the world, the human skull shown on the right was recently unearthed in Victoria County by Texas University anthropologists. The other two are of normal size.

Historical Collections of Virginia, 1845

"On the Wappatomaka have been found numerous Indian relics, among which was highly a finished pipe, representing a snake coiled around the bowl. There was also discovered the under jaw bone of a giant human being (says Keucheval) of great size, which contained eight jaw teeth in each side, of enormous size; and what is more remarkable the teeth stood transversely in the jawbone. It would pass over any man's face with entire ease."

Ohio Democrat November 24, 1892
Burial Place of Giants

"A rich archaeological find was recently unearthed two miles west of Crawfordsville, Indiana in a gravel pit along the high bluffs of Sugar creek. Thus far twenty-five skeletons of Brobdingnagian stature have been exhumed, and the unburying of these mammoth bones is still going on. This necropolis of long ago is filled with exited hunters of curios and scientific students from Wabash college almost continually, and as soon as removed from the gravel their rattling bones carried away to become parts of departments of archaeology, which are being established all over the city.

"The last skeleton taken from the burial ground was a gigantic one, measuring seven feet in length. The femur alone would prove that the skeleton was that of a giant, and the pelvic bones twice as large as those of an ordinary man. The grinning skull of the giant had a perfect set of teeth, not one cracked or decayed, and with enamel as beautiful as polished marble. The bones were perfect in every detail, notwithstanding the fact that they must have interred here for centuries. The entire absence of vegetable matter in the soil and the perfect drainage would account for the preservation of the bony structure.

"Of the whole number of skeletons thus far found only two indicate immature development, the remainder representing the framework of a race of men evidently extinct for centuries. This is certainly the first discovery of skeletons in which the characteristic development of giants has been observed. It is thought by local scientist that these bones belong to a tribe of aborigines, but this theory cannot be fully established by the material structure of the skeleton.

"Although no implements or ornaments were found buried with the bones, yet in close proximity many instruments of warfare and domestic utensils were found. They are mostly composed of stone, though some are composed of copper and a few of shell and bone. The stone implements are flint spears and arrow heads, and appear to be wrought with exceeding great skill. Pottery is found in great abundance. For many years specimens of these pots have been unearthed in this region, especially along the banks of the creek.

"None of these skeletons was found in a separate grave, they being for the most part piled together in one conglomerate mass. Ten were found in one place in close contact, facing the setting sun, and arranged in a sitting posture. Many of the bones found farther down the bank, and in a soil in which there was more vegetable matter, crumbled to a dust as soon as exposed to the atmosphere, and the symmetry of a single bone could not be distinguished.

"Many traditions have been brought out since the discovery. One old settler has called to mind the fact that fifty years ago a tree was uprooted on this same spot, exposing three skeletons of gigantic dimensions, and as they were beneath the trees, it must have sprung up long after the bodies were buried.

"Gen. Lew Wallace says he remembers the sections of a stranger, who several years ago spent many months digging along the banks of Sugar creek in search of a gold spoon supposed to have been buried long ago when this part of the country was inhabited by savage tribes, and the owner of the land on which these remains were found calls to mind a tradition often related by his grandfather that a Spanish treasure had been buried here in the long, long ago, when the country was a wilderness and Chicago a barren waste of impenetrable swamps.

"The excavations are being continued, and it is thought that rich developments are in prospect, for there is not a foot of the soil removed that does not contain some relic or grinning skull."

History of Park and Vermillion Counties, Indiana, 1913

"In March, 1880 while a company of gravel road workers were excavating gravel from the bank on the ridge at the southwest corner of the Newport Fairgrounds, five human skeletons were found... In the gravel bank along the railroad, at the southeast corner of the Fairground, another skeleton was found.

No implements of war were found with the bones but ashes were perceivable...A collection of a dozen skeletons shows by measurements of the thigh bones found that the warriors, including a few women, averaged over six feet and two inches in height...the trochanters forming the attachment of muscles show that they were not only a race of giant stature, but also of more than giant strength."

Collins Historical Sketches of Kentucky, History of Kentucky, Lewis Collins, 1874 – Ohio County

"In 1872, in prospecting for coal in Ohio County, about a mile from Rockport, the complete skeleton of a human body of gigantic size was found, 6 feet below the surface. The lower jaw-bone, when fitted over the lower portion of a man's face in the party of explorers, completely covered it; the thigh bone, from hip-bone to the knee, was 42 inches long, and the fore-arm bone from the wrist to elbow measured 22 inches. This would indicate a giant over 10 feet high."

Prehistoric Giant Skeleton Found
Helena Independent October 10, 1883 (Helena, Montana)

"A farmer named John W. Hannon, found the bones protruding from the bank of a ravine that has been cut by the action of the rains during the past years. Mr. Hannon worked several days in unearthing the skeleton which proved to be that of a human being whose height was twelve feet.

"The head through the temples was eleven inches; from the lower part of the skull at the back to the top was fifteen inches, and the circumference forty inches. The ribs were nearly four feet long, one and three-fourths inches wide. The thigh bones we're thirty-six inches long and large in proportion.

"When the earth was removed the ribs stood high enough to enable a man to crawl in and explore the interior of the skeleton, turn around and come out with ease.

"The first joint of the greater toe above the nail, was three inches long, and the entire foot, eighteen inches in length. The skeleton lay on its face twenty feet below the surface of the ground and the toes were imbedded in the earth, indicating that the body either fell or was placed there when the ground was soft.

"The left arm was passed around backward, the hand resting on the spinal column, while the right arm was stretched out to the front, and right. Some of the bones crumbled on exposure to the air, but many good specimens were preserved, and are now exhibited at, Bernard Medical school.

"The skeleton is generally pronounced a relic of the prehistoric race."

Two Giant Skeletons Near Potosi, Wisconsin

The January 13th, 1870 edition of the *Wisconsin Decatur Republican* reported that two giant, well-preserved skeletons of an unknown race were discovered near the town of Potosi by workers digging the foundation of a saw mill near the bank of the Mississippi river. One skeleton measured seven-and-a-half feet, the other eight feet. The skulls of each had prominent cheek bones and double rows of teeth. One skull was described as being as large as a "half bushel measure." A large collection of arrowheads and "finely tempered rods of copper" were found buried with the remains.

The discovery of these giant bones did not occur in a total vacuum. Native Americans (Indians) who lived in the areas where giant bones had been discovered had legends of fearsome giants who were the original inhabitants when the Indians first arrived. These tales were duly recorded by the white settlers who had no preconceived prejudices on the ancient history of the America's.

David Larkin and Julek Heller in their 1985 book **Giants** wrote that, "The Pawnee believes that the first human beings on the Earth were a race of giants — so large that they could lift a full-grown buffalo bull from the ground and throw it over their shoulders. These giant forebears had no fear of any superior power, had no notion of a life after death and did not believe in Ti-ra'-wa, the all powerful one who watches over the destiny of man. So the giants did as they pleased with no regard for the consequences. Finally, when the deeds they perpetrated had reached unacceptable proportions, Ti-ra'-wa resolved to punish the big men. He caused the waters of the rivers, lakes and seas to rise up until they were level with the land. The ground became soft and the heavy giants sank down into the mud and were drowned. Even today massive bones are still found in remote areas of North America."

America's Strange and Supernatural History

Another example was collected by James Mooney (1861-1921). "James Wafford, of the western Cherokee, who was born in Georgia in 1806, says that his grandmother, who must have been born about the middle of the 18th century, told him that she had heard from the old people that long before her time a party of giants had once come to visit the Cherokee. They were nearly twice as tall as common men, and had their eyes set slanting in their heads, so that the Cherokee called them Tsunil´ kalu,´ 'the Slant-eyed people,' because they looked like the giant hunter Tsul´ kalu.´ They said that these giants lived far away in the direction in which the sun goes down. The Cherokee received them as friends, and they stayed some time, and then returned to their home in the west."

In 1833, while digging a foundation for a powder magazine, a group of soldiers at an army outpost on Lompock Ranchero, in California came upon a layer of carefully placed stone and gravel. Breaking through this with bars and picks, the workers found a stone coffin surrounded by carved shells, a massive stone axe, large flint spear points, and several tablets of porphyry covered with an unknown script.

The coffin was found to contain the skeleton of a man who in life would have stood over 12 feet tall. The Indians in a nearby settlement heard of the find, and the medicine man of the tribe said that the bones were that of an Allegewi.

According to tribal legends, the Allegewi were a race of giants who had occupied the land before the Indians. The Allegewi were extremely fierce and would raid the Indian villages to carry off woman and children to eat. Eventually the local tribes banded together and wiped out the Allegewi in a bloody war.

The shaman demanded that the Allegewi bones, which were believed to still contain the spirit of great strength and cunning, be turned over to the village. In order to prevent a local Indian uprising, the commander of the outpost instead gave the bones and artifacts to a priest at the local mission. The bones were reburied in a secret location, and have yet to be rediscovered today.

The legend of fierce giants living in North America is not an isolated story, but is a tradition found among many Native American nations. The Paiutes of Nevada tell about a race of red-haired, cannibalistic giants called the Si-Te-Cah, with whom their forefathers once fought. Finding no land to expand for their people, and constantly harassed by roving bands of these giants, the Piute allied with other intermountain tribes and attacked the Sitecah. They were chased into a cave near, what is now Lovelock Nevada. The Si-Te-Cah would not come out of the cave, so the tribes put fire to the entrance of the cave. What few giants that did come out were killed with volleys of arrows. The rest suffocated inside the cave as the fire removed all the oxygen from the air.

A few hundred years later archaeologists visited the cave and found skeletons of the giants. Along with the remains hundreds of artifacts were also found. No known Native American tribes had calendars, but allegedly the Si-Ti-Cah giants did. Inside the cave was found a round stone shaped like a donut with 365 notches on the outside, with 52 notches on the inside of the stone. To confirm the finding of the earlier archaeologist, in June 1931 two more giants were found in a Humboldt dry lake bed near Lovelock Nevada.

According to the Indian accounts (as preserved in Volume 12 of **Memoires of the Historical Society of Pennsylvania**, the Lenni-lenape have a legend of escaping from a volcanic explosion and going eastward to find a tribe of giants (Allegewi) who possessed a high civilization. The progress of the Lenni-lenape was stopped, and they were driven back but not discouraged. At the same time, the Iroquois people were trying to find a passage through Allegewi territory, from the north. Two migratory peoples eventually entered into an alliance together, and proclaimed war against the giants.

One by one, the Allegewi strongholds fell, and the giants were forced to become wanderers along the streams and river-systems of the Mississippi. Another tradition affirms that the primitive Indian invaders, because of their great numbers, successfully overwhelmed the ancient gargantuan inhabitants of the north-central states, and that the last great battle in this area was fought at the falls of the Ohio river, where the remnant was driven upon a small island below the rapids where they were slaughtered.

The Indian chief, Tobacco, informed General George Rogers Clark of a legend in which was preserved the memory of a battle fought at Sandy Island, where "the first peoples of this land" had been exterminated. Another Indian chief, Cornplanter, told that Ohio, Kentucky and Tennessee had once been inhabited by a gigantic white-skinned people, who were familiar with the arts of civilization, which his own forefathers knew nothing of.

After a series of battles with the invading tribes, these former inhabitants were completely exterminated. The chief also declared that the old burial places –

the mounds – were the graves of these indigenous giants, and that the great earthen fortresses had not been constructed by his people, but belonged to the "very long ago" people, who were huge, light-complexioned, and skilled in many arts. Other Native Americans say that their forefathers had worked on the great earthworks – but as slaves to the giants, who were the real masterminds.

The Indians also had a superstition concerning the territory of what is now Kentucky. One Indian elder expressed his astonishment that present-day white folk would want to live in a region which had been the scene of such conflicts as had taken place there. An old Sac Indian, in 1800, said that Kentucky was filled with ghosts of its slaughtered giant inhabitants, and wondered why the white man could make it his home.

The giants of North America appear at one time to have been a restless, warlike breed, for several ancient sources describe their invasions of other lands. The last surviving Incan prince, and historian of his people, Garcilasco de la Vega, preserved the legend in his multi-volume opus **Commentaries Reales de los Incas**, that Peru was once attacked by a gigantic race from the North. He recounted that they first arrived by sea upon the northern Peruvian coast in the Manta region: "The giant men were strange to behold; their eyes were large, and their hair was worn long. They were beardless and their skin was light. A few of the giants wore animal skins for clothing ; others walked the land without clothes. They built a settlement near the sea, at a spot along the desert land of the Manta region. They dug enormous wells."

De la Vega further described how the giants, not finding enough to eat, began raiding local villages and cities, killing and pillaging, and striking terror in everyone because of their gigantic size. The Incan historian claimed that the giants were then struck dead from some catastrophe originating in the sky, and that all that is left of their reign of terror are giant bones scattered across the Peruvian countryside.

Mississippi, Texas And Florida Giants

In 1519, a year before Magellan discovered the Patagonians, Alonzo Alvarez de Pineda encountered some giants on the banks of the Mississippi River, not far from where it empties into the Gulf of Mexico. Sent to search for a strait across

Florida, Pineda came first upon the northern gulf coast, reconnoitered it, then sailed south, coasting the western shore of Florida until he reached its southern tip. Finding the peninsula offered no strait, he then retraced his course. Landing at strategic places along the coasts of Florida, Alabama, Mississippi, Louisiana, Texas, and even down to Tampico in Mexico, Pineda made maps and notes of the rivers and bays, established landmarks, and took possession of all these lands in his king's name. That done, he sailed back to the mouth of the Mississippi River. There he "found a large town, and on both sides of its banks, for a distance of six leagues up its course, some forty native villages." These Indians proved friendly, so he remained here forty days while his crew careened their four ships and made necessary repairs. In his report on the country, Pineda noted that it provided the natives with an abundance of food, that many of its rivers contained so much gold that they commonly wore it as ornaments in their ears and noses, around their necks, and over other parts of the body, and that there lived on the banks of this river "a race of giants from ten to eleven palms in height."

On his return from Tampico to the Mississippi, Pineda also, unknowingly, sailed right past a tribe of equally huge Texas Indians. For historian Woodbury Lowery, along with several others, places "the giant Karankawas" nation around Matagorda Bay at that time.

In a report on the Karankawas, John R. Swanton, of the Bureau of American Ethnology, describes the men as being "very tall and well formed...Their hair was unusually coarse and worn so long by many of the men that it reached to the waist. Agriculture was not practiced by these Indians, their food supply being obtained from the waters, the chase, and wild plants, and, to a limited extent, human flesh; for, like most of the tribes of the Texas coast, they were cannibals. Travel among them was almost wholly by the canoe, or dugout, for they seldom left the coast. Head-flattening and tattooing were practiced to a considerable extent. Little is known in regard to their tribal government, further than that they had civil and war chiefs, the former being hereditary in the male line."

The first positive notice of them, adds Swanton, is found in the accounts of La Salle's disastrous visit to this area. They also later engaged in a fierce battle with Lafitte and his band of pirates, who had abducted one of their women. But the Karankawas proved no match for the buccaneers, who, having superior arms

Ceremonial stones, scratched with the sign of the cross, show Spanish influence. Skull is of a giant Indian who was seven feet tall.

Popular Science - October 1932

and firepower, inflicted heavy casualties upon them and forced them to retreat. When Stephen Austin built his settlement on the Brazos in 1823, the tribe began to decline. "Conflicts between the settlers and the Indians were frequent," says the ethnologist, "and finally a battle was fought in which about half the tribe was slain, the other portion fleeing for refuge to La Bahia." By 1840, the Karankawas had been reduced to about one hundred souls living on Lavaca Bay.

In 1528, or almost ten years after Alonzo Alvarez de Pineda's discovery of giants on the Mississippi River, the ill-fated explorer Panfilo de Narvaez put three hundred men ashore at Tampa Bay. His mission was to search the Florida mainland for its riches, while his five ships sailed just off the coast. Only Alvar Nunez Cabeza de Vaca and three companions survived this expedition. Afterward they crossed the North American continent from shore to shore, becoming the first white men to do so. In his history, Cabeza de Vaca mentions some giant Florida Indians who attacked the Narvaez party. "When we came in view of Apalachen," he writes, "the Governor ordered that I should take nine cavalry with fifty infantry and enter the town.

Accordingly the assessor and I assailed it; and having got in, we found only women and boys there, the men being absent; however these returned to its support, after a little time, while we were walking about, and began discharging arrows at us. They killed the horse of the assessor, and at last taking to flight, they left us...The town consisted of forty small houses, made low, and set up in sheltered places because of the frequent storms. The material was thatch. They were surrounded by very dense woods, large groves and many bodies of fresh water... Two hours after our arrival at Apalachen, the Indians who had fled from there came in peace to us, asking for their women and children, whom we released; but the detention of a cacique [the Indians' chief] by the Governor produced great excitement, in consequence of which they returned for battle early the next day, and attacked us with such prompt- ness and alacrity that they succeeded in setting fire to the houses in which we were."

After twenty-five days, Narvaez' army departed Apalachen. But a short while later, as they attempted to cross a large lake, they came under heavy attack from many giant Indians concealed behind trees. "Some of our men were wounded in this conflict, for which the good armor they wore did not avail," continues Cabeza de Vaca. 'There were those this day who swore that they had seen two red oaks, each the thickness of the lower part of the leg, pierced through from side to side by arrows; and this is not so much to be wondered at, considering the power and skill with which the Indians are able to project them. I myself saw an arrow that had entered the butt of an elm to the depth of a span... The Indians we had so far seen in Florida are all archers. They go naked, are large of body, and appear at a distance like giants. They are of admirable proportions, very spare and of great activity and strength. The bows they use are as thick as the arm, of eleven or twelve palms in length, which will discharge at two hundred paces with so great precision that they miss nothing."

Harassment's by these Indian giants continued. So Narvaez decided to head south for the gulf coast and escape by the sea. Arriving there after much hardship, he and his men constructed five crude boats, in order to search along the coast for a Spanish settlement.

Unfortunately, a sudden, fierce storm caught them some distance from land. The high winds drove all the boats, with all their men aboard, far out to sea. All were subsequently lost except Cabeza de Vaca and three companions who managed to reach the shore.

They walked across Texas and northern Mexico, finally reaching the Pacific coast where they linked up with Francisco Vazquez de Coronado in 1541.

Chapter Two

East Bay Walls, Enigmatic Feature or Part of the Remnants of a Lost Civilization in Northern California?

By Olav Phillips

THE journey started quietly enough, I was writing a series of columns for my local paper "The Martinez Gazette" about mysterious features of Contra Costa County and the eastern part of the San Francisco Bay Area. I had already written a number of articles about haunted houses, mysterious spots, even the odd UFO abduction but when I came across the mysterious walls of the east bay I found a true oddity.

The walls of the East Bay traverse some 50 miles in a straight line from the Carquinez Strait to San Jose, and in some places another 20 miles inland to Mt. Diablo. They are generally six feet high and so far have defied explanation, hence the title "mysterious." For nigh on 100 years they have been explored, thought about but today have been largely abandoned. Theories on their origins range from Zheng Hue's exploration fleet, giants, Native Americans, even farmers but so far little or no archeological research has been done on them outside of the trying to document their history which apparently pre-dates western/Spanish activity in the area.

Rough estimates by a geologist put their age older than 400 years or circa late 1500's which puts this anomaly in new territory and forces the dismissal of many common theories about European / Spanish farms. Especially since the greater San Francisco the Spaniards did not settle region until 1769 when an expedition lead by Don Gaspar de Portola and Fr. Juan Crespi began to settle in what is now San Francisco. There was the odd seafarer such as Sir Francis Drake, who was believed to have sailed through the area in 1579, but seeing as he was a privateer the notion that he and his men attempted to settle the region is high suspect.

Conventional research of the mystery walls has pointed towards Native American construction. This is the passively accepted view of this mysterious artifact, but this too seems suspect. To build a wall over 50 miles long running North to South and up to 20 miles East would have been a massive undertaking and is almost unheard of for hunter gatherer cultures. That added to the general lack previously discovered megalithic structures casts serious doubt over the notion that the wall is of Native American origin. In fact to posit that notion we would need to understand what purpose would a massive wall, broken today but one would imagine it was unbroken in the past, serve to a nomadic group? Conventionally walls are used defensively or to define land ownership and keep animals in as pens. In the case of the Coastal Miwok (the indigenous group of the greater San Francisco area) they were nomadic and not pastoralists having no real domesticated animals. So that leaves a defensive wall but what war would be large enough for that size of wall?

That leaves us in a very interesting position and forces the exploration of other options. One possible scenario is the Zheng Hue fleet which set out to circumnavigate the world, and that end there is evidence that the Chinese did reach California. Anchors found in Baja California, mysterious writings from a Buddhist monk in Meso America, even a sunken 17th century Junk found near Chico. Then there is the porcelain found in Drakes Bay.

All these elements make for a true mystery. A 50 mile long wall is odd enough, but what if the wall was not alone? What if there were other walls? A chain of walls all along Northern California because as it turns out, there are other mysterious walls in North California but not just in the San Francisco Bay Area. Instead these series of walls may stretch as far as the origin border.

My first discovery was made while doing research about the East Bay Wall. I found information about a series of walls located in Marin County, just across the bay from the termination point of the East Bay walls. These walls, also apparently dating to the same time period and also rock pile walls have long believed to have been built to pen cattle by an Amish farmer who lived in the area in the 19th century. Wait, I've heard that story before? Yes, you have. A similar explanation has been used to classify the East Bay Walls, an explanation we now have decent evidence is not possible.

The Marin segment of the wall heads out towards the coast, and displays the same characteristics. The rocks are stacked and the wall is about six feet high. There are places where the wall is lower, but as I personally discovered in a exploration the Milpitas section of wall, over three feet of it had been buried due to weather antiquity. Never the less, a very similar wall exists in Marin County which starts and roughly the same position, just west, of the East Bay Wall. But why doesn't the wall connect? The section of land between the Carquinez Straight and Marin, home to the former Mare Island Shipyard, is largely a marsh and wetland. Build a wall in those conditions would have been near impossible. It is also important to note that at many of these locations the rocks seem to show human manipulation, in many cases you can see bore holes where a hole was drilled into the rock for an unknown reason.

So as we move back towards Marin, we continue towards the Coast. At which point we pick up a new segment of wall located in Point Reyes. The mysterious Standing Stones of Point Reyes, bisect the Tomales Point peninsula and are laid out in a straight line with some 400 stones placed to make a wall roughly two feet high. It bears mentioning that although this wall is only two feet high it may in fact be partially buried as I discovered with the Mission Peak segment of wall, but the fact that it is two feet high and laid in a straight line. This has led some to point out that it is directly aligned towards Mt. St. Helens in Washington State but this has not been explored.

So the mystery deepens as we now have a 50 mile long wall with a separate series of walls in Marin leading to another set of walls in Pt. Reyes. To say that is a massive engineering project is somewhat of a misnomer. The construct a series of walls, complete or broken, of that magnitude would have taken a large manual work force probably decades to construct. To allocate resources for such a massive undertaking would also require an equally massive need, something beyond simple celestial alignment or ritual structures.

The interesting thing is that the story does not end there. I also recently came across a rather interesting series of articles about a mysterious wall located in the Shasta Valley. This wall would be located North and East of the Tomales

The walls of the East Bay traverse some 50 miles in a straight line from the Carquinez Strait to San Jose, and in some places another 20 miles inland to Mt. Diablo. They are generally six feet high and so far have defied explanation.

Point structure, but is again of similar design. Roughly six foot walls which seem to stretch on for miles across the valley. What makes this even more interesting is the fact that these walls exist in a fairly remote mountainous, and non Coastal Miwok, zone. In fact in a research study written about the area, the archeologist could find no apparent reason for these walls to have been constructed.

"While it is conceivable that the reason for these stone fences being constructed in the valley proper lies with the obvious need to clear some of the rocks off the land in order to plant crops, the need for fences within the foothills and more mountainous regions is not so readily apparent." ("Archaeological Explorations in Shasta Valley, California", by Hamusek, Blossom, Eric W. Ritter and Julie Burcell, for the California Bureau of Land Management in 1997).

The interesting thing is that the rock walls are not confined to just the San Francisco area, or to just the Shasta are but are actually located throughout the northern part of the state. They stretch, in groupings, south to Fresno and North to the Oregon border. The walls also seem to exist in concentrations, many times around hills or some central landmass. This is also consistent with the East Bay Walls which originally started this line of research. In the case of the East Bay Walls, the wall takes a move inland towards Mt. Diablo, which is the dominant landmass of the area as well as ringing several small hills along the way.

If the East Bay Walls or any of the wall complexes are taken independently they represent quite a mystery, but when taken in the larger context what appears to emerge is order and distribution. It is particularly telling in the region around the Sutter Buttes, which display a massive number of walls, which appear to ring the buttes themselves, but it's the geographical distribution of the wall complexes, which is most telling.

In the Bay Area the walls seem to ring the bay, one would imagine that the original unworn walls would have encircled the bay. In the Sutter Buttes the walls appear to extend out from the central feature and do indeed look like property divisions with fairly small areas enclosed by larger areas. In many ways it looks much like county lines but on a micro scale. This seems to indicate they would have been defensive or property boundaries, but the issue here is boundaries for whom? That is the true question here. This is especially interesting because the structures themselves seem to cross the boundaries of known indigenous groups and in some cases cross the boundaries between groups which had historically held a high level of animosity towards each other. This would also seem to discount the notion that native groups built these walls.

What has emerged from this exploration is the possibility of a heretofore unknown, large scale, and distributed culture. There appears to be several fairly large population centers where the walls seem to concentrate and divide less land. While in other lower population density areas there seems to be larger chunks of land divided up. This can be seen in the Sutter Butte complex vs. Burney Rock Lines. In the Northern area there seems to be another large complex in the area surrounding Mt. Shasta.

The interesting thing about the distribution of these large complexes seems to exist around large landmasses and to ring them. Another interesting element of this culture appears to be the propensity to ring bodies of water. This is seen at the Hog Hill location as well as in the Shasta complex.

So the fifty million dollar question is who built this? It would appear to be a distributed group since the construction technique is similar as well as the position of the geographic zones (around hills), with large concentrations around larger landmasses such as mountains then smaller groups around lower hills.

Who built these is something, which could be open for debate, but it would seem with such a geographic distribution the ancient Chinese would need to be ruled out since their fleet would not provide the population size for such a level of construction. The apparent age, based on samples examined at the East Bay Wall, would rule out European incursion since the samples inspected would indicate a settlement pattern hundreds of year pre-dating the Spaniards. It is also important that the relative age estimate is older than 400 years, but based on conversations the actual age is probably more in the 500 to 600 year range maybe even older. Further analysis is needed before a better dating of the rocks can be done.

This ancient, potentially pre-contact, civilization could also account for the persistent stories of Lemurian and survivors of Mu landing in California post cataclysm. There are stories dating back some time which seem to recall survivors

Whether the walls were built by Lemurians or some other pre-contact culture, better and more defined research needs to be conducted. It is disappointing that conventional archeology has refused to investigate a historical anomaly of this magnitude.

of a great cataclysm settling in California, especially around Mt. Shasta which also appears to have the highest density of these mysterious walls.

Whether the walls were built by Lemurians or some other ancient pre-contact culture this would appear to be the source of the story and begs for better and more defined research to be done. It represents a massive failure on the part of conventional archeology to not investigate an anomaly of this magnitude.

What we can see is a large population, geographically dispersed which had a fairly sophisticated concept of resource division as well as defense, but what is really interesting is the apparent lack of ruins in these areas. We can see the walls, we can see the concentrations, but there don't seem to be any other ruins. This would suggest either extreme antiquity meaning the ruins of the settlements are buried or that while this apparent civilization did build walls on a massive scale their structures were temporary or at least made out of non stone/non age resistant material such as stone. The third possibility is that the walls themselves are not the population centers but maybe agricultural centers with the bulk of the population living in settlements close by.

No matter which way you take the discussion there is an anomaly here which needs further intensive interest and investigation. Not enough has been done to understand the true nature of what has emerged as a lost civilization. Not only a lost civilization but fairly large lost civilizations which could pre-date European contact and could also account the long standing myths of Lemurians and survivors of a lost island in the Pacific and that is a story that has been in doubt for sometime by conventional historians.

Maybe they were Lemurians or maybe some unknown group built these structures, either way the mystery of the California Walls needs further exploration and still persists as a true enigma.

Chapter Three

Weird Stuff From the Sky

CHICKEN Little may not have had his facts quite straight when he assumed that the sky was falling when an acorn hit him on the head. However, to give Chicken Little a little credit, throughout our weird history there have been all sorts of unusual things falling from the sky.

As strange as it may seem, it has not been all that unusual for living things such as fish or frogs to be seen tumbling down during a rainstorm. Meteorologists normally attribute such sky falls as the end result of a tornado sucking animals up into the clouds. What they can't answer is why the tornados are so choosy as to gather up only one species of water critter, and why mud, sand and other debris is suspiciously absent during these incidents.

Assuming that little creatures such as fish and frogs can fall from the sky because of tornados, this does not explain the appearance of other, even weirder stuff that clearly does not belong in the sky. It seems that, at one time or another, practically everything at one time or another has been spotted falling from the heavens.

The July 24, 1851 edition of *The San Francisco Herald*, troops on the drill ground at the Benicia army station near San Francisco were showered with blood and pieces of meat, apparently beef. Specimens "from the size of a pigeon's egg up to that of an orange" were given to the post surgeon and he described some of the slices as being slightly spoiled, as if they had been left out in the sun too long.

The *San Francisco Evening Bulletin* reported that on August 1, 1869, flesh, blood and short, fine hairs fell from the sky over a three minute period and covered over two acres of Mr. J. Hudson's farm near Los Nietos California. The day was clear and windless, and flesh fell as fine particles as well as in strips from one to six inches long. It was also reported that flesh and blood had fallen in Santa Clara County some two months earlier.

One of the best researched cases of weird falling flesh occurred on March 3, 1876 in Bath County, Kentucky. According to Troy Taylor in his article *Mysterious Falls from the Sky*, flakes of meat fell from a clear sky over an area 100 yards long and 50 yards wide near the home of Mr. and Mrs. Allen Crouch, who lived two or three miles from the Olympian Springs in the southern portion of the county.

Mrs. Crouch was out in the yard at the time, engaged in making soap, when meat which looked like beef began to fall around her. The sky was perfectly clear at the time, and she said it fell like large snowflakes, the pieces as a general thing not being much larger, but some were as large as three to four inches. Particles of meat were found scattered over the ground and stuck to fences. The meat when it first fell appeared to be similar in appearance to beef and perfectly fresh.

Within a 10 minute period, a "horse wagon full" of meat fell over the area. Chickens and hogs devoured the substance with relish and "two gentlemen" who tasted it determined that it was either venison or mutton. Several large samples were gathered for study by a group of faculty members at Transylvania University. Other samples, collected by Alexander Tenney Parker (a freed slave living as the head of a household in Lexington), were shipped around the country. The scholars who received these samples shared their findings in several publications.

Mr. Leopold Brandeis, whose article appeared on the strange fall in a July issue of *The Sanitarian*, theorized that the alleged "meat" was nothing more than "nostic" – "a low form of vegetable substance." What was left unexplained was how it managed to fall from the sky.

A letter from Dr. Allan McLane Hamilton was posted to the *Medical Record*, saying that along with Dr. J.W.S. Arnold, Dr. Hamilton examined the material from the Kentucky meat shower under a microscope. The material was identified as being lung tissue from a human infant or a horse. According to the letter, "the structure of the organ in these two cases" was apparently "very similar."

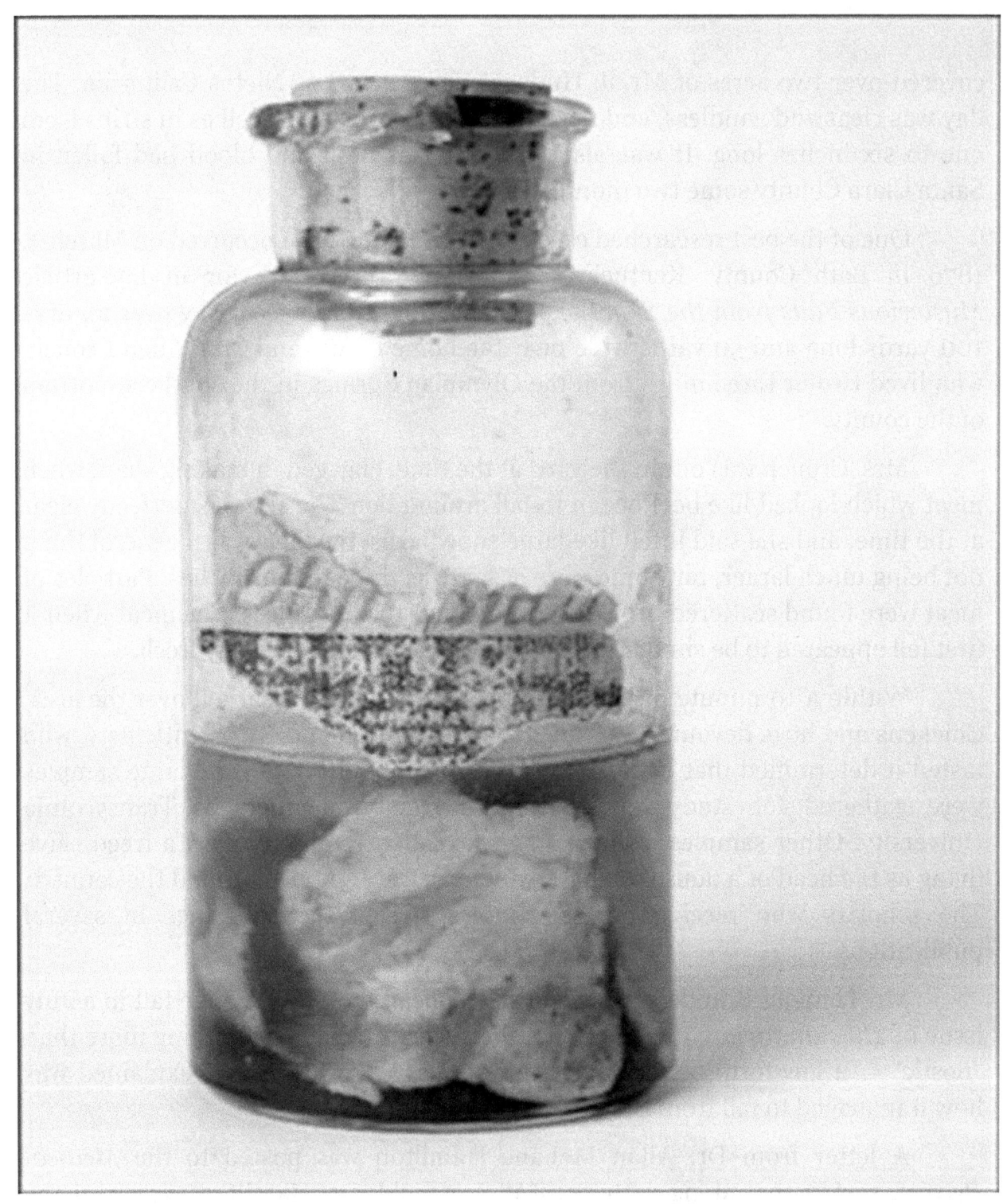

Tissue sample of the flakes of meat that fell from a clear sky at the farm of Allen Crouch, three miles south of Olympia Springs in Bath County, Kentucky

Locals believed that the meat was the result of "vomiting buzzards, who, as is their custom, seeing one of their companions disgorge himself, immediately followed suit." Be that as it may, it would take a lot of stuffed buzzards to be able to disgorge the amount of meat that fell over Bath County, Kentucky that day. As far as it can be said, there has not been a situation where people have actually seen buzzards engaging in such a case of mass heaving.

Not all things inexplicably falling from the clouds has to be as gruesome as the previous stories. On the nights of September 2 and 11, 1857, a shower of candy fell over some sections of Lake County Calif. According to **History of Napa and Lake Counties, Calif.** (Lyman L. Palmer), "It is said that on both these nights there fell a shower of candy or sugar. The crystals were from 1/8th to 1/4th of an inch in length and the size of a goose quill. Syrup was made of it by some of the lady residents of the section."

At one time the idea that rocks could fall from the sky was considered the stuff of fantasy and fairy tales. Now, it is known that outer space is full of cosmic debris raining down on us practically every second of the day. But how do you explain showers of stones that obviously originate from the far reaches of space?

On March 12, 1922, it was reported in the *New York Times* that rocks fell from the sky in Chico, California. They were reported to be "large smooth stones" that fell from the clouds and were warm to the touch. In the *San Francisco Chronicle*, it was reported in issues dated March 12 to the 18 that there were accounts of the stones falling for four months on and off. The storm of stones seemed to center on a warehouse located in Chico. The stones fell with enough force to break windows, crack boards and collapse roof shingles.

It was said that when crowds gathered on March 17th, a deluge of rocks fell upon the crowd injuring one. Reportedly, a large boulder came of out nowhere and struck a wall right behind the spot where Fire Chief C.E. Tovee and Traffic Officer, J.J. Corbett had been standing. It hit so hard, it dented the wood. The police could not come up with an explanation.

An eye witness, Miriam Allen deFord from San Francisco, went to investigate and saw the event take place. The quote reads, "While I was discussing it with some bystanders, I looked up at the cloudless sky, and suddenly saw a rock falling straight down. This rock struck the roof with a thud, and bounced off on the track beside the warehouse, and I could not find it. I learned that the rocks had been falling since July 1921, though no publicity arose until November."

Prof. C.K. Studley, vice-president of the Teachers' College, Chico, is quoted as saying: "Some of the rocks are so large that they could not be thrown by any ordinary means. One of the rocks weighs 16 ounces. They are not of meteoric origin, as seems to have been hinted, because two of them show signs of cementation, either natural or artificial, and no meteoric factor was ever connected with a cement factory."

Stephen Wagner, of paranormal.about.com, notes other examples of weird rock falls over the United States.

Harrisonville, Ohio, 1901 - The stone attack on this small village began on the Sunday afternoon of October 13 when, as the Buffalo Express reported, "A small boulder came crashing through the window of Zach Dye's house." No culprit could be found around the isolated house...and this was just the beginning. The next day, dozens of stones rained down in the heart of the village, breaking windows and striking citizens. Were mischievous kids to blame? The next day, all of the male children of the village were gathered together (how could girls do such a thing?), and stones fell for a third day. None of the villagers could detect where the stones were coming from.

Oakland, California, 1943 - In August of that year, Mrs. Irene Fellows finally called the police after two weeks of stones pelting her house at various times of the day. At first skeptical, the police inquiry became serious when their investigation clearly identified the pockmarks of the falling stones on Mrs. Fellows' roof and walls, and by the litter of stones on her lawn. Mrs. Fellows and members of her family were frequently hit by the stones, although to no serious injury. The thorough police investigation could offer no explanation for the stones, which seemed to materialize out of nothingness.

Skaneateles, New York, 1973 - Most often, a particular house is the target for this phenomenon, but in this highly unusual case, two fisherman became the victims of the falling stones - a paranormal storm that followed wherever they went! The rain of pebbles began as they were finishing their fishing expedition and followed them as they made their way to their car. The shower ceased for a while, then resumed when they stopped briefly on their way home. Deciding they needed a drink, they went to a bar, and when they came out some time later, the rain of pebbles began again. As they were about to go their separate ways in their hometown of Liverpool (about 25 miles northeast of Skaneateles), the little stones dropped on them one last time.

Arizona, 1983 - The attack on the Berkbigler family began in September, just as they moved into their new home. Large rocks crashed down on the house every night, usually between the hours of 5:30 and 7:00 p.m. The local sheriff's department could determine no assailant, even with helicopter surveillance. The authorities became reluctant to visit the Berkbigler home when they too were struck by the falling rocks. This went on for weeks, culminating on December 4 while two newspaper reporters were interviewing the family. Rocks slammed into the side door of the house for two hours. What's most mysterious here is that to strike this door, the rocks had to pass through the garage where a van was parked, through a narrow two-foot space.

Corn From The Sky

Since 1892, kernels of corn have been falling on houses along Pleasant Acres Drive in Evans, Colorado, just south of Greeley. Gary Bryan, who lives there, says, "I'd probably have a ton of it if I picked it all up." Once in a while a pinto bean appears amid the corn.

The problem is that there are no cornfields near the houses, and the nearest grain elevator is five miles away. Nobody can figure out where the corn could be coming from. All the witnesses can say is that from time to time it is seen falling from the sky.

When the press heard the story in September 1986, reporters from the area newspapers and television channels came to the site and saw the bizarre phenomenon for themselves. As the corn was falling, they searched for a prankster with a slingshot but found none.

People who hadn't seen the fall with their own eyes didn't believe it - until they saw it themselves. As one convert, Eldred McClintock, told the Rocky Mountain News, "It really came down. I've seen it now and I believe it."

Unidentified Hunk of Metal Hits Home

In Middletown, Ohio, according to the *Cincinnati Enquirer*, Kristy Blair and her 7-week-old son, Josiah, were half-asleep in bed on a Monday afternoon March 10, 2003, when a hunk of metal, larger than a softball, burst through their ceiling.

Crumbled plaster rained down. Startled and confused, Blair grabbed the baby and rushed out of the room. They avoided injury as the metal bounced from the bed and landed on the floor with a thud.

The unidentified object left a 6-inch-diameter hole in the ceiling - and a mystery that has involved the Federal Aviation Administration and even NASA. "We're holding it (the object) for NASA," said city Police Sgt. John Magill. "They'll come and examine it. They'll probably take it."

Blair, 27, laughed and said, "I feel like I'm in the middle of an X Files."

A police report gives this description: "some type of metal, silver or aluminum in color, having a circular hole through the center...damaged and possibly burnt with discoloration." That appearance, coupled with what appears to be the letters, "U.S.," make Blair and her husband, Scott, wonder whether the metal could have fallen from an aircraft - or if it could be space junk.

Golf Balls Over Florida

Local authorities were left baffled on Sept. 1, 1969, when a seemingly routine rainstorm got pretty weird and began depositing golf balls in the gutters, lawns and streets of Punta Gorda, Florida.

The St. Petersburg Times reported that "dozens and dozens and dozens" of golf balls fell from the sky, though no explanation was ever given. Located on Florida's western Gulf coast, Punta Gorda regularly experiences severe weather, which often causes waterspouts. The region is also home to many golf courses, so a logical explanation might be that a passing storm sipped up a ball-filled pond, then dropped its catch on the town.

Once again though, no explanation is given why a passing storm would only pick up golf balls leaving other pond debris behind.

America's Strange and Supernatural History

Falling Alligators

There are just some things that you don't want to experience falling from the sky. Snakes come to mind...a lot of people would be somewhat uncomfortable if spiders started raining down on them...but I think that practically everyone would agree that they would not want to be anywhere near a place where alligators would come plummeting out of nowhere.

On December 26, 1877, *The New York Times* reported the following: "Dr. J.L. Smith of Silverton Township, South Carolina, while opening up a new turpentine farm, noticed something fall to the ground and commence to crawl toward the tent where he was sitting. On examining the object he found it to be an alligator. In the course of a few moments a second one made its appearance. This so excited the curiosity of the doctor that he looked around to see if he could discover any more, and found six others within a space of two hundred yards. The animals were all quite lively and about twelve inches in length. The place whereon they fell is situated on high sandy ground about six miles north of the Savannah River."

A similar story surfaced in 1957, courtesy of writer John Toland, who wrote about the U.S. Navy airship Macon. In 1934 the Macon had participated in maneuvers in the Caribbean and was sailing westward on its return trip. As it was nearing California on the afternoon of May 17, the commander, Robert Davis, heard a loud splashing over his head from one of the ballast bags.

Concerned, he climbed into the rigging as the splashing grew louder and louder. He opened the ballast bag and looked in. Swimming around excitedly was a two-foot alligator. No one had any idea where it came from. They had been in the air for several days and it seemed highly improbable that this large, and now angry creature could have been with them all that time without being noticed.

The only possible explanation - though it made no sense at all - was that the reptile had fallen on the ballast bag from above.

Another tale comes from Mr. and Mrs. Tucker of Long Beach, California, who heard a loud thump in their backyard in 1960. Immediately following that, they heard a loud grunt. When the couple stepped outside, they were astonished to encounter a five-foot alligator. Their only conclusion, no matter how improbable, was that it somehow had dropped from the sky.

America's Strange and Supernatural History

A Rain of Insects

In a letter printed in the 1932 edition of *Science Magazine*, John Zeleny described how in a in 1897 he observed a luminous, cumulus-type cloud that drifted over Hutchinson, Minnesota from the east.

"It shone with a uniform, steady, vivid, whitish light and passed directly over the town," Zeleny wrote. "When the cloud was overhead, a great shower of insects descended to earth covering the ground all around to the number of about 50 to 100 per square foot."

Upon examination, the insects proved to be a common type of bug of the species hemiptera. This is an order of insects most often known as the true bugs, comprising around 50,000–80,000 species of cicadas, aphids, plant-hoppers, leafhoppers, shield bugs, and others.

A Rain of Fire

The universality of myths involving fire raining out of the sky is remarkable. Was it actual fire - or great heat as in a blast caused by a falling meteor? The Egyptian goddess Sekhmet, a variation on Isis and Hathor, specifically caused fire to fall out of the sky - somewhat like the Indian goddess Kali. The deprecations of Sekhmet seem to occur on the last memorable occasion in the time of Ramses III - and the sea peoples fled towards Egyptian territory (in the Levant as well as the delta) as a result of 'the flame of Sekhmet' - which is otherwise described as the star of Anath (which destroyed the Libyans).

The writers of the Bible loved to scare their readers with tales of an angry, vengeful God who, at times, would punish his flock by raining down brimstone and fire. In Genesis 19, God destroys Sodom and Gomorrah with a rain of fire and brimstone, and in Deuteronomy 29, the Israelites are threatened with the same punishment should they abandon their covenant with God. Elsewhere, divine judgments involving fire and sulfur are prophesied against Assyria (Isaiah 30), Edom (Isaiah 34), Gog (Ezekiel 38), and all the wicked (Psalm 11).

An interesting side note, the breath of God, in Isaiah 30:33, is compared to Brimstone: "The Breath of Jehovah, like a stream of Brimstone, doth kindle it."

America's Strange and Supernatural History

Volcanic eruptions can certainly make it appear that fire is falling from the heavens themselves. Meteorites can also lend credence to that particular concept with occurrences such as the Tunguska event, or the great meteor blast over Chelyabinsk, Russia on February 15, 2013 that damaged hundreds of buildings and injured more than 1,000 people.

The Great Chicago Fire of 1871 has gone down in history as one of the greatest disasters in the history of the United States. Yet, there has been no satisfactory explanation on the cause of the fire. Pop culture puts the blame on poor old Mrs. O'Leary's cow for knocking over a lantern and setting her barn on fire. But, what has been forgotten is the fact that Chicago wasn't the only victim of the unforgiving fires that started on October 8, 1871. Peshtigo, Wisconsin, over 200 miles to the north of Chicago, was destroyed by wildfires along with a dozen other villages. Estimates of those killed range upward from 1200 to 2500 in a single night.

Large areas in Lower Michigan were also destroyed, killing hundreds and leaving thousands homeless. *The Detroit Post* on Oct. 10, 1871 reported, "In all parts of the state, as will be noticed by our correspondence during the past few days and also today, there are numerous fires in the wood, in many places approaching so near to towns as to endanger the towns themselves."

The fire destroyed the city of Holland, Michigan, and in Lansing, flames threatened the agricultural college. In the upper part of Michigan, farmers trying to establish homesteads tried diving into shallow wells to escape the "The Fiery Fiend." Many did not escape.

Fires threatened Muskegon, South Haven, Grand Rapids, Wayland and reached the outskirts of Big Rapids. A steamship passing the Manitou Islands reported they were on fire.

Most historians point to the dry weather of the summer and the poor logging practices of the day for creating conditions ripe for a hot dry wind from the southwest that blew into the area whipping up small fires already smoldering and carrying destruction throughout the region.

In 1883, Ignatius Donnelly, author of **Ragnarok: the Rain of Fire and Gravel,** suggested that in early historic times our Earth suffered great catastrophes from cometary intruders. To this claim he added: "There is reason

America's Strange and Supernatural History

The Great Chicago Fire, October 1871

to believe that the present generation has passed through the gaseous prolongation of a comet's tail, and that hundreds of human beings lost their lives." He was referring to the conflagration of 1871.

Robert Wood, a retired McDonnell-Douglas physicist, takes Donnelly's theory a step further by suggesting that fragments of Biela's comet, discovered in the early 1820s, possibly caused the fires. Biela's Comet was only the third comet ever proven to be periodic, joining Halley's Comet and the less well known Comet Encke. Unlike the 76-year gap between Halley's Comet sightings, Comet Biela came around once every 6.6 years, and it was named for Baron Wilhelm von Biela, an officer in the Austrian army who determined in 1826 that a particular comet was the same one that had been observed in 1772 and 1805. He successfully predicted the comet's return in 1832.

The comet was next spotted in 1845, but was observed to have split in half. Comet A and Comet B were seen one last time in 1852, but then they both vanished, never to be seen again despite searches in 1859, 1865, and 1872. Biela's Comet became suspect as the true cause of the 1871 fires. The timing wasn't utterly impossible - October 1871 would have been a bit of an early return for Comet Biela, but not totally beyond the bounds of possibility. This theory was probably helped along by the comet's previous close approaches to Earth, which had triggered some panics about the comet actually hitting Earth - one 1877 newspaper illustration in Chile rather offhandedly captioned that there would be an "inevitable impact of the Earth with Comet Biela."

Robert Wood theorizes that small pieces of frozen methane, acetylene or other high combustive materials from what was left of Comet Biela hit the Earth sparking the fires that simultaneously devastated Chicago and parts of Minnesota, Wisconsin, Michigan and Ontario. Wood cited eyewitness reports of spontaneous ignitions and "fire balloons."

Wood's theory is certainly controversial. However, the characteristics of the fires are so abnormal that from the very day they occurred they have been considered mysterious. Stone buildings were reduced to calcinated ash. One large house was observed to burst into flame and rise 85 feet in the air on its own updraft. Large numbers of victims had no burns or injuries; they simply suffocated in the oxygen-less air. The largest number of survivors escaped into the woods. A total of nine towns in four Wisconsin counties were essentially exterminated at the same time. In one town of 260, the death rate was 100%, no one survived.

In Chicago, a "solid wall" of fire advanced "upwind" in the face of a 40 mph wind, buildings, blocks from any visible flames, burst into flame instantaneously, and ingots of iron stored on the banks of the Chicago river downtown melted and ran into the river (requires temperatures in excess of 2700 degrees F).

Mel Waskin, who at one time was the creative director of Coronet/MTI Film & Video, in his book **Mrs. O`Leary`s Comet!**, says the story about Mrs. O`Leary`s cow is a lot of bull, and agrees with Robert Wood that a much better explanation for the conflagration was Comet Biela.

"A comet, "he says, "is a dirty snowball. It`s basically a rock surrounded by hard-packed snow and ice containing a lot of frozen gases. What probably happened was that chunks of frozen gases broke away from the main body of Biela and were heated to their gaseous states as they plunged through the atmosphere, fueling existing fires or igniting new ones."

Waskin says that there are enough strange, documented events and coincidences that happened in October, 1871 to make it a very convincing possibility that a comet was responsible for the mysterious rain of fire.

Whirlwinds of Fire

During the great 1871 fires, numerous reports came in of "whirlwinds of fire," great spinning pillars of fire that stretched hundreds of feet into the sky, destroying everything it their path. Fire whirls come about only under specific conditions, a combination of air currents and temperature. A fire on the ground forms a whirl which can rapidly reach great heights, though mercifully most never last for long. Just like a tornado, the fire rises in an almost vertical rotating column.

However, the strange and supernatural history of the United States shows that fire tornadoes can occur without any apparent source of combustion. It is almost as if the tornado spontaneously heats up and ignites all on its own.

Symond's Monthly Meteorological Magazine reported that in Tennessee "...a remarkably hot day in 1869...a sort of whirlwind came along over the neighboring woods, taking up small branches and leaves of trees and burning them in a sort of flaming cylinder that traveled at the rate of about five miles per hour, developing size as it traveled. It passed directly over the spot where a team of horses were feeding and singed their manes and tails up to their roots; it then swept towards the house, taking a stack of hay in its course. It seemed to increase in heat as it went, and by the time it reached the house it immediately fired the shingles from end to end of the building, so that in ten minutes the whole dwelling was wrapped in flames. The tall column of traveling calorific (i.e. energy) then continued its course over a wheat field that had been recently cradled, setting fire to all the stacks that happen to be in its course. Passing through the field, its path lay over a stretch of woods which reached the river. The green leaves on the trees were crisped to a cinder for a breadth of 20 yards, in a straight line to the Cumberland River. When the 'pillar of fire' reached the water, it suddenly changed its route down the river, raising a column of steam which went up to the clouds for about half-a-mile, when it finally died out. Not less than 200 people witnessed this strangest of phenomena."

Another interesting case occurred in Americus, Georgia in 1881, as reported by the *Marietta Journal* on July 28: "Mr. Zack T. Baisden gives us the following story of a whirlwind that visited his place about 12 o'clock on Monday, scaring all his hands and some visitors very badly. A whirlwind occurred in a twelve acre cornfield that was about four feet in diameter and sometimes a hundred feet high. The body of it was perfectly black, with fire in the centre and emitted a strong, sulphurous vapor that could be smelt three hundred yards from it. The whirlwind would divide into three and move rapidly over the field, twisting up the corn stalks by the roots and carrying them up. These three minor whirlwinds would then come together with a loud crash, cracking and burning and shoot high up into the heavens. Three young ladies who were visiting Mrs. Baisden went in about 150 feet to observe it, but received such a shower of burning sand upon their face and necks that they ran affrighten to the house. Mr. Baisden says that he cannot account for this strange phenomenon, and it certainly frightened all who saw it. The strange part was that it contained fire, yet did not appear to burn the corn that it did not tear up, and its sulphurous vapor sickened and burnt all who got close enough to get a full breath of it."

In the book, ***The Evidence for the Bermuda Triangle***, a couple by the name of Wingfield, encountered something strange while they were on a fishing trip in Florida. About four miles off Boca Raton, Florida, Jean Wingfield noticed a stream of smoke along the horizon. Thinking that a ship was on fire, they rushed towards the source, only to see that it was not a burning ship, but a column of thick smoke and fire, roaring up from the surface of the water, high into the sky. The smoke was an odd, yellowish colored and was odorless. Even more bizarre, the strange phenomenon was completely silent. After they watched it for some time, the smoke and flames gradually subsided.

Ball Lightning

One aspect about whirlwinds/tornadoes is that they are usually highly energized with electricity and are accompanied by fantastic displays of lightning. Lightning has long been a source of fear and mystery. It is violent, unpredictable, and potentially deadly. It was often seen as an indication of divine judgment or displeasure. Lightning is better understood in modern times, but there are still aspects of lightning that remain a mystery. Take for example ball lightning, an exceedingly rare phenomenon in which luminous balls of energy suddenly appear, move about erratically, and in some cases, cause injuries or even kill.

The September/October 1985 issue of *Science Frontiers* reported that in the summer of 1977, Patricia Townsend of Haymarket, Virginia, was standing in front of her kitchen counter talking on the telephone.

"Several things happened at the same time and the whole incident probably lasted no more than a few seconds at the most. While I was on the phone, I heard a tremendous crack, something like the report of a high-powered rifle or the sound of a bat hitting a baseball. At the same time the outside of my house, meaning the outdoors, lit up brilliantly. A split second later or perhaps at the same time, I heard a loud swooshing or hissing noise and the phone seemed to come alive in my hand. Then my whole kitchen lit up like a floodlight. Lightning or electricity or whatever it was seemed to flow rapidly from the open kitchen door across the expanse of the far end of my kitchen at ceiling level. Almost at the same time as the lightning zoomed across my kitchen and the phone started vibrating in my hand, a large red ball (with yellow and white somewhere) appeared in front of me and hit me on the chest with the force of a large man hitting me with his fist. I fell to the floor and I believe the phone was still in my hand. I'm still not sure if I was knocked unconscious or not. I couldn't

Ball lightning has been reported to appear during violent storms for centuries. The phenomenon has generally been described as being a luminous sphere and there are a number of reports of ball lightning injuring or even killing people and setting buildings on fire. Pictured is a 1901 depiction of ball lightning.

swear I was and couldn't swear I wasn't. The ball hit me with the accompanying sounds of smacking and crackling, kind of like a string of firecrackers being set off."

The telephone was dead and Townsend suffered chest pains for several days. The ball seemed to be made of a soft burlap-type surface with a fuzzy texture. Almost exactly a year later, June 21, 1978, Townsend was once again in her kitchen during a thunderstorm when a fireball entered the kitchen. It was about a foot across with jagged yellow and white edges. It hit Mrs. Townsend in the face, with the sensation being like a slap with an open hand. The ball possessed a surface like that of a textured fabric as before. The witness collapsed and when recovering found herself with slurred speech and neck pains. She soon regained full faculties and health.

Another case of human/ball lightning interaction occurred in 1960, when Louise Matthews of South Philadelphia reported that while she was lying on her living room sofa, she glanced up to see a large red ball of fire come through both the closed window and the venetian blinds without harming either. At first Matthews thought that an atomic bomb had fallen, and she buried her face in the sofa. But the ball of fire passed through the living room, into the dining room, and drifted out through a closed dining room window. Matthews said that it made a sizzling noise as it floated through her house. And she was able to exhibit visible proof of her experience: As the ball of fire had passed over her, she had felt a tingling sensation in the back of her head. Her scalp was left as smooth and clean as her face.

Ball lightning has sometimes been used as an explanation for reported cases of spontaneous human combustion. John Abrahamson, a chemical engineer at the University of Canterbury in Christchurch, New Zealand, says that ball lightning could account for some cases of spontaneous human combustion.

"This is circumstantial only, but the charring of human limbs seen in a number of ball lightning cases are very suggestive that this mechanism may also have occurred where people have had limbs combusted," says Abrahamson. (*New Scientist*, December 2001, "Ball lightning scientists remain in the dark," by Hazel Muir).

In their 1969 book, **The Taming of the Thunderbolts; The Science and Superstition of Ball Lightning**, authors C. Maxwell Cade and Delphine

Davis, site several instances of spontaneous human combustion being connected to ball lightning. In one incident, a man was awoken at about 5:00AM by the screams of his wife who was in their living room. He ran to her and found her lying on the floor, burning fiercely, while a blazing ball hovered above her. The man was badly burned while he attempted to put out the fire. Calling for help, those who came to assist him poured buckets of water over the woman, but sadly, this was to no avail because she soon died in the hospital.

A similar fatality dates from 1886: "At Crawford, Indiana, on August 9, during a slight shower, a ball of fire was seen to enter the window of a house occupied by one of the most prominent citizens of the town. Shortly afterwards, Mr. Riley was observed lying on the floor, his body was burnt almost to a cinder and unrecognizable. A black streak was traced upon the carpet from the window to the fireplace, in which line the body was found. The family, who were sitting outside the house, witnessed the ball of fire enter the window and apparently disappear up the chimney."

At the close of this chapter we are left puzzled to the fact that weird things does fall from the sky...where as far as we know, there shouldn't be weird stuff in the sky to begin with. Charles Fort in his **Book of the Damned**, speculates, with his tongue firmly planted in his cheek, that perhaps high above the Earth is a "Super-Sargasso Sea," a region somewhere above this earth's surface, in which gravitation is inoperative, a place where things caught up in storms and hurricanes stay up indefinitely, but may, after a while, be shaken down by storms.

Fort's explanation is as good as any as this point. So watch your head when you venture outside...you never know what strange beastie or hideous madness may suddenly fall upon you.

Chapter Four

Mysterious Fumes! Poisonous Gas Warfare From Outer Space?

"**OFFICE** Workers Sickened by Mysterious Gas." "Fumes From Meteorite Crater Have Sickened 600." "Fumes From Corpse Cause Evacuation." News reports from all over the world have shown a drastic increase in cases in which people are sickened and harmed by mysterious gases. Many reports have come from seemingly common, normal buildings and schools. Dubbed "sick buildings" by the press, explanations on the causes range from chemicals used during construction, to mass hysteria.

All across the U.S. recent suicides using household chemicals and the possibility of terrorist attacks using poisonous gas has focused attention to the frightening scenario of gas attacks on large population centers. However, little attention has been paid to the evidence that mysterious fumes have already been responsible for sickening hundreds, maybe thousands of innocent people. Reports of unexplained gas attacks go back a number of years; some seem to indicate a disturbing connection with the frequency of attacks and an increase of UFO sightings.

One of the more familiar cases of reported gas attacks was the 1944 series of incidents in Mattoon, Illinois. However, there have been other, similar cases, such as the gas attacks of Botetourt County, Virginia in 1933. These episodes have been completely written off as classic cases of mass hysteria. However, there were elements to these cases, most notably in the form of physical evidence, that have been repeated constantly in the mysterious fumes and gas attack reports that continue to this very day.

America's Strange and Supernatural History

Cold War Fears and Flying Saucers

Starting in July 1950, reports of UFOs associated with mysterious fumes began to trickle in. The July 1 edition of *The Cincinnati Post* ran the front page headline, "Saucers whirl over city."

"Flying saucers were reported over Cincinnati at widely separated points. At least three reports were received around noon. The first saucer was sighted around 11 a.m. by Mrs. Katherine Willis at 25 Murray Road, St. Bernard, and her daughter, Beverly Ann. A few moments later, Jack Earls of 4713 Paxton Road, reported seeing saucers over Mt. Lookout and Lunken Airport. Control tower operators at the airport said they saw no saucers, and nothing unusual.

"Saucers also were reported at the same time by a Mt. Washington resident. 'Beverly saw it first and watched it for about two minutes,' said Mrs. Willis. 'It was white, way up in the sky, and I could tell that it was spinning,' said Mrs. Willis. 'I couldn't tell how high it was. It looked like it was going as fast or faster than the airplanes.' In the past two days, flying saucers have been reported by officials in Cairo, Ill., and Louisville, Ky."

The reports of UFOs coincided with reported low-flying aircraft leaving a noxious exhaust, causing an outbreak of mystery fumes throughout the Cincinnati area. The press at the time did not make the obvious correlation. The *Cincinnati Enquirer* reported on July 9th a similar incident in Illinois.

The *Cincinnati Enquirer's* headline reflected the Cold War fears that were on the minds of everyone during the decade. "Only a horrible nightmare. Fears of Russian gas bombing arise when foul odor from passing truck spreads through seven towns near Moline, Ill." The article goes on to report that a foul smell choked seven towns, sending some residents into hysterics and raising fears of a Russian gas bombing.

The noxious odor crept through Moline, East Moline, Silvis and Rock Island, Ill., and then spread across the border into Muscatine, Bettendorf and Davenport, Iowa. No injuries were reported aside from upset stomachs. Some residents, in hysterics, called police. One man insisted to Silvis police that "the Russians are flying over and gassing us."

The evil-smelling fumes routed citizens from the beds and from taverns, almost forced the closing of two farm machinery factories, jammed police

Photograph of UFO emitting a gaseous contrail taken on July 19, 1951, in the Madre de Dios section of Peru. UFO researcher Jim Moseley was given a print of the photograph by agricultural engineer Pedro Bardi. The Project Blue Book report by Col. McHenry Hamilton, Jr. states that the photograph is a hoax created for "commercial reasons."

switchboards and kept firemen on a near-emergency basis. An official of the Iowa-Illinois Gas and Electric Co. said the odor probably resulted from a leak in a tank of Pentalarm being hauled through the area on a truck headed west. He said the truck was seen passing through Moline shortly before midnight. Pentalarm is an odorant used to inject a smell into natural gas, normally odorless, to permit detection of leaks. The official said the odor is not injurious but can cause nausea.

Several taverns in Silvis and East Moline lost their patrons in a hurry when the smell entered. Some 20 persons jammed the East Moline police station. Police at Muscatine, Iowa, said anxious citizens jammed the switchboard with calls. Some became hysterical and left town. Others just closed all their doors and windows and tried to go back to sleep.

In Moline, a reporter said, "The police are being run ragged, calls are coming in from all over the town, and the squad cars are going all over the place. People are heading for the high ground away from the river." The smell was strongest in the lowland areas along the Mississippi.

The utility company, flooded with calls, dispatched more than 30 repairmen to find what was first believed to be a leak in a gas main. The men hunted for three hours but found no leaks. Authorities at the Rock Island arsenal said, "Everything is in order here," in response to queries on whether the smell might have originated there. The smell lingered in the Illinois area for three hours, then hit the Iowa cities. It disappeared at daylight.

Subsequent attempts to locate the mysterious leaking truck failed. Some residents said the gas was nothing like the smell of Pentalarm. The gas they smelled was incapacitating, and felt like, "the air was being sucked out of the lungs." On July 7th and 8th, newspaper and police switchboards were flooded with reports of UFOs flying overhead. The Moline/Davenport area also had an unusually high amount of UFO reports during the week of the 8th.

The Return

Sometimes the mysterious fumes inexplicitly return years later to the same location. *The Cincinnati Times-Star* reported on October 24, 1949 that mystery fumes that gave off an offensive odor in south Reading, Ohio, damaged paint on more than 100 homes and made at least three persons ill. The article also reported that silverware in the affected area was strangely tarnished by the gas.

An 18 to 20 block area was affected by the fumes, whose odor was described as "like rotten eggs" and like "a burning brake band." Police Chief William Martin and Safety Director Harry Veddern said there was no evidence of the source of the odor. Martin added that he would have, "a chemical analysis made of the rain drippings from an affected house."

Officials at the Carlisle Chemical Works, which has a plant in southeast Reading, told city officials they did not believe their plant was responsible and offered their facilities to assist in the investigation. The odor was first reported to police at 3:00AM by patrolman William Appenfelder, who was cruising in south Reading. He told the dispatcher "the smell is so strong I can hardly breathe."

Newsmen said the paint on houses in this area apparently had dissolved, and was washed away by the rain. They noted that spots not struck by the rain appeared unaffected. Most serious damage was at the home of Mr. and Mrs. Charles Ringo, 219 Reading Road, where the south side of the house was left entirely bare of paint. Another resident, Mrs. George Bradford, 266 Burkhardt Avenue, said the side of her house looked as though "it was plastered by a mud shower."

In the same neighborhood forty-seven years later, on April 18, 1996, The *Cincinnati Enquirer* reported that a mysterious odor caused the evacuation of a local plant. About 600 Employees at the Hoechst Marion Roussel Inc. complex were ordered out shortly after noon when an odor was detected there and at the nearby Standard Textile Co. plant.

Toni Sweeney, spokesperson for Hoescht, said workers reported smelling propane or sulfur, and the building was evacuated as a precaution. Employees were kept outside for about an hour, she said. After firefighters arrived, they and members of Hoechst's Environmental Safety and Health Team toured the facility and found no source for the odor. Tests found no levels of dangerous chemicals or gases.

Mrs. Sweeney said the smell probably originated outside the plant, particularly because it was also reported at Standard Textile, east of Hoechst. "It may have been brought in through the ventilation system," she said.

Another strange gas incident happened at 11:30 PM, October 13, 1996, according to a WLW radio news update. The odor was detected in the Lockland region. The complaint originated from an area around the business, Office Depot. Eleven people were treated at the scene during the early morning hours. Lockland Fire Dept. Captain Bill Welchans said that there is no explanation for the fumes. All industries initially thought responsible were ruled out, and Welchans stated that there were no industrial operations within the vicinity of the odors.

Sick Buildings

The phenomenon of "sick buildings" has some people worried that a new, though subtle form of terrorism is taking place. An alarming increase of UFO sightings in the same areas as reported sick buildings has lead some investigators to suggest that there could be a connection. More mundane explanations such as chemicals used during construction, to outgassing from new carpets have taken the brunt of the blame when mysterious fumes are reported. However, air checks usually can find no trace of any potentially hazardous chemical or gas to account for the strange symptoms reported by stricken individuals. Other, less credible attempts at an explanation generally leans towards cases of mass hysteria, or workers suffering from the "blue flu."

In Margate, Florida on April 7, 1997, a grocery store was forced to close because of a strange gas that made at least 30 ill. Officials say about 100 people were in the store when workers and customers began complaining of sore throats and watery eyes. Hazardous materials investigators say noxious fumes that caused the apparent respiratory problems among store customers had dissipated by the time they arrived, making it difficult to trace their origin.

Of the people who complained about symptoms, 11 were taken to area hospitals, but all were released following treatment for what were described as "minor" problems. Some customers said the fumes smelled like chlorine, while others described them as smelling like pepper.

Tamarac, Fla., Fire & Rescue Battalion Chief Dennis Peloso said the varied descriptions made it difficult to determine the source of the smell. "We've checked for chemicals, gas, Freon. We looked at the refrigeration system. Nothing," said Peloso, who called the negative tests "a little weird."

Schools also seem to be a favorite target of "sick building syndrome." On January 14, 2008, St Helens, Oregon High School was evacuated after students and faculty fell ill after noticed a strong odor like "rotten eggs." Nearby, people at the local Safeway store, and at the bank, also became ill. Several people had to be treated for nausea, dizziness, burning of skin and eyes, and respiratory complaints.

After some initial speculation that it was a natural gas leak, it was finally determined that it was, instead, a mystery. There was no leak anywhere on the school grounds, and chemical sniffers detected no natural gas. Local officials promised to look into the matter, but no investigation was ever conducted.

Mysterious fumes circulating through a classroom in Jamaica triggered a school evacuation and sent five children to the hospital gasping for breath, on January 25, 1997. Traces of the fumes were detected inside Room 315 of PS 37. Children were complaining of headaches, chest pains, watery eyes and breathing difficulties, Fire Department spokesman Luis Basso said.

Taking emergency precautions, the Fire Department evacuated the building immediately. Basso said 25 people from Room 315 - 23 children and two adults were treated at the scene for inhaling the mysterious fumes. Five of those were taken to a nearby hospital for further treatment.

Superintendent Celestine Miller of Community School District 29 said she did not know the exact source of the children's discomfort. However, the investigation by environmental authorities and the city Health Department was unable to trace any hazardous materials released into the school environment.

So far no explanation has satisfactorily answered the questions concerning the causes of "sick building syndrome." If the culprit is a mélange of "common" chemicals, then air tests should have found the suspected contaminants. The same goes for deliberate gas attacks. Air tests should be able to determine what the fumes are. There is also no good reason for the fumes to suddenly appear, and then disappear just as quickly. Chemicals in the carpet or in the structure of the building would leak slowly and evenly into the atmosphere. Making it easy for modern air check systems to find and fix the cause of the problem. Easy answers however, are not forthcoming.

Unknown "Fumes" Sicken Wal-Mart Customers and Employees

A "mysterious illness" that caused nausea, vomiting, and upper respiratory issues caused the evacuation and shut down of an entire Wal-Mart shopping center in Pennsylvania on February 12, 2013, and officials still have no idea what caused the strange event.

Firefighters from Center Township were called to the store at around 7:00 PM after both employees and customers began vomiting and having trouble breathing. Wal-Mart employees believed the cause of the odd event was emanating from the grocery section, roping it off from customers before the sickness began overtaking the rest of the store.

Center Twp. Fire Chief Bill Brucker mentioned feeling his airways close up when called to investigate, but couldn't explain it.

"I wasn't back there long before I started to feel something in my throat," Brucker told the Beaver County Times. "I couldn't pinpoint a smell or a cause, though."

At least two customers were affected so badly that they were rushed to the hospital in ambulances, with at least another three driven by car.

When the firefighter's own air quality tests didn't turn up anything odd, they called in the county's hazmat team who also came up empty handed, though Brucker wondered if that might have anything to do with the fact that the store's air conditioning had been reversed to filter the air by the time the team had arrived.

Not too long afterwards the store re-opened without any further incidents of unexplained sicknesses. Wal-Mart did not issue a statement, and no medical test results from those who fell ill were ever released.

"I don't know if we'll ever find out the cause," Brucker said.

Around the same time as the Wal-Mart incident, several faculty members from a school in Shawnee, Oklahoma started to experience strange symptoms while in the building, but reasonable explanations for the sickness were never pinpointed.

"I think it raises alarms when you have more than one experiencing problems," Shawnee Superintendent Dr. Marc Moore told Oklahoma News 9.

The issues came to a head at a January 11 meeting where teachers all began to complain of a "different kind" of headache, dizziness, and a "fogginess" clouding their minds, leaving them a tired mess when they get home from work.

The first thing the faculty did was call in the air quality testers from Oklahoma Natural Gas to check for leaks, but when they came up empty handed, they moved on to installing carbon monoxide detectors. Those, too, came up clean.

"If it is something here, we're doing everything we can to find it," said Taylor.

The school employees believed the source of the strange sickness emanated from the kitchen, however, just as mysteriously as it appeared, the cause quickly vanished.

The mysterious fumes made another appearance in February, 2013 when residents of the Autumn West apartment complex in Bangor, Maine began complaining of a "God awful" smell that they couldn't quite put their fingers on. Some thought it smelled a bit like burning rubber, others like a kind of musty, dirty smoke. One resident, Laurie Baker, even began to notice strange symptoms that coincided with the appearance of the odors; a sunburn-like skin rash appeared all over her body and her dog, Bella, began to experience respiratory problems.

The strange smells and their accompanying side effects eventually got so unbearable that many of the renters had to be evacuated to a local hotel.

Both the police and local fire department were called out to the location on separate occasions, and while the air tests showed elevated levels of ethanol or other chemicals often found in "clandestine laboratories" (read: meth labs), each investigation came up empty handed for a source of the mystery fumes. The housing authority and an air quality testing company have also conducted their own tests which have yielded similar dead ends.

"I wish we could have found something," housing authority director Mike Myatt told The Bangor Daily News. "We're hoping that it's resolved quickly and that we can get these people back in their homes."

Mystery Remains Over Fumes That Sickened 60 People

In Springfield, Massachusetts, over 60 people were sickened and 10,000 workers and students were forced to evacuate a two-block area when mysterious fumes blew through the western Massachusetts city on Thursday, May 29, 1986.

People fell to their knees complaining of dizziness, shortness of breath and nausea. Eight people were hospitalized for the night, including a young man who suffered seizures.

Officials were uncertain what tests to perform on blood and urine samples taken from those who were stricken, said Dr. John Santoro, chief of emergency medical services at Baystate Medical Center.

"You can't put them in a magic machine and get an answer. We need some clues from the chemists working on what the possible toxin was," he said.

Officials examined sewer lines for substances that could have reacted after being dumped down different drains, investigated an old supermarket being converted into offices, sampled air and looked into an old refrigeration system inside the store for possible ammonia leaks. None of these has yielded any clues, they said.

The fainting spells began at about 10:00AM Thursday in the first floor of the old grocery. Two employees of Kavanagh Furniture Co., which rents part of the building, fainted.

Authorities said they could find no connection between Thursday's events and a report two weeks ago from city workers who said they smelled a strange odor while planting trees in front of the store.

"It's possible that we may never identify the source," said Robert Terenzi, a member of a state environmental emergency response team.

America's Strange and Supernatural History

Georgia McDonald's Toxic Fumes a Deadly Mystery

Fire officials in Pooler, Georgia were stumped about what toxic chemical or chemical mixture knocked two women unconscious and sickened eight others at the local McDonalds restaurant on September 7, 2011. One of the women, Anne Felton, 80, of Ponte Vedra, Fla., died after going into cardiac arrest. Firefighters administered oxygen to Carol Barry, 56, of Jacksonville, Fla., before she was admitted to a Savannah hospital, Pooler Fire Chief G. Wade Simmons said.

"Every one of the 10 people that had some sort of symptoms...had been or were in that restroom," Simmons said.

No one anywhere else in the restaurant was affected.

Among other confounding aspects of the case was how quickly the gas disappeared. "It was there, and then it was gone in the next hour to hour and a half we were doing things at the scene," Simmons said.

By the time a Savannah hazardous materials analyzed air samples from the restroom, they found nothing detectable.

That left law enforcement officials and toxicologists to speculate about what the victims might have inhaled, and how it ended up in the women's room. "We've heard everything from terrorist attacks to carbon monoxide to sewer gas to God knows else," Simmons said.

Much of the speculation centered on the possibility that the women were sickened by a noxious combination of cleaning chemicals. Labels on toilet bowl cleaners, drain openers, window and glass sprays and scouring powders usually caution against using more than one product at a time.

Simmons said that based on employees' routines at the Pooler McDonald's, workers would have cleaned the women's room early in the day, before serving up Egg McMuffins to the morning breakfast crowd. But the initial report of someone choking didn't get called in until just before noon, further deepening the mystery of why people suddenly became ill so much later. None of the products on the cleaning cart had spilled, he said, and the cart wasn't even near the bathroom when patrons began developing symptoms.

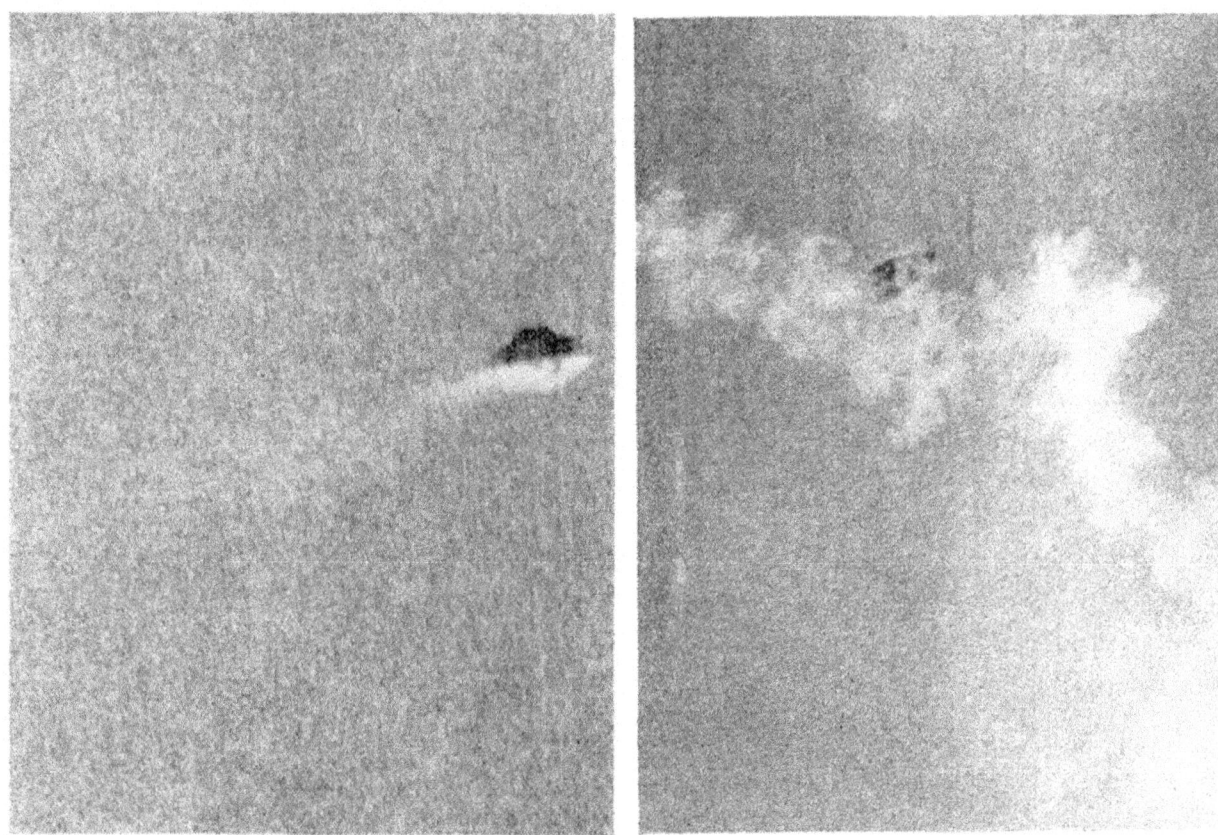

Namur, Belgium, picture set taken by the "Belgian repairman" on June 5, 1955. The witness stated that he saw the object arrive swiftly in the area and then slow down to a hover. The UFO looked to be silvery grey and had four "legs" on its underside. The witness took photographs as the craft emitted a gaseous vapor trail and slowly sank towards the ground. Finally, the object rose up and passed through its own trail, disappearing into the sky.

"Cleaning chemicals are common culprits in bathrooms," said Dr. Kelly Johnson-Arbor, a medical toxicology specialist at Hartford Hospital in Connecticut.

"Perhaps the people in the bathroom mixed together bleach and ammonia," which would produce chloramine gas, an irritant. "It doesn't usually cause people to die, but if it's in a high enough concentration and/or the person had underlying cardiopulmonary disease (such as asthma), it could certainly be potentially fatal."

Despite all of the possible explanations, no cause for the gas was ever determined.

Toxic People

The case of Gloria Ramirez remains one of the most baffling events in modern medicine. On February 19, 1994, 31 year old Gloria Ramirez, who had been recently diagnosed with cervical cancer, fell ill at her home in Riverside, California. Her family comforted her as she began to vomit and her condition worsened. In the evening, they called for an ambulance.

Ramirez was brought into Riverside General Hospital's emergency room at 8:14 p.m., suffering with severe cardiac distress. Her blood pressure was dangerously low because her heart was beating too rapidly, a condition highly unusual in someone so young. The ER staff administered drug treatment and pumped air into Ramirez's lungs. When her heartbeat suddenly began to falter, they tore open her shirt to use defibrillation paddles. Nurse Sally Balderas recalls seeing an odd, greasy film on Ramirez's skin, like a puddle of oil on pavement. Some witnesses recalled a scent similar to ammonia that suddenly began to fill the air.

Registered nurse Susan Kane drew a blood sample from Ramirez, and she immediately noted a strong odor coming from the syringe. She handed the syringe to respiratory therapist Maureen Welch, who sniffed it and reported an ammonia smell. Welch in turn gave the syringe to medical student Julie Gorchynski, who observed specks in the blood which have been described as "white crystals" and "manila-colored particles."

America's Strange and Supernatural History

Within seconds of drawing the blood, Kane collapsed. Trying to maintain consciousness, she complained of burning pains on her face and was taken away on a gurney. Soon after, Gorchynski reported lightheadedness and then passed out. She had severe difficulty breathing and was the most severely affected member of the ER staff. Dr. Mark Thomas next felt ill, although he was able to remain standing. Welch was the third to faint, thrashing her limbs involuntarily on the ER floor. Nurse Sally Balderas experienced a burning on her skin and began to vomit. Balderas spent ten days in hospitalization, while Gorchynski, remained in intensive care for two weeks. Out of 37 ER staffers present, 23 reported an affliction of some kind. The total number of complainants would later reach thirty-two.

Dr. Humberto Ochoa, emergency room director, ordered an evacuation of all patients from the ER as he continued the effort to save Ramirez. He and three other staffers remained well enough to continue the struggle for the better part of an hour. In fact, Ochoa never felt ill at all, and could smell nothing unusual. Unable to revive her, Ochoa pronounced Ramirez dead at 8:50 PM. Her body was sealed in an airtight bag and left for the Riverside County hazardous materials team and the coroner's office to investigate. However, it would yield no easy answers.

From the start, the truth of the Ramirez incident has been clouded in confusion. In the instant media frenzy, some news reports blamed Ramirez's chemotherapy as a possible catalyst for the toxicity, when in reality she had never undergone chemotherapy. The first investigation into the Ramirez case came from the Riverside County hazardous materials (HAZMAT) team, which arrived at the scene two hours after Ramirez's death. The HAZMAT team tested the air in the ER and in other parts of the hospital for poisonous chemicals, and found nothing.

An autopsy was also inconclusive. Led by Riverside coroner Scotty Hill, a team of pathologists conducted the examination inside airtight contamination suits. They collected blood and tissue samples, as well as air that had been sealed in Ramirez's body bag. Apparently mystified by the case, Hill did not announce the autopsy results until April 29, 1994, over two months after the fact. The official cause of Ramirez's death: cardiac dysrhythmia as a result of kidney failure, which had been brought on by her cervical cancer. Hill had found no identifiable toxic substance that might have played a role in her death or in the illnesses of those present in the Riverside General ER.

As for how toxic fumes may have originated from Ramirez's body, no reasonable explanations have been suggested. The most complex theory, albeit a highly controversial one, comes from the Lawrence Livermore National Laboratory in a California. Livermore investigators found that Ramirez's body contained a high concentration of the harmless compound dimethyl sulfone. Its presence may be explained; they felt, by the use of DMSO, a common folk remedy for ailments such as cancer pain.

With two oxygen atoms added, dimethyl sulfone becomes dimethyl sulfate, an enormously deadly chemical. Livermore offered the theory that such a reaction had occurred within Ramirez's body, resulting in the mystery fumes.

Most scientific authorities call the Livermore hypothesis impossible. Dimethyl sulfate causes eyes to tear, does not take effect immediately upon exposure, and would most likely cause death, none of which was true of the alleged Ramirez toxin. Furthermore, proper conditions for dimethyl sulfone to gain two oxygen atoms do not exist in the human body. To add to the confusion, the Ramirez family denied that she had ever used DMSO.

The official explanation issued by Riverside County Department of Health, and the one most widely accepted, is that the incident was the result of "mass hysteria." Given the lack of a physical explanation and the inconsistent reactions of those present, stress and anxiety were judged the true source of the spontaneous afflictions. This mass hysteria could have been triggered by an incidental odor in the environment, such as cleaning chemicals or smelling salts.

Two of the stricken ER staffers, Dr. Julie Gorchynski and Maureen Welch, forcefully objected to this conclusion. Dr. Gorchynski in fact suffered from a degenerative condition to her knees after being contaminated by the mysterious fumes. She also suffered from breathing difficulties, muscle spasms and other symptoms. "I had chemical burns in my throat and nose," Gorchynski told reporters. "My lungs are working at half capacity, biopsies show my knees are dead, there has been a drop of my enzyme levels and crystals in my blood as well, and it's all medically documented. You don't get these kinds of symptoms from mass hysteria."

Possibly in deference to Gorchynski's $6 million lawsuit pending against Riverside County, the health department later revised its opinion to state that Gorchynski, Welch and Sally Balderas were in fact not casualties of mass hysteria. Ultimately, there have been no conclusive answers to the Ramirez case, and for the time being at least, it will continue to remain a baffling medical mystery.

A week after the Riverside incident there was another outbreak of mysterious fumes at the Mercy Hospital in Bakersfield, California. The emergency room was evacuated after doctors inserted a breathing tube in the trachea of a 44-year old woman suffering with shortness of breath. As at Riverside, emergency room personnel noticed a gaseous cloud rising from the patient. They complained that a potent chemical odor originating with the patient's blood left them with burning eyes, nausea and headaches. Fortunately, no serious injuries resulted from the exposure.

What could be the cause of the mystery fumes? Can we blame modern industry for their continued use of dangerous chemicals? Should we point a finger at the strange reports of UFOs that seem to coincide with an increase of people sickened by strange unknown gases? Or is the human mind to blame, with doctors and other health professionals assuring the panicked populace that the shortness of breath, vomiting, paralysis, unconsciousness, and long term physical damage is nothing more than mass hysteria?

The mystery continues.

Chapter Five

Who Was The Mad Gasser of Mattoon?

FOR two years, Scott Maruna has researched leads, interviewed witnesses and pored over every bit of information he could dig up on the Mad Gasser of Mattoon. He has studied police reports, pondered newspaper accounts and constructed criminal profiles.

"I think I have been almost obsessed with this case for a long time," Maruna said. "I have probably read everything ever written about the Mad Gasser of Mattoon."

After countless hours of hard work and investigation, Maruna said he has made some startling discoveries, unlocking secrets surrounding the case that have been buried for the last sixty years.

Maruna, said he has uncovered the true identity of the Mad Gasser of Mattoon, and while the name of the gasser may come as no surprise to some long-time Mattoon residents, he believes most people will be shocked by what he calls "the other half of the story."

According to Maruna's book, ***The Mad Gasser of Mattoon: Dispelling the Hysteria***, the real mad gasser was not an escaped Nazi, a crazed ape-man or a figment of the imagination, as many other publications have reported over the last several decades.

Instead, Maruna's theory suggests the gasser was actually a well-known resident of Mattoon – someone from an influential family who had a grudge against many area residents and desired revenge against a town that would not accept him.

That person, according to Maruna's book, was Farley Llewellyn, the son of a grocer who was considered "a pillar of the community." Although his father was highly respected, Farley never "fit in" to the Mattoon community.

"When I spoke with people who knew him, the same words would keep coming up over and over – odd, different, recluse, loner," Maruna said. "Although he was highly intelligent and excelled in school, no one ever really understood him."

When Farley returned to Mattoon after attending the University of Illinois as chemistry major, Maruna's sources report that he became even more introverted and distant.

Spending most of his time in a full-scale cellar chemistry laboratory on his family's property, Farley began drinking heavily. Only days prior to the first mad gasser attack, one neighbor recalls an explosion that resulted from one of Farley's experiments in the secret lab.

Maruna said he has no doubt that the explosion occurred while Farley was testing the gas he would later use to torment local residents. "I believe his true motive was to blow up the town," Maruna said.

Maruna, a Jacksonville chemistry and physics teacher who grew up in Charleston, said the gas Farley used could have been nitromethane, a sweet-smelling, clear and highly volatile liquid that can cause nausea, burning of the mouth, swelling of the lips and minimal eye irritation.

Because nitromethane evaporates quickly, little to no evidence would often be left by the time police arrived at the scene of the attacks. Following almost all of the attacks, victims described the gas as smelling "sweet," with one person comparing it to the smell of cheap perfume.

It was not long after the gasser attacks began during the first week of September 1944 that Farley became a suspect. In fact, Maruna said many Mattoon residents told him that they knew Farley was the true mad gasser all along. Why, then, have police and others remained silent for so long?

"It was purely out of respect for Farley's family, primarily his father," Maruna said. In fact, it is only because all members of the Llewellyn family are now dead that many area residents are finally willing to speak out.

America's Strange and Supernatural History

September 2, 1944, edition of the Mattoon Daily Journal-Gazette described a mysterious attack by an "Anesthetic Prowler" the previous evening

In addition, Maruna said a "twist" in the case cast a shadow of doubt on police suspicions that Farley was the mad gasser. Farley was placed under constant police surveillance following the first several gassings, however the attacks continued to occur, baffling police and giving the appearance that Farley was innocent.

Maruna believes that, in an attempt to clear their brother's name, Farley's two sisters, Florence and Katherine Llewellyn, assumed the role of the mad gasser for the final series of attacks.

According to Maruna's book, the later gassings became sloppier and were markedly different from the earlier attacks. While Farley had preyed on couples and families during the early gassings, his sisters targeted younger victims, often single women.

The final victim of the gasser reported that her sons chased the culprit down a back alley behind her house and later found a set of footprints under the window where the paralyzing gas had been sprayed - prints that were made by a pair of women's high-heeled shoes.

Although Farley was no longer considered the prime suspect in the case, the Llewellyn family placed him in a state mental institution following the final mad gasser attack, where he lived out the remainder of his life. The Llewellyn sisters were never considered as suspects and remained in Mattoon until their deaths.

So there you have it, the truth is finally out – at least one version of it. "That is what I love so much about the mad gasser case," Maruna said. "There are so many opposing viewpoints and I think there is a little bit of truth to all of them."

Not too long after Maruna's book was published, he heard from several individuals throughout the country about similar suspected gas attacks in their family's or town's history. Maruna believed most of the stories could be easily explained through natural phenomena or industrial error, but one story stood out. He sat on the story for a couple of years, not certain as to what to do with it.

The Fortean world is by now well familiar with the "Mad Gassers" of:

* Mattoon IL, 1944

* Botetourt County, VA, 1933-34

America's Strange and Supernatural History

* Coatesville, PA, Feb. 1, 1944
* Canastota, SD, early 1950s
* Houston, TX, 1961
* Strongsville, OH, 1962...

However, a new and significant addition to that list needs to be made. This story was sent to Maruna by Lee Holliway, now of Florida. It is a telling from his family history: The West Bainbridge, GA "Gas Man"

There was a full moon Nov. 30, 1944, and there was record cold toward the end of November, so the first gas attacks probably began Dec. 4-5 and lasted through Dec. 14-15. Following are the names of the principals:

* W. D. "Will" Dean, late 40s and in poor health. He died in 1948 of kidney problems. At the time of the incident, he worked on the local military training base (Bainbridge Army Air Field) where he checked employees & visitors in and out of some facility on the base.

* Edna Dean - his wife, age 44 at the time. She was working on the assembly line at a local factory that produced packing crates for the military.

* James A. Dean, son of Will & Edna, born Oct. 27, 1927 (died June 21, 1998). He had just turned 17 at the time of the "gas man" incident. He was attending West Bainbridge High School and working part-time in the packing and shipping department of the factory where his mother worked.

* Elefair Poitevint, Edna's mother, age 67. Her husband had died in 1937 and she took turns living with her three children. She was suffering from pellagra (a niacin deficiency caused by a diet high in corn products and common in the South at that time), but looked after two or three children of women who were working at the military base and/or the factory. One of the children, was a member of the Allen family who were victims of the mad gasser.

* Myrtie Dean, 14-year-old daughter of Will & Edna, but, at the time of the attacks, she was living with female relatives in another part of the county where she helped with housework, etc. while the man of the house was overseas.

America's Strange and Supernatural History

* Addie Poitevint and Claudia Poitevint, nieces of Edna "Poitevint" Dean, around 13 & 11 at time of incident. Their parents lived in a neighboring county, way out in the country, and the girls were visiting in order to go Christmas shopping. They arrived by train and James met them at the depot to help carry their bags the several blocks to the house. (People didn't mind walking a few blocks back then and even if they owned automobiles, gasoline was rationed.)

* Norman Dollar (early 40s) was working on the military base and living with the Deans. (It was common for people to share houses during the war.)

* Vedah Dollar (early 60s). Mother of Norman. Vedah cooked and kept house. Everyone else in the house either worked or attended school. Hazel Dollar (6-or 7-years-old), daughter of Norman.

Incident: Norman, Vedah and Hazel Dollar traveled by train to visit relatives for Thanksgiving. There was a record cold that November, but after a few days, it was fairly warm again and everyone was sitting on the front porch after supper when they heard screams coming from down the street. Naturally, everyone went out into the street to try to see what was happening. Other people had also come out of their houses and Dean, Dollar, James and an elderly man who lived next door, walked down the street. There, they learned two women and some children had smelled something sweet that made them sick while they were sitting at the kitchen table having supper. No one thought much about it.

The following day, the family learned a woman and her elderly father had also gotten sick from smelling something sweet. In this instance, the woman was in bed asleep and was awakened by the sweet smell which made her ill. Concerned about her father, she opened the adjoining bedroom door and his room was filled with the same odor. She got him out of bed and out into the backyard where they were both sick.

Of course, the entire neighborhood was talking about what happened and I remember my grandmother saying "somebody had sprayed gas in through the window screens," so I don't think there was any doubt the kitchen window of the first house and the two bedroom windows of the second house were at least partially open.

America's Strange and Supernatural History

I think the first incident must have been in the earlier part of the week because by the weekend of Dec. 8-10, when Addie and Claudia Poitevint arrived, the entire neighborhood was in a panic. I'm sure there were some false reports because everyone was alarmed and some people may have imagined smelling a sweet substance, but as with the Mattoon incident, I think most reports were genuine.

In addition to the two attacks the first night, other incidents—before Addie and Claudia arrived—included, among others, a woman and her granddaughter and an elderly couple and their middle-aged, mentally-handicapped son. All those attacked were either female, elderly, a child, or disabled. Of course, most able-bodied men were away fighting but not a single incident occurred in a house that included an able-bodied man or teenage boy, i.e., someone who could come out and chase the attacker.

By the time Addie and Claudia arrived, Mrs. Dean was keeping all the doors inside the house open at all times and had candles burning throughout the night. (The candles probably weren't such a good idea if, indeed, someone was spraying gas into houses.) People were also apparently closing their windows at night because there were reports of gas being sprayed under doors (houses in warm, humid climates aren't always well-constructed), through broken windows, and through small openings around water and gas pipes, etc.

I'm not sure how many attacks occurred prior to the weekend, but I gather there had been at least six or seven. On Friday night after Addie and Claudia arrived, following supper, the entire family walked several blocks, or farther, to what was either a small carnival or some type traveling show. I remember this particularly because there was a gypsy fortuneteller there who told Addie she would marry twice and have seven children—she did. The fortuneteller must have been quite good because everything she said apparently came true and everyone talked about it for the remainder of their lives. However, while they were at the carnival, or whatever, Mrs. Dean developed a headache and realized she didn't have any aspirin in her purse and she, Mrs. Poitevint and Vedah Dollar decided to leave.

There weren't any streetlights (this was during a time people had blackout shades in their houses and lights were discouraged because people feared being bombed by the Japanese and/or Germans). As the three women passed what my grandmother always referred to as "the woods" on the way home, Vedah said she heard someone walking behind them. (I always imagined the situation something like one sees in the movies where a person hears footsteps behind him and when he stops, the footsteps also stop.) Whether anyone was actually following them or not, I don't know—perhaps they just scared themselves—but they started running. I remember my grandmother saying, "Ma couldn't keep up and we kept having to stop and wait for her." I think they ran at least two or three blocks because according to what I was told, they were all out of breath by the time they got home and collapsed on the front steps. While they were sitting on the steps, all three heard footsteps and the screen door to the back porch opening and closing. Naturally, they were afraid to go into the house and instead ran next door to the elderly neighbor's house where they remained until the others arrived home from the carnival.

After everyone went to bed and was, apparently, asleep, Addie, who was sleeping on the living room sofa, was awakened by the front porch swing creaking. Assuming a cat had jumped up onto the swing, she thought nothing of it and was just about asleep when she was startled awake again, this time by a noise outside the window. Then, she saw what she always described as a "shadow" move across the window and she screamed. Dollar and James, who were sleeping in the "front bedroom" right next to the living room, jumped out of bed and ran outside in their pajamas but did not find anything.

On that same night, a woman awakened by her barking dog went out onto the porch and saw what appeared to be a man wearing dark clothing running between her house and that of her next-door neighbor. Concerned, she grabbed a rifle, went next door and awakened her neighbors who were convinced there was gas in the house even though they did not become ill. Perhaps the attacker was scared off before he had a chance to spray more than a very little gas through the window.

It was the following afternoon that people of the neighborhood got together and decided to patrol the streets at night. I think, but am not absolutely sure, they met at a nearby church. Some of the men had guns, some had baseball bats, and some carried "loaded sticks" (a wooden walking cane in which a hole is bored and filled with lead to make it exceptionally heavy at one end).

Norman Dollar had such a stick. Even though men were walking the streets, the Moore family returned home from the carnival and smelled something sweet inside the house. They all left and went to a house where there was a telephone—I don't think many people in the neighborhood had phones—and called the sheriff. However, by the time a deputy arrived, if there was any gas in the house, it had dissipated and nothing was found. To my knowledge, this was the only time the sheriff was called to investigate any of the gas attacks.

It doesn't seem the street patrols were much of a deterrent because there were several attacks afterward, including the attack on the Allen house where one of the children Mrs. Poitevint looked after lived. The incidents leading up to the attack on the Allen house are interesting. Shortly before the attack, while Mrs. Dean and Vedah Dollar were cooking supper early one evening, Mrs. Poitevint and little Hazel Dollar walked to the Allen house to trade sugar for coffee (sugar and coffee were rationed and people often bought one and then traded it for the other).

I believe my grandmother, a coffee drinker, traded almost all the family sugar allotment for coffee and used sugar cane syrup for sweetening. As they were leaving the Allen house, Hazel thought she saw someone watching them from the bushes and—afraid to get close to whatever was hiding and return to the Allen house—they ran home screaming. Mr. Dean was sleeping on the sofa before starting patrol duty which began at 8 p.m., so the incident probably happened around 7 p.m. Mr. Dollar and James hurried to the Allen house and thoroughly checked the house and yard. Nevertheless, later that night, the gasser attacked the Allens.

There were no menfolk in the Allen household and the night following the attack on the family, Mrs. Poitevint and James began spending the night with Mrs. Allen and the children. I always had the impression Mrs. Allen was a young woman, probably no more than in her 20s, which would explain why Mrs. Poitevint felt compelled the stay there at night. The gas, or whatever it was, didn't have any permanent effects but made people ill. One person who suffered an attack told my grandmother the gas smelled sort of like the sickly sweetness of the banana shrub (michelia figo), a plant with exceptionally fragrant creamy yellow flowers, which I have seen growing only in the South. Its scent gives a lot of people a headache. One woman, I don't know which, who was attacked by the gasser, told people that after smelling the gas, she vomited and had a headache that wouldn't go away for the next two days.

According to my uncle, while the men were taking turns patrolling the streets, he, another boy about his age, and Norman Dollar, caught a glimpse of what appeared to be a man in the yard of a house where a woman and child lived. The other boy entered the yard from the street while Mr. Dollar and James ran around the other side of the house. I had not thought of it before, but this particular house must have been close to the "woods" because my uncle said whoever it was must have run into the woods. Although Mr. Dollar and James only saw "movement" in the yard, the other teenager claimed he shined the light onto the attacker who turned toward him before running away. Unfortunately, he couldn't identify the man except to say he had "strange-looking eyes." Norman Dollar always claimed the boy told him it was "like looking into the eyes of the devil." (Although I think Mr. Dollar had a tendency to exaggerate, the boy may have very well said this.)

The last attack—or at least the last reported attack— took place a few days after Addie and Claudia left. They stayed only for the weekend, so it must have been the following Wednesday or Thursday. I'm not certain of which was the final attack, but one of the last attacks involved an elderly woman and her two adult daughters. One of the daughters was in a wheelchair from polio and the other (whose husband was away in the Army) had two or three young children. I recall this incident particularly because they had difficulty getting the wheelchair-bound lady out of the house quickly and my uncle said she had vomited all down the front of her clothes. While James and others were helping the three ladies and children, Dollar and a neighbor went into the house. When they came out, they said it was "full of gas" and the following day, Dollar had a headache which he attributed to whatever was in the house. The foregoing attack would have likely occurred between midnight and 2 a.m. because I recall my uncle always saying he and Dollar went on duty at midnight. I believe Mr. Dean, who wasn't in good health, was always on the 8 to 10 p.m. watch.

As I mentioned before, there was a lot of speculation as to who or what was responsible for these attacks. I believe most people thought it was either the Germans or some new gas the military was testing. However, there were those, including Mrs. Poitevint and Norman Dollar, who apparently believed the attacker might be supernatural in origin. Remember, Dollar was present when the boy identified the gasser as having "strange-looking eyes" and instead of running into the woods, Dollar always claimed whatever it was "disappeared into thin air."

Scott Maruna finishes this amazing account by noting: "The fact that this story seems to have been ignored by the major media outlets of the area is not all that surprising in that it follows so closely on the coattails of Mattoon 'Gasser' incident being labeled as a case of 'hysteria' (a shameful term at the time). The town of Mattoon was ridiculed nationally (even world-wide) for their claims of a 'gasser' and the West Bainbridge area may have feared similar retribution."

Sources: *The Journal Gazette and Times-Courier;* Biofort/Scott Maruna

http://biofort.blogspot.com/2006/10/mad-gasser-of-west-bainbridge_24.html

Chapter Six
Return to Sleepy Hollow
By Timothy Green Beckley and Circe

RECENTLY, we deployed our company ghoul and likeable horror movie host Mr Creepo (aka "Mr UFO" - Tim Beckley) along with sexy vamp hunter and Creepo henchwoman Circe (or is that wenchwoman?) to check out rumors of a revival of paranormal activity in the dreamy village of Sleepy Hollow, New York, and neighboring Tarrytown.

Though our budget was small, the researchers managed to drink and eat – mainly drink—themselves into a tizzy as if possessed by glutinous spirits. Very much, we fear, like the early farmers whose wives accused them of "tarrying" to long on market day at the local tavern, thus the name Tarrytown was born. In any respect we present their - pardon the expression – "sobering" – report.

The cool autumn air sets in just before twilight and a breeze starts to drift in from the Hudson River, just down the road a bit from where legend has it Ichabod Crane was chased by the headless horseman.

Indeed, the bridge and adjacent brook where Crane soiled his pants in an attempt to run for his life still stands, albeit part of the main drag that goes through town, a road now used by truckers, buses and SUV's coming up from Manhattan a scant 40-minute drive away.

Many commuters unwilling to drive in the midst of quite ghostly (I mean ghastly) traffic take to the rails, hopping onboard one of the numerous commuter trains that make the trip from the Big Apple all day and well into the evening hours.

The cool autumn air sets in just before twilight and a breeze starts to drift in from the Hudson River...just down the road a bit from where legend has it Ichabod Crane was chased by the headless horseman. To quote Irving: "A drowsy, dreamy influence seems to hang over the land, and to pervade the very atmosphere. Certain it is, the place still continues under the sway of some witching power that holds a spell over the minds of the good people, causing them to walk in a continual reverie."

America's Strange and Supernatural History

Folding back the pages of the *New York Post* (we are much too blue collar to read the Times) and gazing out the window one would hardly guess that the area is particularly rich in paranormal lore. But as you pass White Plains and the office buildings start to diminish in height and number you can start to be thankful that Circe is your traveling companion as ghouls know well to leave her be. We figure it has to be the garlic in her bag, but she insists it is the lovely charms she makes and wears to ward off negativity and things that go bump in the night.

But, indeed the truth sometimes can be very strange. For it is along this very route to Sleepy Hollow back in 1982 that thousands craned their necks out of car windows to watch as a silent, giant, black-shaped triangle filled the sky, much like the cloak of the headless horseman is said to have done as the phantom glided through the thickets and glades of this same community in the early eighteen hundreds.

One of our first destinations was the Sleepy Hollow cemetery to visit some of the communities founding members. Circe (made infamous for her role of Muffy in my low budget vampire flix, "The Curse of Ed Wood") was perched on a tombstone while I frolicked with the angels near the grave of Washington Irving.

Switching into a serious mode, I remarked how I could recall numerous conversations with fellow researcher Philip Imbrogno whose book **Night Siege: The Hudson Valley UFO Sightings** fairly well documents the numerous close encounters in the area. I told Circe how Phil, a teacher by profession (strange, wasn't Ichabod Crane also a teacher?) had started out as a conservative investigator of unexplainable aerial phenomena only to end up photographing ghost lights and confronting time distortions (to find out more order my book **Our Alien Planet: This Eerie Earth** in the Conspiracy Journal bookstore). All within a few square rural miles of where we were now standing.

During the course of our investigation in the area, we drove over into Connecticut to hunt down giant Jack 'O' Lanterns known to be harassing residents near an outdoor farmers market. This was pretty much the same trek truck drivers had been on that fright filled night in 1982 when they rubbed 18 wheelers with a "thing" the size of a 747 that tailed them at less than a thousand feet in the air. Around the same time the mysterious men in black showed up to persuade witnesses to back off from telling of their encounters with the unknown.

The bridge and adjacent brook where Ichabod Crane soiled his pants in an attempt to run for his life still stands, albeit part of the main drag that goes through town, a road now used by truckers, buses and SUV's coming up from Manhattan a scant 40-minute drive away. One of our first destinations was the Sleepy Hollow cemetery to visit some of the community's founding members.

America's Strange and Supernatural History

Many similar tales exist from the time of Washington Irving who also spoke of nightmarish figures cloaked in black who staked those who dared discuss their own paranormal misadventures.

Those who have followed such matters will be able to confirm that often times places that have a reputation for being "haunted" have a long history of paranormal phenomenon.

Indeed, it was Circe that reminded me that Washington Irving had, himself, speculated on this very "coincidence" in his Legend of Sleepy Hollow tale. To prove her point, she cracked opened a copy of Irving's book just purchased at the Kyjuit gift shop on the Rockefeller Foundation estate, scene of the annual Halloween activities that tourists flock to this region along the Hudson every fall season.

To quote Irving: "A drowsy, dreamy influence seems to hang over the land, and to pervade the very atmosphere. Some say that the place was bewitched by a high German doctor during the early days of the settlement; others, that an old Indian chief, the prophet or wizard of his tribe, held his powwows there before the country was discovered by Master Hendrick Hudson. Certain it is, the place still continues under the sway of some witching power that holds a spell over the minds of the good people, causing them to walk in a continual reverie. They are given to all kinds of marvelous beliefs, are subject to trances and visions, and frequently see strange sights and hear music and voices in the air. The whole neighborhood abounds with local tales, haunted spots, and twilight superstitions; stars shoot and meteors glare oftener across the valley than in any other part of the country..."

One almost has to scratch their head in disbelief that this paragraph was written two hundred – give or take – years ago. It seems like something a contemporary ghost hunter like our pal Joshua Warren might write in one of his scripts for the Discovery Channel.

As we hunkered down for the evening – after hours of paranormal musings – we couldn't help but reflect on how the area seemingly abounds in the macabre. In fact, all around us were signs and symbols that a spooky October was in the works for the area just up the river from our vampiric crypts.

America's Strange and Supernatural History

The Great Jack 'O Lantern Blaze

Three thousand hand-carved pumpkins are the decidedly spooky backdrop for a spine tingling event set on the grounds of the 18th Century Van Courtland Manor. You might be a bit too scared to nip away at those pumpkin cookies or sip down that warming cup of hot apple cider, as you experience the SCARECROW AVALANCHE and PUMPKIN PROMENADE.

The Horseman Still Rides!

Join Jonathan Kruk for a lively reading and reenactment of the Legend of Sleepy Hollow at the Philipsburg Manor. For Legend Weekend (October 28-30) there will be candle lanterns and bonfires, and a haunted landscape to set the mood. Say doesn't that fellow with the crooked nose over there look like??? Nah, it can't be!

Sponsored by the Historic Hudson Valley Society, more information can be found at: www.hudsonvalley.org or for ticket information call 914-631-8200.

Where To Stay

Numerous bed and breakfasts dot the scenic area. The Doubletree right on the Hudson offers a breathtaking view, but we were stopped at the entrance by the burly ghoul in charge who informed us before we even had time to twist our heads around, that the palatial estate was being renovated and thus closed to all. So I guess even the Horseman won't be staying there on Ole Hallows Eve.

If your budget is up to it and you are looking for really lavish grounds, go ahead and plop yourself down on one of the beds at the Tarrytown House. The restaurant wasn't open when we where there so we had to venture out into the crisp autumn air. This slight inconvenience was offset by the use of the heated indoor pool (just call me Creepo the prune) and the fact looking out the window at around 3 AM I thought I saw a specter under the flood lights in back of the complex where we should have been fast asleep and not watching the SyFy Channel.

America's Strange and Supernatural History

Where To Eat

For lunch there is the Horseman saloon and the Sleepy Hollow Cafe (service is fine but if your seated outside you notice the sidewalk slants more than it does in one of those mystery vortex spots).

For about the best meal ever in an absolutely superb setting stop by Harvest-on-the Hudson in Hasting on the Hudson. Its right on the Hudson (boy isn't that repetitive) and outdoor dining for lunch will be a treat you won't forget for a long time. Lots of indoor seating as well, and a bar that goes on for miles (thank you, but we had our Bloody Mary's on the lawn).

Thus ended our little adventure...Being psycho – I mean psychic – I asked Circe about the vibes. She didn't appear to be scared out of her wits despite the traffic headed home, so I guess the spirits weren't as restless as they might have been.

So do we plan to return to Sleepy Hollow and Tarrytown to search for more spirits? It could well be that sometime in the not too distant future we might set up shop to film our own version of Sleepy Hollow – except it will be called CREEPY HOLLOW.

Chapter Six

An Unnatural History of Indiana

BECAUSE of its bucolic setting and undeserved reputation for being strictly agrarian, few people realize just how strange and unusual the state of Indiana can be. Lake monsters, reports of Bigfoot, anomalous big cats, UFOs and more, fill the hills and cornfields of the Hoosier state with a rich Fortean tradition. It's a shame that little attention has been given to these wonderfully weird stories of high strangeness in Indiana.

Located in the southern great lakes region of the United States, Indiana was once covered with a vast, shallow sea some 300 million years ago during the Paleozoic era. This sea was home to corals and other sea creatures that created the huge deposits of limestone reefs so valued today by builders worldwide. During the last ice-age, Indiana was almost completely covered with the Wisconsin glacial sheet that smoothed out the landscape resulting in the rich, flat farmlands we see today. The southern half of Indiana however, escaped the bulldozers of ice, leaving a hilly, forested terrain.

No one really knows when humans first encountered the lands that would later be known as Indiana, since no written history exists of this ancient period. Artifacts and physical evidence indicates that the first inhabitants of Indiana were an aboriginal people who relied on hunting and gathering to survive. These aborigines, commonly called "the Mound Builders" lived throughout the state, usually along rivers and streams.

These prehistoric people built a vast array of earthworks, primarily mounds, cones and ditches. Some can still be seen today in Mounds State Park near the city of Anderson, and the Angel Mounds state historic site in southern Indiana.

The Mound builders are commonly divided into four cultures: The Shell Culture (400-500AD), The Adena Culture (700-800AD), The Hopewell Culture (800-900AD) and the Middle-Mississippi Culture (1000-1200AD). The societies that built these impressive structures lived throughout Indiana, Ohio, Illinois, Missouri and Kansas.

Oral traditions of Native Americans who populated the area after the Mound Builders, state that these areas were part of a sophisticated civilization whose religious influence reached down into South America. Reportedly, a vast trail leading from south and Central America existed to enable pilgrims to journey to their spiritual Mecca located within the Mound Builders societies. In fact, recent evidence has shown that the earthworks had been built not as burial sites, as historians believed, but as religious sites aligned with various celestial bodies and events.

After the collapse of the Mound Builders society, much of Indiana became uninhabited, and was used by several Native American tribes as hunting areas. Permanent villages were not established in Indiana during this time because of legends of hairy, cannibalistic "wildmen" who allegedly lived in caves along streams and rivers. However, around the year 1170 AD, Southern Indiana may have been the final home to a group of Welsh explorers who died at the hands of hostile native Americans.

The Legend of Prince Madoc

Of all the legendary stories told of pre-Columbian visitors to the American continent, the story of Prince Madoc of Wales is probably the most fascinating. The Madoc tradition says that a colony of Welshmen immigrated to America in 1170AD and found their way to the Falls of the Ohio River in what is now Clark County Indiana. There they lived for many years before being routed from the area and almost exterminated in a great battle with "Red Indians."

Prince Madoc is believed to have been born at Dowyddlan castle between 1134-1142AD. His father was Owain Gwynedd who ruled Wales from 1137 until his death in 1169AD. Prince Madoc was reputed to be a brilliant naval commander during his father's reign, using his men and ships tactfully to repulse or devastate the seaward invasions that were sent by King Henry II. Julius Caesar had reported that the Welsh used large ships and were skilled navigators. Celtic vessels were able to travel on the open ocean and were far superior to Caesar's own Roman fleet.

Madoc supposedly made three expeditions to the Americas, reaching the South American coast sometime around 1165. Madoc's last expedition left Wales in the year 1170 and this voyage was recorded as lost at sea in the ancient maritime log of missing ships of Britain in 1171.

Prince Madoc might have faded into history had it not been for the curiosity of John Sevier, the first Governor of Tennessee. In a letter written to Amos Stoddard in 1810, Sevier wrote about his discoveries of ancient though regular fortifications extending up through Alabama and into Tennessee.

In 1782 he inquired about the forts to the ruling Chief of the Cherokee nation, Oconostota. The old Chief told Sevier that the works had been made by the first white people who came to their lands via the Gulf of Mexico, into what is now Mobile bay, and up the Alabama River. Sevier asked Oconostota if he knew from where these white men came and the Chief stated that "he had heard his grandfather and father say they were a people called Welsh, and they had crossed the Great Water in ships." The Welsh, or "White Indians" as they were later called, moved into the interior of the country using large tributaries and creeks. Along the way they built stone fortresses incorporating natural features to protect them from hostile natives.

The trail of the Welsh and their stone fortresses leads directly to the Falls of the Ohio, where, according to local traditions, the white Indians made their last stand against the attacking native Americans. A historical marker in Clarksville, Indiana reads: "A prehistoric Indian village site. According to legend, was peopled by white Indians, who descended from 12th century Welshmen led by Prince Madoc and destroyed by red Indians."

Since the early days of Clarksville, the Native Americans who lived in the area told arriving settlers that the "white Indians" were led by chiefs who were "yellow haired giants." They also said that when one of these kings died, the body was buried with great ceremony in a stone grave.

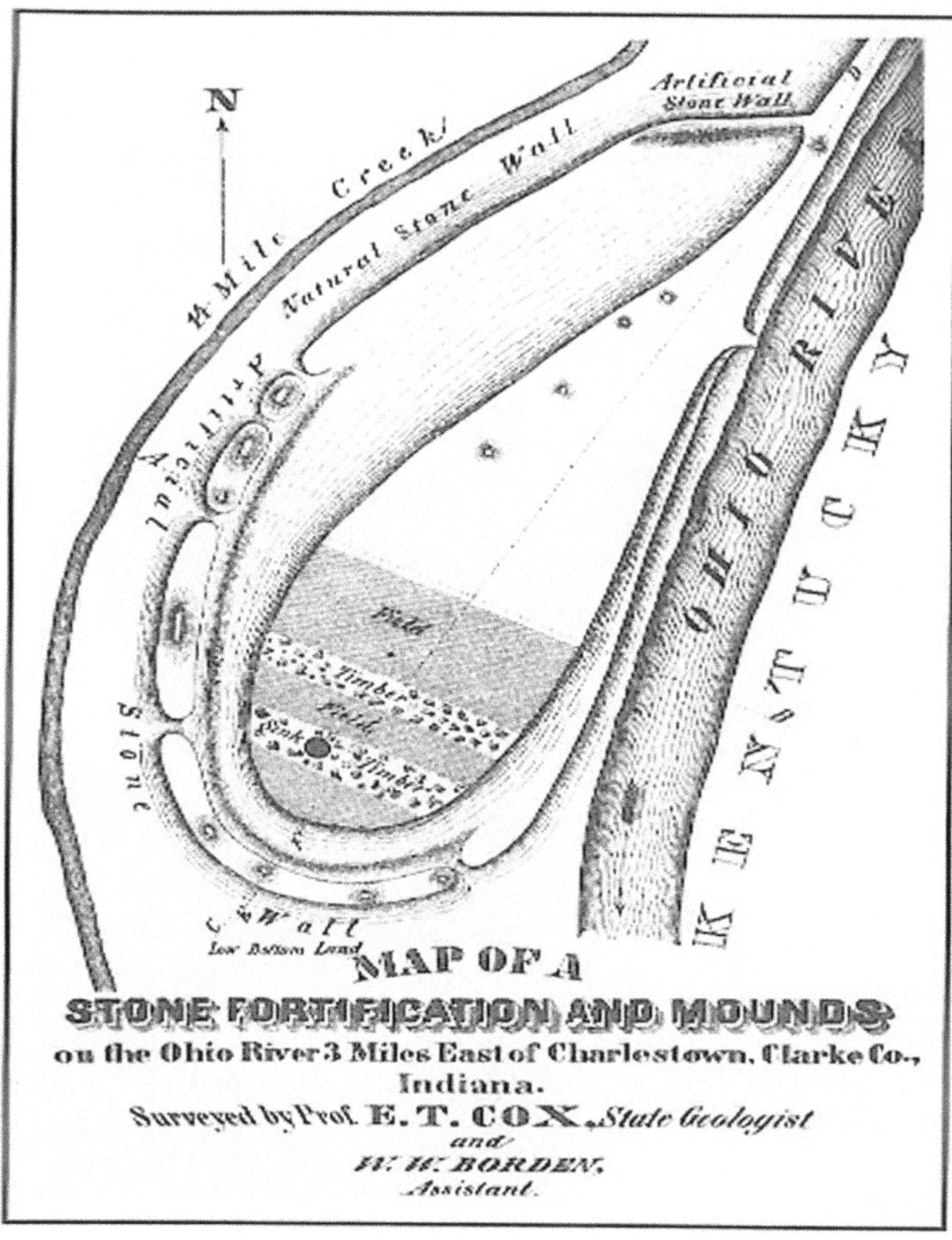

Madoc's proponents believe the earthen fort mounds at Devil's Backbone along the Ohio River to be the work of Welsh colonists.

America's Strange and Supernatural History

In 1898, a man named John Brady uncovered an ancient bronze helmet and shield in a vacant lot on the Kentucky side of the Falls of the Ohio. The helmet was found near a site where in 1799, six skeletons were found wearing brass breastplates adorned with the Welsh coat of arms.

Outside of Clarksville, an extensive graveyard of ancient origin existed on property once known as the Kelly farm. On this site, thousands of human bones were found. They had been buried in such a way as to indicate that the dead were left there after a battle, and that silt from flooding of the Ohio River had covered them as the battle had left them. These bones, all of large stature, were identified as "not Indian." Unfortunately, massive floods in 1907, 1913 and finally in 1937, completely washed out the site, removing any traces of what might have been the final resting place of Indiana's White Indians.

The Shape-Shifters of Old Vincennes

In the early 18th century, French fur traders making their way south from Canada, settled in what is now South-Western Indiana. The area was rich with game such as beaver and buffalo, and even after the French lost their claim on the territory following the French-Indian wars, the settlers remained and founded the town of Vincennes.

Because of its early French heritage, which is robust with supernatural-based folklore, Vincennes, Indiana has become a focal point for mysterious creatures straight from the shadowy corners of the human mind. For the 18th century settler, the dark, endless forest that surrounded Vincennes was filled with all manner of unknown dangers. But it was threats of the supernatural that produced the most terror, and the most horrifying of these paranormal nightmares was the Loup-garou.

The Loup-garou, also known as the Rougarou, which haunted the dreams of early French settlers, could appear as a monstrous wolf, but it could also be someone who transformed into a cow, horse, or any other animal. Once under a spell as a Loup-garou, the unfortunate victim became an enraged animal that roamed each night through the fields and forests for a certain period of time, usually 101 days. During the day, he returned to his human form, though he was continually morose and sickly and fearful to tell of his predicament lest even a worse sentence should befall him.

According to some legends, a person could become a Loup-garou by breaking lent seven years in a row. As well, the cursed shape-shifter was especially fond of hunting down and killing Catholics who did not follow the rules of Lent. The main way the Loup-garou could be released from its spell was for someone to recognize him as a cursed creature of the night and injure him to the point of drawing blood. Only this would effectively remove the curse. However, both the victim and his rescuer could not mention the incident, even to each other. Anyone who defied this taboo could find themselves possessed and transformed into the Loup-garou.

One could also be possessed by the spirit of a Loup-garou if they were unfortunate enough to encounter a Feu Follet in the forest. A Feu Follet, also known as a will-o'-the-wisp, was a bright ball of light that would be seen flying and hopping around trees and brush. It was thought that the Feu Follet could bewitch both man and horse to lead them off the trail and into the dark forest.

By the beginning of the 20th century, memories of the Loup-garou began to fade with each passing generation. Fortunately, many of these folk tales were recorded in the 1920's by Anna C. O' Flynn, a teacher in the old French section of Vincennes. As well, in the 1930s a group of writers with the Federal Writers' Project of the Works Progress Administration also managed to record some of the old tales from a handful of Vincennes French descendants. These people, who at this point were in their seventies and eighties, clearly remembered the stories of the Loup-garou told to them on dark nights in front of the flickering fire of the family hearth.

One story, as recalled by Pepe Boucher, involved a man named Charlie Page who one night, as he was going home, encountered a large, black dog with gleaming red eyes. Page, a large man who feared nothing, at first tried to shoo the dog away. When the dog refused to move, Page attempted to kick it in its face. However, the dog with a stealthy, panther-like movement sprang at his throat and knocked him to the ground.

Boucher recalled: "You bet this time he tried to kick and get his knife to finish the dog whose hot breath was singeing his hair—whose great paws were tearing his shoulders and whose fangs were near his neck. With one of his

In Vincennes, Indiana, it was believed that a person could become a Loup-garou by breaking lent seven years in a row. The main way the Loup-garou could be released from its spell was for someone to recognize him as a cursed creature of the night.

powerful arms he grab the neck of the dog until his tongue hant out. The shaggy hair on the dog's neck be lashing his face and his eyes blazing with madness. The Loup-garou be trying to bewitch Page. He know now it be Loup-garou. He know that nothing but blood could save him. Struggling to use his knife the beast pushed the point against Page to make him draw his own blood. Now had Page not been almost a giant he would have turned right into a Loup-garou."

Throwing his whole strength into the struggle, Page managed to push his knife through the shaggy fur, deep behind the forelegs of the savage creature. As its blood spurted from its wound, the Loup-garou vanished in a flash of light and flames. In its place stood Page's best friend, Jean Vetal.

"They look and look at each other," Boucher said. "Mais they spoke no word. Soon they part, each going to his own home. The knife had cut Jean Vetal's arm near the elbow, he doctor it and soon it be well, and then he be delivered from the Loup-garou power."

According to tradition, for 101 days Page and Vetal never spoke of the horrible animal. After the 101 days had passed the two men were free to tell their friends what had happened.

Boucher told the researchers that Jean Vetal gave Page a horse and a cow in gratitude from being freed of his curse.

The Loup-Garou Cow

Another tale, as recalled by Pepe Boucher, shows that the traditional Loup-garou was not always a wolf or dog. Around 1780, shortly after Gen. George R. Clark and his troops took Fort Sackville from the British, Vincennes saw an increase in American settlers coming from the east in search of homesteads. The Americans had no time for tales of ghosts, witches and Loup-garous and openly mocked the French and their superstitions.

Soon, however, one of the new American settlers, a man who had been especially mocking of the French and their belief in the loup-garou, started disappearing from his home every night. When questioned by his friends, he claimed that he had lost his cow and was simply out trying to find it. This story sounded suspicious to Jean Vetal, who, remembering his own misery as a cursed Loup-garou years before, was certain that supernatural forces were at work.

Feeling that God had presented Vetal this opportunity to further cleanse his accursed soul, he secured a large, sharp knife and went out into the night in search for the possessed American.

After searching most of the night, Vetal heard the moan of a cow. Gathering up his courage, Vetal crept softly to the spot where the moaning came. There, lying in a clearing, was a cow moaning like a person in great pain.

Vetal was convinced that this cow was the missing American, now a Loup-garou. The unearthly moaning made Vetal tremble in fear as he reached out with his knife to draw blood and deliver the cursed man. Unfortunately, before Vetal could plant his knife, the cow jumped up, swung her head and knocked the man onto the ground.

For over a mile the Loup-garou ran with Vetal chasing close behind. Finally he was able to get close enough to stick his knife deep enough into the cows shoulder to draw blood.

"Oh! Oh!," Boucher said, "The blood spout out and the cow tumble down as Vetal tumble over on the grass in the common right by the side of the American what always make fun on the French loup-garou."

As the two men walked back to town the American begged Vetal not to tell anyone until he had died or moved away. Shortly afterwards, he moved back east and was never heard from again.

Boucher concluded his story with: "When the American be gone Vetal tell, mais some not believe, pourquei. Et quelquesunes ne pas eroire! (It is so whether you believe it or not!)

Curses of the Cauchemars

In Old Vincennes, shape-shifters did not necessarily have to be Loup-garous. According to an article published in the January 8, 1891, issue of the *Vincennes Commercial* newspaper, there were also witches around to cast evil spells upon the early settlers of Vincennes.

It was believed that witches--called "cauchemars" (nightmares)—could turn men into horses so that they could ride them along the Wabash River

Bottoms. In the morning, when the French woke up feeling all worn out and "hag-ridden," they would say, "C'est mon cauchemar!" (It is my nightmare!)

One old man always claimed that this had happened to him. The next day he said he could see where he had stood and pawed the earth, at the place where the witch had dismounted and tied him.

And there were marks on the fence rail where he had gnawed as an impatient horse. Even the day after, he still was picking some pieces of wood out of his teeth, the bewitched man said.

It was also believed that witches could shape-shift themselves into anything that they desired, and in that shape they would torment their neighbors.

One old French farmer said that for years he had experienced nothing but bad luck because of an old hag that had been persecuting him. At length he made a silver bullet, loaded his gun, and went to a deer-lick. There he killed the witch that had taken the form of a deer. After that he was not bothered again.

Nowadays the vast, wild forests that once surrounded Vincennes have been cut down to make way for shopping malls, housing developments and highways. In the harsh light of modern society, the old superstitions of the early French settlers have been all but forgotten. Nevertheless, the shape-shifters, witches and other monsters of times past still remain, quietly waiting for their chance to live once again in the nightmares of those foolish enough to travel alone into the dark, forbidding night.

The Little People

The Native American tribes who later settled in Indiana believed that they shared the land with several other types of wild forest people. These wildmen, the natives thought, straddled the line somewhere between living, physical men and mystical creatures of the spirit.

One group that was considered very real was a race of little people called the Pa-i-sa-ki by the Miami tribe, and the Puk-wud-jies by the Delaware. The names translate as "little wild men of the forest" and both the Miami and Delaware believed that the little people had occupied the areas before the arrival of Native Americans.

America's Strange and Supernatural History

Described as being about two feet tall, with white skin and light brown hair, the Pa-i-sa-ki wore shirt like garments woven with long grasses, bark and sometimes fur. The little wild men of the forest lived in caves along the river banks, but would sometimes build small huts out of grass or tree limbs when they were away from their caves on hunting trips.

Paul Startzman of Anderson, Indiana believes that the Native American stories are true. In fact, he believes that the little wild men of the forest have survived into present times because he has seen them himself. Startzman was already familiar with the legends of the Pa-i-sa-ki. His grandmother, Mary Gunyan, was a Native American and used to entertain his mother and her sister with tales of the little people who lived along the banks of the nearby White River.

Startzman told about his personal encounters with the Pa-i-sa-ki on the popular TV show, ACROSS INDIANA, seen on WFYI-TV 20.

In 1927 when Startzman was ten years old, he was hiking along an overgrown gravel pit when he came face to face with a little man who was no bigger than two feet tall. "We stopped about ten yards apart and looked at each other, he had thick, dark blond hair and his face was round and pinkish in color, like it was sunburned." Startzman also observed that the little man was barefoot and wearing a long, light blue gown that came down to his ankles.

Before Startzman could move, the little man turned and quickly moved away into the underbrush. Later, Startzman claimed that he and a school chum spotted another Pa-i-sa-ki following them as they walked near the same gravel pit. This little person again, wore a long gown that Startzman speculates could have been a man's shirt that the Pa-i-sa-ki might have stolen from a clothes line.

Paul Startzman believes that the Pa-i-sa-ki was a race of pygmy-like men that existed in Indiana long before the first Native Americans occupied this part of the world. The Native American tribes believed it best to maintain friendly relations with the little people. Food and other gifts were left out in the forest, and the little people in return would warn the tribes of enemies or the whereabouts of game animals. The Pa-i-sa-ki was considered to be very shy and usually avoided contact with people. The little people are said to communicate with each other by making tapping sounds with rocks or sticks, or by imitating the whistles of songbirds.

Startzman considers it possible that the Pa-i-sa-ki could have survived into modern times. "Wild deer and other animals still live along the wooded sections of the White River, why not small, intelligent humans with an old, well established society?" Paul still hikes along the banks of the White river with his camera, hoping that someday he'll finally catch a shot of the elusive, little wild people of Indiana.

The Hairy Ones – Bigfoot and Big Cats

While Bigfoot is generally thought of as living in the mountains and forests of the northwest coast, a surprising number of incidents involving large, hairy ape-like creatures have taken place in Indiana.

The strange creatures seen in Indiana superficially appear to resemble flesh and blood animals. However, the chances that large, wild, human-like creatures could live in Indiana is extremely small. Some researchers have suggested that Bigfoot could migrate throughout the country by using rivers and creeks to remain hidden. In fact, Indiana's Bigfoot does seem to have a fondness for appearing in areas with such waterways nearby.

On the evening of May 19, 1969 near the southern Indiana town of Rising Sun, George Kaiser walked through the family farmyard, when he was startled to see a strange figure standing about 25 feet away. George had the chance to observe the creature for a few minutes and noticed that it stood in a fairly upright position, although it was bent over at about the middle of its back.

The creature was around five feet, eight inches tall and was very muscular in build. The head sat directly on the shoulder and the face was dark, with hair that stuck out on the back of its head. It was covered with a dark brown hair that covered its entire body, except for the face and the back of its hands. When it noticed the young Kaiser watching it, the animal "made a strange grunting-like sound," turned, leaped over a ditch and disappeared down the road. The next day, large footprints were found in the dirt by the ditch, when plaster casts were made, they showed a foot with three toes plus a large big toe that stood out like a thumb.

Rising Sun Indiana, in Clark county, sits along the banks of the Ohio river. Perhaps the Ohio is a favorite river of Bigfoot, because on April 13, 1977 Tom and

America's Strange and Supernatural History

Connie Courter spotted something that looked like the traditional Sasquatch in an area between the towns of Aurora and Rising Sun. The Courter's arrived home in their car around 11:00PM. Tom got out of the car and heard a strange noise which sounded like an "UGH." When he looked up, he saw a large hairy animal about a foot away from him. The creature appeared to be over 12 feet tall, black and hairy, with large red eyes. Its head appeared to resemble a human, but its arms were long and hung to the ground.

Tom quickly jumped into his car and spun the tires, as the creature swung its arms and struck the car, denting it. The couple quickly left the area and spent the night at their mother's house. The next night Tom and Connie returned to their trailer with a .22 rifle and again saw the large creature standing near a tree next to the road.

Tom fired one shot at the animal, but missed. He fired several more shots, but they, too, had no effect. Tom and Connie both said that the animal seemed to dive to the ground and vanish. Connie Courter said that the creature was so large that "If my husband stood on my shoulders he'd still have to look up at it, and it wasn't a bear."

This Bigfoot story seems to indicate that the creature might not be a flesh and blood animal. The large, glowing red eyes are a common report with unnatural creature sightings. Point Pleasant West Virginia's Mothman sightings all involved a large creature with hypnotic red eyes. Also, the fact that Tom Courter shot several rounds from a .22 rifle into his creature with no effect, and its mysterious vanishing act seem to indicate that something more unusual than a physical creature was walking the night in southern Indiana.

In west-central Indiana, in the town of Roachdale, another ghostly Bigfoot type creature made itself known after several nighttime UFO sightings were reported in the area. Mrs. Lou Rogers was the first person to hear the unusual intruder in August, 1972.

She had stepped outside of her house one evening when she was startled by a noise somewhat like a growl which was followed by a "boo" or "oo." Turning around, Mrs. Rogers looked in the direction of the sound, but due to the darkness, could see nothing. She did have the feeling though that something was watching her and she quickly retreated back into her house.

The following evenings the strange sounds returned followed by something banging on the doors and windows. Lou Rogers commented that "whatever it was, it must have gotten braver because the noise got louder and louder each night. It would always come around ten to eleven thirty each night, you could feel it coming, I don't know how to explain it, and then the knocking would start."

When the Rogers would go outside they would sometimes catch a glimpse of a large, broad-shouldered "something" running away through the cornfields. Mrs. Rogers commented, "We tried to think of a rational explanation, maybe an ape had gotten away from a zoo or circus. It would stand up like a man, but would run on all fours, even bent over on all four feet it was still taller than my husband, and it stank, like rotten garbage." Mr. Rogers continued, "The funny thing is that it never left footprints, even in mud, and when it ran through tall weeds you couldn't hear anything. And sometimes when you looked at it, it looked like you could see through it, like it was a ghost or something."

The Rogers weren't the only people in Roachdale to sight the mysterious animal. On August 22, around nine o'clock in the evening, Carter Burdine and his uncle, Bill Burdine, discovered at Carter's farm, the remains of over sixty chickens that had been ripped apart and scattered along a path from the chicken coop, to the front yard of the house. None of the chickens had been eaten, just torn apart and dropped.

After Town Marshall, Leroy Cloncs arrived, the men stood outside discussing what could have attacked the birds in such a strange way. Suddenly, they heard an unusual noise nearby. Cloncs got into his patrol car and slowly went down the road while Bill Burdine walked behind. After the car passed, something large jumped out of the roadside ditch and ran between Bill and the patrol car. "It ran so fast I couldn't get a good look at it in the dark," Bill said. "Whatever it was, it was big. The fence it ran over was mashed all the way to the ground, and you could see where it had trampled the weeds when it ran away."

After the Town Marshall had left, Carter and Bill returned to the chicken coop to find the creature standing in the chicken-house doorway. "The thing completely blocked out the light in the chicken-house," Bill said. "The door is six feet by eight, its shoulders came to the top of the doorway. It looked like a gorilla with long brownish colored hair. I never saw its face, but it was making an awful groaning sound."

The creature ran from the coop with Bill shooting at it with a pump shotgun. Like other ghostly Bigfoot encounters, the Roachdale creature seemed unharmed by the hail of shotgun pellets, and once again disappeared into the nearby fields. This time the animal had killed one hundred and ten chickens, all had been ripped apart and drained of blood. Out of two hundred chickens, Carter Burdine lost all but thirty. After this incident, reports of the strange beast subsided. Whatever the monster of Roachdale was, it vanished as mysteriously as it had arrived.

Other strange animal sightings have been reported over the years in this rural part of the state. Indiana used to be home to a large population of predators including bears, wolves and pumas. The puma, or mountain lion, has been declared extinct in Indiana for over one hundred years, yet reports of big cat sightings still turn up every now and then.

In 1877 a young couple walking home near Rising Sun were chased and attacked by a large cat "as big as a good sized calf." The animal ran along the top of a roadside fence and caught the girl with its claws.

Mary Crane was pinned to the ground and the cat proceeded to lick the girl's face. Her friend ran ahead, alerting men in the nearby village who quickly came to Mary's rescue. Hearing the approaching men, the cat gave a piercing shriek and fled into the night.

Mary Crane was uninjured. The next day cat footprints were found at the scene. The prints reportedly measured 6 inches wide. The footprints were tracked for several miles through the woods, but no cat was ever found.

Indiana's Lake Monsters

Located in the town of Rochester, Lake Manitou was once considered forbidden to the Potawtomi who lived in the area. The reason for their fear was their belief that the lake was inhabited by a great monster called, Meshekenabek. In his "Recollections of the Early Settlements of the Wabash Valley," Sanford C. Cox reported that, "The Indians would not hunt upon its borders, nor fish in its waters for fear of incurring the anger of the evil spirit that made its home in this little woodland lake." In fact, the Native Americans would later warn settlers against building a mill on the lake, said Cox, fearful that the monster would "rush forth from its watery dominions and take indiscriminate vengeance on all those who resided near the sacred lake."

Perhaps the Lake Manitou monster wasn't all Native American superstition because during construction of the mentioned corn mill in 1827 several men who worked surveying the lake for the mill reported seeing the monster. They claimed the creature was dark colored, and over thirty feet long with a long neck and a head like a horse. News soon spread of the lake monster, making it difficult to find men to finish the job. The area's first blacksmith described the monster like this: "The head being about three feet across the frontal bone and having something of the contour of a beef's head, but the neck tapering and having the character of the serpent. Its color was dingy, with large yellow spots."

On July 21, 1838, the *Logansport Telegraph* reported that two men spotted the monster which was "sixty feet long, and looked like a huge snake." Using the eyewitness descriptions, George Winter, noted painter of Native Americans, sketched his conception of the monster for the newspaper. Over the years sporadic sightings of the "Devil's Lake Monster" were reported. However, in 1849 the Logansport Journal reported that a huge buffalo carp that "weighed several hundred pounds" was caught in the lake, the fish's thirty pound head was exhibited at Logansport. People thought that the monster had been caught at last, but in 1888 a 116 pound spoonbill catfish was pulled from the lake by four men. The monster sized fish was placed in a horse trough by the county courthouse in Rochester and people were charged ten cents for a peek. Eventually, the catfish was butchered and sold at ten cents a pound. In recent years reports of the lake Manitou monster have waned. Today when the northern Indiana winters freeze the lake over, the ice shifts and emits booming and roaring noises. Residents around the lake smile and say that it is the monster trying to force its head above the ice.

The Monster Turtle of Churubusco

The Lake Manitou Monster was reportedly a large serpent. In the Whitley county town of Churubusco, the lake monster was a giant turtle. The story of "Oscar" as the turtle would later be known, starts in 1898 in a seven acre lake about one mile east of town. The owner of the lake, Oscar Fulk, first spotted the turtle when it unexpectedly surfaced in front of him just a few yards from shore.

The turtle was huge; Fulk estimated the animal to be at least five feet wide with a big, ugly head like a snapping turtle.

"Oscar" the turtle would remain unseen for almost fifty years when, in 1947, it would once again be sighted, capturing the attention of the national media. By then the lake was called "Fulks Lake" and was about 100 yards behind the plowed fields and small, white farmhouse owned by the Gale Harris family. Helen Harris would later write about her family's encounters with the "Beast of Busco" and the unwanted attention they received.

"My brother, Charles Wilson, and his son-in-law first saw the turtle while fishing in the lake. We thought at first he was kidding us, but he said he was serious. He had never seen a turtle that big. Later, my husband Gale and our minister, the Rev. Orville Reese, were repairing the roof of the barn when they saw the turtle surface."

The two men estimated that the turtle was as big as a large dining room table and could weigh as much as 400 pounds. Gale Harris was determined to catch "Oscar" and he would watch the lake to try and study the beast's habits. An unverified story says that Gale managed to get a rope around the turtle with the other end attached to a hitch with four horses. But "Oscar" wasn't about to be caught in such a undignified fashion. The beast dug its claws into the mud and the rope broke allowing the turtle to escape.

Unfortunately for the Harris family, the newspaper reports about "Oscar" led to a steady stream of uninvited guests to the farm. According to Helen Harris, "We couldn't sit down and eat a meal in peace or get our work done on schedule. We had no privacy in our home. People came by the hundreds and would walk into our home without knocking. They used our bathroom, sat in the living room or did anything else they wanted to do without asking."

What finally happened to the "Beast of Busco" is anybody's guess. Gale Harris thinks the turtle went underground, through springs and channels to another lake. Others think he walked out of the lake in order to find a more peaceful home. The road just 100 yards from Fulk Lake caved in around 1954, some say because of "Oscars" great weight when he walked across it.

"Oscar," however, has not been forgotten. Every year the town of Churubusco celebrates its "Turtle Days" festival with a parade and other turtle

In Churubusco, Indiana, crowds would gather in hopes of catching a glimpse of "Oscar," the 400 pound giant turtle that allegedly lived in Fulks Lake.

oriented activities. Although the Harris family didn't enjoy the fame "Oscar" brought them. Churubusco, (or Turtle Town USA as they like to be called) still enjoys the attention brought about by the mysterious "Beast of Busco."

Hoosier UFO Reports

UFOs have enjoyed a long and often tumultuous relationship with Indiana over the years. In fact, UFOs have been reported over the skies of Indiana long before the so-called "modern era of UFOs" which began in 1947. The Hoosier state, like the rest of the country was caught up in sightings of the Great Airship that was supposedly making its way eastward from California starting in 1896. In 1897 reports started to trickle in from the northern counties with sightings in Hammond, Gary and South Bend. Soon, however, local newspapers all across the state started reporting Airship sightings in the skies above their communities. On the night of Friday, April 16, residents of Vincennes twice sighted a mysterious airship that passed slowly over the city.

According to the *Vincennes Morning Commercial*, the airship first appeared about nine o'clock, traveling along the extreme eastern portion of the horizon. A sphere of golden light was first seen in the vicinity of the Union Depot, from down in the city. Those near the ship claimed they could clearly see the dark lines of its car, although no passengers were observed.

Many reputable citizens witnessed the flight. From his home on Burnett's Heights, Sam Judah said he could plainly see the ship with its fluttering wings, its movements resembling a side wheeler steam-boat, sailing through the air with incredible velocity.

From his doorway, where he had gone to look at his thermometer, Col. Ewing saw the light, which he at first thought was a falling star, but as it moved so slowly, soon became convinced that it was the inevitable airship. Ewing watched it for about four minutes. Anton Simon noticed a ball of fire, moving in a northwesterly to southeasterly course, which he later realized was an airship.

Victor Schonfeld, somewhat of an expert observer, having made airships and balloons, a lifelong study, and having even made several ascensions in his time, testified that this was a genuine airship. Among many others who saw the

On the night of Friday, April 16, 1897, residents of Vincennes, Indiana, sighted a mysterious airship that passed slowly over the city. Sam Judah said he could plainly see the ship with its fluttering wings, its movements resembling a side wheeler steam-boat, sailing through the air with incredible velocity.

airship were Col. M.P. Ghee, Thomas Eastham, Judge DeWolf, Will Mason, Scott Emison, Jesse Foulks, all highly reputable witnesses.

The airship first passed rapidly overhead in a southwesterly direction. An hour and a half later, it was seen again, passing over the northern portion of the city, traveling in a northwesterly direction. The last time it seemed to pass directly over the fairgrounds (present-day Gregg Park) and traveled more slowly than in its first swift passage straight over the city.

It is thought that the navigator turned his flying machine around and started back, or that the ship landed near the city and started back. Some say voices could be heard in the airship, and one gentleman, who saw it from Burnett's Heights says he could see a man moving about in the ship and that he appeared to be adjusting the machinery.

In fact, the Vincennes encounter was only one of some 200 sightings made by thousands of people in 19 states, during the Great Airship flap of 1896-1897.

UFO or Sky Serpent Over Crawfordsville?

Citizens in Crawfordsville witnessed an unusual object in the heavens above their town in September 1891. The late researcher and author Vincent Gaddis attended college and worked as a reporter in the vicinity of Crawfordsville and had the opportunity to interview surviving witnesses and to read the original on-the-scene newspaper accounts of this amazing visitation. Gaddis detailed this sighting in his book ***Mysterious Fires and Lights***.

Eyewitnesses described the thing as self-luminous, surrounded by an aura of dim white light; the appearance resembled "a white shroud with fins." No clear-cut shape or outline could be observed. It was about 18 or 20 feet long, eight feet wide, and no head or tail was visible. It moved rapidly "like a fish in water" with the aid of "side fins." At times it flapped its fins violently, emitting a wheezing, plainting sound. It hovered about 300 feet above the town, but on several occasions it came within a hundred feet of the ground.

All the reports refer to this object as a living thing. A flaming red "eye" was noticeable. At times it "squirmed as if in agony." Once it swooped low over a group of witnesses who said that it radiated "a hot breath."

This strange creature made its appearance on two successive nights, September 4-5, 1891, first coming into view about midnight on both nights, and disappearing upward about 2:00AM. On the first night witnesses included the Rev. G.W. Switzer, pastor of the local Methodist Church, and his wife, who watched the sky phantom for more than an hour. On the second night hundreds of residents watched the monster as it moved slowly over various parts of the business district for two hours. The next evening the entire town stayed up to see the strange visitor, but it failed to reappear.

UFO Occupants Seen in 1923

A young boy by the name of Norman Massie was leading a team of horses into a pasture near his Mount Erie home, when he happened to look up and saw what he is convinced to this day was a spaceship.

"You can call me anything you want, but I know in my heart and in my mind what I saw that evening, and it was some kind of spaceship," Massie said.

Massie, 85, was ten years old when he encountered the object. The retired high school math teacher and coach said he kept quiet about the incident until 1990 because his father told him never to breathe a word about what he saw because "people would talk." Massie's UFO sighting happened in June 1923 on the family farm in northern Wayne County (east-central Indiana, near Richmond).

"I opened the gate to let the horses into the pasture. I let them through, and as I was closing the gate I looked back down the field and there was an object with lights all around it," Massie said. "I kept walking closer to the object until I got about 50 feet away. I stood there and watched the five men who were on board."

Massie described the men as being about four feet tall with blond hair. "I got close enough that I could hear them talk," Massie said. "One guy sat in a chair and the others called him the commander. Four others made trips back and forth in the ship. I didn't know what was going on until the end."

Massie claims he heard one of the crew members tell his commander that "the repairs had been made."

"The machine was metallic and stood on three legs. The top was a dome with holes in it. The best way I could describe the top was it looked like melted glass," Massie said.

The encounter lasted only about five minutes, Massie said. "In a minute, it came to a hovering position. The tripod legs telescoped up into the belly of the thing, and it went straight up about 200 feet and whizzed off to the west like a bullet," he said. Startled by what he saw, Massie says he ran home and told his parents, Grover and Laura Massie, and his 8-year-old brother, Lyveere.

"Mom and Dad tried to convince me that I really hadn't seen anything, and was making up the whole thing," he said.

He says his dad announced he wanted no member of his family mentioning the incident to anyone because they might think Norman was "crazy in the head, or an idiot."

Massie broke his silence on the matter in 1990 when he told his son, Jerry, who was a colonel in the Air Force at the time:

When I got done telling him the whole story he told me there was nothing wrong with me, that the Air Force files are full of pictures of UFOs. He accepted my story as the truth.

Massie says he's convinced the object had to come from somewhere other than Earth. "It doesn't bother me one bit that people might think I'm a crazy old man. In my own mind and my own heart, it existed and I saw it with my own two eyes."

That same year, two college students in Greencastle spotted a strange revolving red object that passed quickly and silently overhead from the northeast to the southwest. The two young men describe the object as round and glowing like a "red hot piece of molten metal."

UFOs and Airlines

An early airline sighting involved the crew and passengers of a TWA DC-3 on the evening of April 4, 1950 over Goshen, Indiana. The DC-3, piloted by Capt. Robert Adickes and co-piloted by Capt. Robert F. Manning, was at about 2000 feet and heading for Chicago when, at about 8:25PM, Manning spotted a glowing red object aft of the starboard wing, well to their rear.

It was similar in appearance to a rising blood red moon, and appeared to be closing with the airliner at a relatively slow rate of convergence. The co-pilot watched the UFOs approach for about two minutes, trying to determine what it might be. Then Manning attracted Adickes' attention to the object asking what he thought it was. He rang for the hostess, Gloria Henshaw, and pointed it out to her. At that time the object was at a relative bearing of about 100 degrees and slightly lower than the airliner.

"The object was seemingly holding its position relative to us, about one-half mile away," Manning reported. Capt. Adickes sent the stewardess back to alert the passengers, and then banked the DC-3 to starboard to try to close on the unknown object. "As we turned, the object seemed to veer away from us in a direction just west of north, toward the airport area of South Bend," Captain Adickes said. "It seemed to descend as it increased its velocity, and within a few minutes was lost to our sight."

In July, 1952, Captain Richard Case was flying an American Airlines Convair near Indianapolis when he became one of several people who sighted a UFO that startled the residents by making a low pass over the city. He commented that it seemed to be a controlled disc-shaped craft moving at some 1,000 miles per hour and he witnessed it dropping from approximately 15,000 to 5,000 feet before heading in over the city.

Mr. John Michael of Bedford wrote a letter to WTTV-4 detailing his UFO sighting on October 16, 1956:

"I was aroused from sleep by a noise buzzing over my house. I went to the front door to look and as I stepped out on the darkened porch, I found myself directly under the beam of a white light from an object in front of the house...its nose was pointed directly at me as it approached. Missing the power lines and the house, it flew on south.

"The object circled back and its searchlight was again being focused directly upon me, then it pulled sharply up again to miss the power lines and the house. It headed south and again began a sharply cut circle back. As it did, I could see the shape of it. The wings sat back at dead center and many lights were flickering off and on, from the wings, the tail and the front. There were at least four colors of lights, red, blue, yellow and the white of the searchlight.

"Now it was headed back and as it stood on the east side of the house it again pointed the light and the nose of the ship at me. I expected it to land on the vacant lot in front, but suddenly it stopped as if powerful brakes had been applied. It then flew away to the east, making considerable noise from some sort of power plant. A person living near the airport had also seen it, but had taken it for a navy plane."

At least two control tower operators at Bunker Hill Air Force Base near Peru (now known as Grissom Air Base), and the pilot of a Mooney private airplane spotted a UFO hovering near the base on September 13, 1959. The UFO was described as pear-shaped and white colored with a definite metallic sheen. The UFO also had mist or smoke coming from underneath. It showed little movement during the over three hours in which it was seen both visually and on radar. A USAF T-33 jet trainer was sent up to try and intercept the UFO which then shot straight up and disappeared.

Numerous sightings of a UFO were reported in eastern Indiana and western Ohio on the night of October 10, 1973. The object was said to blink a red and blue revolving light, and hovered near the ground. The UFO was tracked for hours by Delaware County police officers. Military radar controllers operating in the tower at Baer Field, Ft. Wayne, confirmed that their radar sensors had tracked an object that could not be identified.

Airport communications personnel said they couldn't get the object to respond. More than 750 calls were received from law enforcement switchboards. Delaware County officers received calls from 15 different areas of the county. A light plane was dispatched, but failed to find the object.

One of the better reports that evening was in Martinsville where Morgan County Sheriff's Deputy Robert Williams said he saw a UFO take off from the ground.

"It looked like a clear, bright light," Morgan said, "and it looked like it took off from the ground toward the east and got so far off the ground and disappeared."

America's Strange and Supernatural History

More Strange Stuff

Some of Indiana's strange stories cannot be as easily categorized as the tales of lake monsters or Bigfoot. Take for instance the story of the weird animal seen living in a well on a farm in eastern Indiana. The farm belonged to Dan Craig of Lynn, Indiana. *The Indianapolis News* first wrote about Craig's strange guest on June 8, 1960.

Craig told the newspaper he had been aware of his well's unusual visitor for about a year. He described the animal as "an eerie beast with a dome-shaped head, two bulbous eyes, and eight flailing tentacles as long as a man's arm." Dan Craig's wife said the animal looked like "a mushroom as large as a plate, with long legs and feet."

Craig decided to drain the well to find out once and for all what kind of creature was in there. After the well had been drained, a 12-year-old friend of the family, Craig Lee, descended into the well and said that he saw something about the size of a dinner plate that looked like a yellowish sponge mushroom with eyes on the top of its head and with eight legs with claws on the ends. Dan Craig decided that enough was enough and had the well filled in. Naturally the creature was never seen again.

In 1974, the Midwest was hopping with reports of mysterious kangaroos. Indiana contributed its fair share of reports with the November 17th sighting of a kangaroo in Carmel, Indiana. The animal was seen by Amos Miller and his wife while they were driving to church. The kangaroo was sitting on its haunches near the Cool Creek Bridge at Indiana 234 and Keystone Avenue.

In Sheridan, Indiana, on November 25th, farmer Donald Johnson was driving his pickup down a rural road when he saw an unusual animal. Donald said it was a "kangaroo running on all four feet down the middle of the road." When the kangaroo saw the farmer it jumped over a four-foot-tall barbed wire fence, and disappeared across a field. Police speculated that the kangaroo could have escaped from a private owner, however no missing kangaroo reports were ever filed, and no further sightings were ever reported.

In 1876, people were drawn to Jim Bailey's well located near Plymouth, Indiana. The reason was that the water from the well had magnetic properties. Knives, shears, scissors, hooks, and small bars of steel became magnetized when placed in the water. From two feet away the water could totally control a compass needle.

The well's output was an estimated 500 gallons a minute; however it was not what Bailey had wanted. His firm had been trying to open a seam to operate a mill wheel by underground streams. Instead they got the gusher whose waters sparkled strangely with the tints of the rainbow. People came for miles around to bathe in the magnetic waters, believing that magnetism would restore health, treat rheumatism and dyspepsia. The crowds soon became a nuisance to Jim Bailey who covered up the well, much to the disappointment of the devotees of Bailey's magnetic waters.

Strange stories, unnatural creatures, mysterious occurrences – the supply of fascinating information about Indiana is inexhaustible. Hoosiers, however, take these stories in stride. Tall tales and folklore, entertainment since the early pioneer days, have never lost their charm to Hoosiers. An expression used since the early days of Indiana best describes the wondrous stories and events that make Indiana's unnatural history so compelling: "will wonders never cease?" Let's hope that they don't.

SOURCES
Ray Boomhower, "The Father of Indiana History and the Devil's Lake Monster," *Traces Magazine*, Volume four, Issue one, Indiana Historical Society, 1992

The Churubusco Chamber of Commerce, B.J. Heath, Director

Janet and Colin Bord, **Alien Animals**, Stackpole Books, 1981

Fred D. Cavinder, **Indiana's Believe it or Not**, Indiana University Press, 1990

Sanford Cox, **Recollections of Early Settlements of the Wabash Valley**, Courier Steam Book and Job Printing House, 1860

Arville L. Funk, **A Sketchbook of Indiana History**, Christian Book Press, 1969

America's Strange and Supernatural History

The Indianapolis News, June 8, 1960.

Dana Olson, ***Prince Madoc: Founder of Clark County, Indiana***, 1987

Mysterious America, By Loren Coleman, Published by Faber & Faber, Inc. 1983

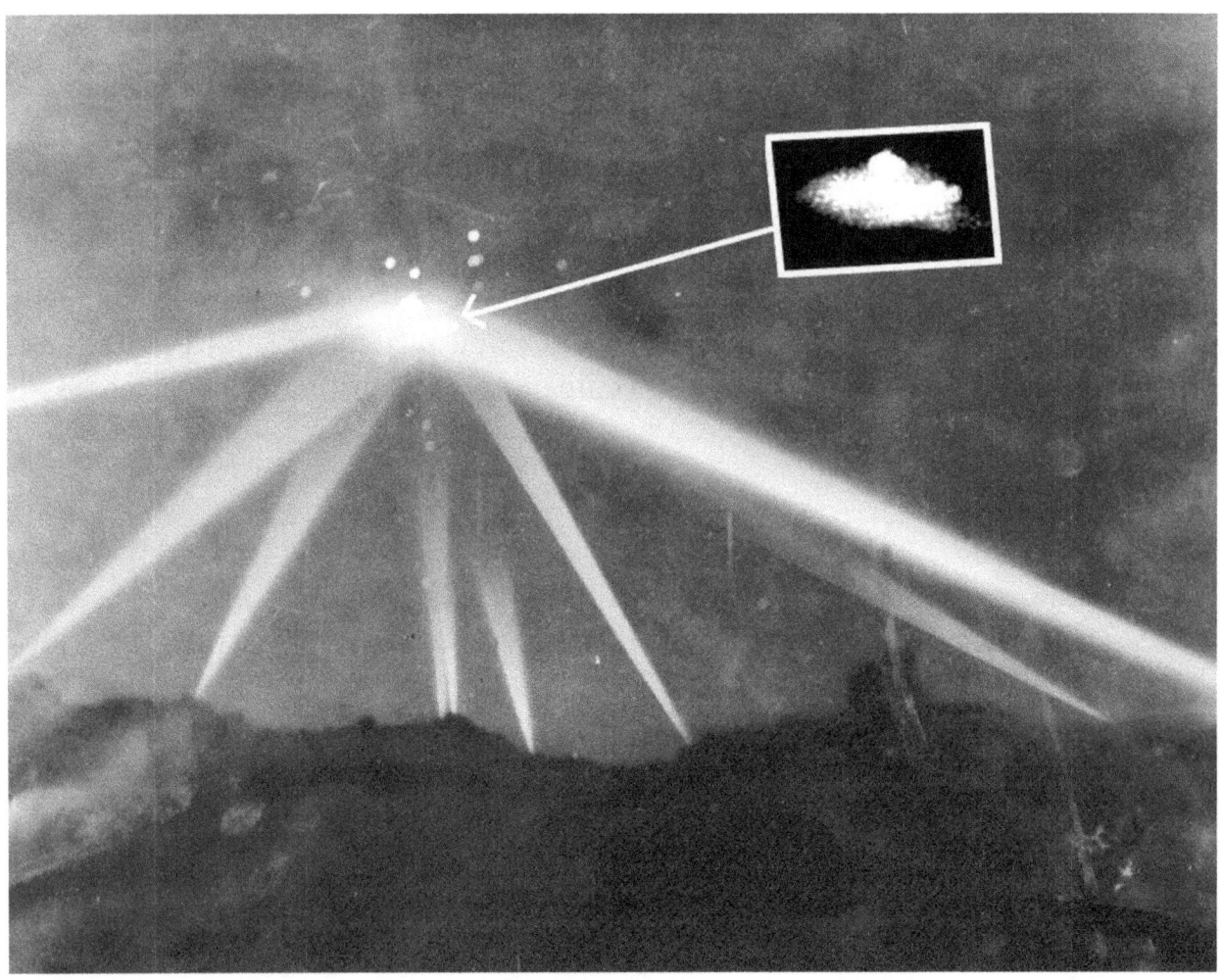

On Feb 25, 1942, a massive UFO appeared over Los Angeles and was shot at by the military. The unknown craft eventually disappeared over the ocean, apparently unscathed, despite the constant barrage. According to the Los Angeles Times, five people died from heart attacks and car accidents, and there were a number of injuries and property damage from falling debris.

Full assessment by witness C. Scott Littleton at www.UFOChronicles.com

Chapter Seven
Cannibalism and Ghosts in American History

By Sean Casteel

JUST how strange does American history get? Many truly bizarre events are concealed from the average American's knowledge of our collective past simply because the weirdness factor surrounding some events goes off the charts and makes the telling too unpleasantly indigestible even for those who prefer to believe they can handle the harshest of truths and look unblinkingly at the most grotesque of historical warts.

Jamestown and the "Starving Time"

For example, there have been the unfortunate occurrences of what is called "survival cannibalism," a horror recorded even in such unlikely places as Jamestown, the oldest permanent English colony in the Americas. The tragic history of what is eerily known as the "Starving Time," the harsh winter of 1609, has generally been conceded by historians. But in May 2013 it was announced that a team of archeologists led by William Kelso had excavated a trash pit at the Jamestown colony site in Virginia and discovered the first physical evidence of cannibalism among the desperate colonists. The skull and skeleton of a 14-year-old girl were unearthed that bore cut marks indicating that her flesh and brain had been removed, clearly to feed the starving people, according to forensic anthropologist Douglas Owsley of the Smithsonian Institution.

The colonists found themselves in such dire straits due to extreme drought in the region coupled with the fact that their relations with the neighboring Native-Americans, the Powhatan Confederacy, who had initially welcomed and

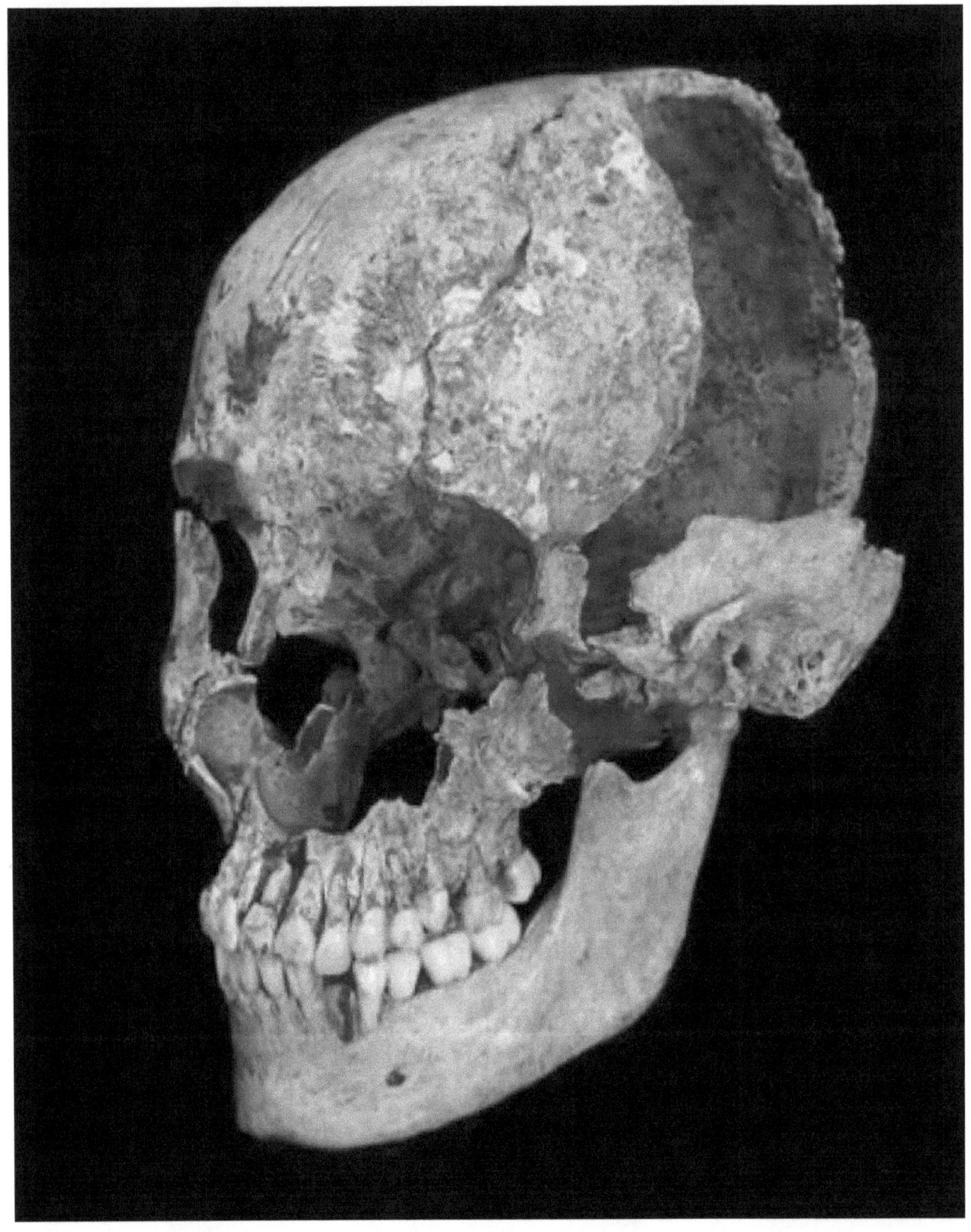

Skull found at Jamestown showing evidence of cannibalism.

provisioned the colony, had deteriorated to the point that the local natives were unwilling to help them. A supply ship the colonists had been counting on was lost at sea, and most of the settlers were not adept at even rudimentary farming.

George Percy, who had been the president of Jamestown during the "Starving Time," wrote a letter in 1625 describing the colonists' diet during that miserable winter. The letter is written in the archaic English of the time, but what follows is an excerpt converted to more modern English:

"Having fed upon our horses and other beasts as long as they lasted," Percy writes, "we were glad to make shift with vermin, such as dogs, cats, rats and mice, as well as to eat boots, shoes or any other leather. And now famine beginning to look ghastly and pale in every face, nothing was spared to maintain life and to do those things which seem incredible – to dig up dead corpses out of the grave and to eat them. And some have licked up the blood which has fallen from their weak fellows."

The Jamestown colony was rescued in May of 1610 when settlers who had been marooned in Bermuda arrived to find 60 skeletally thin survivors. In June, more relief ships arrived, led by Lord De La Warr, after whom the state of Delaware was subsequently named. His men swept the grisly remains of the ordeal, which included the bones of dogs and horses and at least one human, into the refuse pile archeologists later found and excavated and which included the remains of the cannibalized teenage girl. It is impossible to determine whether she was murdered for the sake of food or eaten after she had died naturally from starvation or disease, said Owsley.

The Donner Party

Most Americans grow up with a proud, sentimentalized view of the pioneers who went west and bravely settled the American wilderness. Who doesn't have in their mind deeply engrained images of covered wagons and rudimentary log cabins built with sweat and grit and an unshakable optimism in a uniquely American future? It would be difficult to count the Hollywood movies that have so firmly fixed these icons of guts and faith in our collective consciousness.

However, the story of the Donner Party, pioneers reduced to survival cannibalism, still casts a grim shadow over that normally inspiring historical period.

The Donner Party set out for California in a wagon train, but in the winter of 1846-47, delayed by a series of calamities, it became snowbound in the Sierra Nevada mountain range. The journey typically took four to six months, but the Donner Party had attempted to reach the Promised Land of California by a new route called Hastings Cutoff, which led them across the Wasatch Mountains of Utah and the Great Salt Lake Desert. Along the way, they lost several cattle and wagons. When they arrived in the Sierra Nevadas, they were trapped by an early and heavy snowfall near Truckee Lake (since renamed Donner Lake). High in the mountains, with their food supplies quickly dwindling, some of the group set out on foot in mid-December to get help. The first relief party did not arrive until the middle of February 1847, nearly four months after the wagon train became trapped.

As they awaited rescue, members of the group began to die, most often due to malnutrition, overwork and exposure to cold. While there are conflicting historical accounts, Georgia Donner, who had been four years old during that bitter winter, wrote to author Charles McGlashan that human flesh was prepared for people in the Donner Party, but given only to the youngest children. She also recalled that Elizabeth Donner said one morning that she had cooked the arm of one Samuel Shoemaker, a 25-year-old teamster. Another member, Jean Baptiste Trudeau, at one time spoke of eating Jacob Donner as well as claiming to have consumed a baby raw.

Nevertheless, these stories continue to be disputed by historians, archeologists and especially by descendants of the Donner family. In 2003 and 2004, excavations of the campsite at Alder Creek, near to the Truckee Lake site, found no clear evidence of cannibalism, but did turn up 16,000 bone fragments. The remains of rodents, rabbits, deer, horses, oxen and cattle were found, as well as canine bones that supported survivors' accounts that they ate their pet dogs. It is also apparent that the Donner Party members went to great lengths to avoid eating their own dead and had at one time survived on a glue-like substance made from boiled animal hides, along with charred bones, twigs, leaves and bark.

Yet, while there is so far no conclusive archeological evidence of the Donner Party's admitted cannibalism, accounts like the 1879 book "***History of the Donner Party***," by the aforementioned Charles McGlashan, and later interviews with survivors conducted by other writers make it apparent that the tragic events indeed took place, though many of the more morbid details were omitted from the historical record.

Alferd Packer, The Big-Headed Cannibal

Another cherished image from the Old West in America is that of the hardy, enterprising prospector. In the case of Alferd Packer, however, such treasured clichés do not apply.

Alferd Packer was born in 1842 in Allegheny County, Pennsylvania. He enlisted in the Union Army during the Civil War but was given a medical discharge after eight months because he had epilepsy. He decided to seek his fortune as a prospector.

In November 1873, Packer was among a group of 21 men who departed Provo, Utah, to look for gold in Colorado. Two months later, Chief Ouray, known to be friendly with the white man, recommended to Packer that the group put off its expedition until spring and thus avoid the inevitable dangerous weather in the mountains. Packer, along with five others in the original group, ignored the chief's advice and struck off for Gunnison, Colorado, on February 9, 1874. The group was soon completely lost and, with the provisions exhausted, found itself snowbound in the Rocky Mountains.

Packer would eventually confess three times to the cannibalism that followed, changing his story every time. In his last account, he claimed that he had left the encampment to explore the surrounding country and returned to discover that one of his companions was roasting the flesh of another companion. The man tending the cannibalistic fire then rushed Packer, wielding a hatchet, and Packer shot him in what he said later was self-defense. Packer said the "cook" had gone mad in Packer's absence and murdered the rest of the party.

In April, Packer found his way back to Gunnison and began to tell his story in a local saloon, including to some members of the original group of 21 prospectors he had left Utah with. No one believed his protests of innocence, and

America's Strange and Supernatural History

Alferd Packer

he was sentenced to die by presiding judge M.B. Gerry. Packer escaped imprisonment in the Saguache, Colorado, jail but was later arrested in Cheyenne, Wyoming, where he had been living under an assumed name. He was again tried, found guilty of manslaughter, and sentenced to death. The Colorado Supreme Court commuted his sentence to 40 years, and he was paroled in 1901. He died in 1907 at age 65, and his death was attributed to "senility, trouble and worry."

The American Occultist Cannibal

The cannibalism discussed so far in this chapter involves cases of what is called "survival cannibalism," but there are other forms of cannibalism to be considered. In occult terms, cannibalism may serve as a form of ritual, a kind of offering or sign of obedience to "the gods" or some demonic entity that requires it. There are also occult overtones when cannibalism is intended to invest the cannibal with the qualities of his victim, such as courage, wisdom or strength.

Occultism would come to play a role in the life of William Seabrook, part of the American "Lost Generation" romantically portrayed by writer F. Scott Fitzgerald and others. The Maryland-born Seabrook worked as a reporter and editor of "The Augusta Chronicle" in Georgia before becoming a partner in an advertising agency in Atlanta. After serving in World War I, he moved on to become a reporter for "The New York Times" as well as to write books and work freelance for publications like "Cosmopolitan" and "Vanity Fair." His travels as a writer to third-world countries and modern metropolises like London and Paris exposed him to Satanism and various facets of the occult, a fascination that would last throughout the rest of his life.

In autumn 1919, English occultist Aleister Crowley spent a week with Seabrook at Seabrook's farm, which Seabrook later recounted in his book "Witchcraft: Its Power in the World Today." A few years later, Seabrook journeyed to Haiti and subsequently wrote a book called "The Magic Island," which is said to have introduced the notion of zombies to popular culture.

While on a trip to West Africa, Seabrook asked a cannibal tribal chief what human meat tasted like but did not receive a satisfactory answer. Seabrook subsequently obtained a chunk of human meat from the body of a healthy person who had recently died in an accident by bribing a hospital intern in Paris.

Seabrook cooked the meat sample and ate it. It tasted like good, fully developed veal, Seabrook reported, a little stringy and tough, but not to an unpalatable degree.

Along with Seabrook's absorption in the occult, his comments on ingesting human meat also touch on another form of cannibalism, "epicurean cannibalism," which refers to a person's simply enjoying the taste of human flesh. Seabrook's wife divorced him in 1941, accusing him of drunkenness and sadism. He committed suicide by drug overdose in September 1945.

More Recent Cases of American Cannibalism

In addition to famous cases of criminal cannibals/serial killers like Jeffrey Dahmer, dubbed "The Milwaukee Monster," and Albert Fish, who infamously roasted one of his victims with bacon, a spate of high profile instances of cannibalism briefly made headlines in 2012.

In June of that year, 31-year-old Rudy Eugene was eating a homeless man's face before being shot dead by Miami police. Reports surfaced a few days later that a New Jersey man threw pieces of his own intestines at the cops after stabbing himself. Shortly after, it was reported that Alexander Kinyua, a university student in Maryland, had confessed to cutting up and ingesting his roommate. Another case followed quickly, that of Luka Magnotta, suspected of hacking a man to death with an ice-pick and eating his flesh. A father under the influence of the drug PCP ate his son's eyeballs, and a popular rap artist named Big Lurch was serving a life sentence for killing his roommate and consuming part of her lung, which was also attributed to PCP use.

The fact that all these cases of cannibalism followed each other in such rapid succession created a "zombie/apocalypse" furor at the time, which many did not find entirely humorous, since it fueled fears of the End Times already present in many nervous observers of disturbing social trends. The situation prompted the New York newspaper "The Village Voice" to publish "A Brief History of Cannibalism in America," an article intended to allay such fears by explaining that cannibalism had been with mankind since the Neanderthal period and pointing out that "we're all still here" in spite of the then current outbreaks.

America's Strange and Supernatural History

It may interest the reader to know that there is no law on the books in the U.S. declaring cannibalism to be illegal. What is illegal, of course, is the murder and corpse abuse that typically precede the ingestion of human flesh, but there have still been instances of "consensual" cannibalism, where a person volunteers to have some part of him eaten, that continue to be a kind of legal gray area both here and abroad. The scientific term for consumption of a fellow human being is "anthropophagy," but defining it in criminal terms varies considerably from culture to culture.

The very term "cannibalism" also originated in America. When Columbus encountered the ritually cannibalistic West Indies Carib tribe in 1492, the explorers mispronounced their name as "Canibs" instead of "Caribs." According to Merriam-Webster, the first known use of the word "cannibal" was in 1553.

The Bell Witch Haunting

Another prime example of historical American weirdness is a 19th century poltergeist haunting in Adams, Tennessee, often called the Bell Witch Haunting. The Bell family, headed by farmer John Bell, Sr., allegedly came under attack by a local witch named Kate Batts. The family suffered events similar to other poltergeist hauntings, such as noises in the walls and other unusual sounds, people being slapped and pinched, objects being thrown and animals being spooked without visible cause.

Author Martin Van Buren Ingram, in his 1894 book "***An Authenticated History of the Bell Witch***," claimed that the poltergeist's name was Kate and that she often cursed the Bell family out loud. The ghost focused on Betsy, the family's youngest daughter, and the disturbances grew worse after she became engaged to a man named Joshua Gardner. The idea of an adolescent female being at the center of a poltergeist haunting is familiar to ghost researchers.

It is said that Andrew Jackson, while still serving in the military, investigated the Bell home and was frightened away, though some historians point out that this is nowhere noted in any of Jackson's papers. According to other stories, the family began to hear scratching noises outside their door shortly after John Bell discovered a half-dog, half-rabbit creature on the farm. It

One evening Betsy and Drewry Bell were walking through the orchard when they noticed an old woman walking next to them. When Betsy tried to talk to her, the woman vanished.

was variously speculated that the witch was someone whom Bell had cheated or perhaps a male slave he had killed.

The Bell Witch is described in "History of Tennessee," a book published more than 60 years after the events, as "some spiritual being having the voice and attributes of a woman. It was invisible to the eye, yet it would hold conversation and even shake hands with certain individuals. The feats it performed were wondrous and seemingly designed to annoy the family. It would take sugar from the bowls, spill the milk, take the quilts from the beds, slap and pinch the children and then laugh at the discomfort of its victims."

Another historical work about Tennessee, the 1913 book "A History of Tennessee and Tennesseans," said that, "In 1817, the family heard or imagined queer knockings at night on the walls of the house. Later on, disturbances commenced within the house – sounds as of rats gnawing the bed posts, then as of dogs fighting, and then as of chains dragging over the floor. As soon as a candle was lighted to investigate the disturbance, the noise would cease in the lighted room, while the daughter in another room would scream in fright because of similar noises there."

Neighbors also reported witnessing strange events on the Bells' farm and as news of the haunting spread people came from considerable distances to learn more about the bizarre happenings. Local residents were convinced the Bells were the focus of a "bewitching." The incident has since become a part of Tennessee legend and folklore and is said to have inspired the movies "The Blair Witch Project" and "An American Haunting." The Bell House no longer stands, but there are several Bell Witch attractions in and around Adams, Tennessee.

Haunting the White House

The White House has a history of haunting incidents, and even membership in the exclusive domain of presidents does not render one immune to becoming a ghost.

Dorothy "Dolley" Madison was the wife of James Madison, the fourth president of the United States, who took office in 1809. She is credited with turning the new nation's capital at Washington, D.C., from a dull swamp into a high society social scene. But she never liked to be crossed or contradicted, as the legend of her ghost demonstrates. When the second Mrs. Woodrow Wilson lived in the White House, in the early 20th century, she told her gardeners to dig up the iconic Rose Garden, which Dolley Madison had both planned and built some hundred years prior. Mrs. Wilson's gardeners never even started to carry out the First Lady's orders because Dolley arrived in all her 19th century finery and harshly scolded the men, who quickly fled the scene, having disturbed not a single flower.

The White House's Rose Room, which contains the bed of Andrew "Old Hickory" Jackson, is said to be one of the most haunted spots in the presidential home. It is claimed that Jackson still dwells in his former bed chamber and that his presence has been felt there on more than one occasion. Twenty years after Jackson's death, Mary Todd Lincoln, a devout believer in the spirit world, told friends that she'd heard Jackson stomping through the White House corridors, cursing and swearing bitterly, perhaps still brooding over slights and political defeats he had suffered while still among the living.

President John Adams and his wife Abigail were the first occupants of the White House. Adams served from 1797 to 1801, and the couple took up residence when the home was only half finished. Abigail reportedly cheerfully tolerated the noise and confusion of workmen coming and going, but was confronted with the problem of where to hang the family wash. The White House was not yet properly heated, leaving many of the rooms cold and damp.

Having finally decided the East Room was the warmest and driest space available, she strung her clothesline there. Her ghost is now sometimes seen hurrying toward the East Room with her arms outstretched, as though carrying a load of laundry, and she can be recognized by the cap and lace shawl she favored in life. One could view Abigail Adams' ghost as acting out an eerie illustration of the old adage, "A woman's work is never done," as she labors in eternity, struggling to finish what should be a mundane chore.

* * *

America's Strange and Supernatural History

This has been a brief overview of incidents in American history that clearly demonstrate what we should have already known but may not have taken to heart. We can in a sense be said to have been partially descended from eaters of men, and even a few of our most celebrated leaders apparently do not rest easy in the grave. Collectively, we could be said to stand on a shaky foundation and to be upheld only by some form of divine grace we are too enshrouded in darkness to understand. Will America's ultimate fate be decided by the ability to recognize and reject the demons that have been so firmly entrenched among us for so long?

Sources For This Chapter

Starving Settlers in Jamestown Colony Resorted to Cannibalism

www.smithsonianmag.com/history/starving-settlers-in-jamestown-colony-resorted-to-cannibalism-46000815/?page=1

Girl's Bones Bear Signs of Cannibalism by Starving Virginia Colonists

www.nytimes.com/2013/05/02/science/evidence-of-cannibalism-found-at-jamestown-site.html

Donner Party

http://en.wikipedia.org/w/indexphp?title=Donner_Party

Did the Donner Party really resort to cannibalism?

www.history.com/news/ask-history/did-the-donner-party-really-resort-to-cannibalism

Alferd Packer

http://en.wikipedia.org/w/indexphp?title=Alferd_Packer

America's Strange and Supernatural History

William Seabrook

http://en.wikipedia.org/w/indexphp?title=William_Seabrook

A Brief History of Cannibalism in America

http://blogs.villagevoice/runninscared/2012/06/american_cannibalism.php?

10 Things You Always Wondered About Cannibalism

www.businessinsider.com/10-things-you-always-wondered-about-cannibalism-2012-5?op=1

Bell Witch

http://en.wikipedia.org/w/indexphp?title=Bell_Witch

A 19th Century Haunting

www.exploresouthernhistory.com/bellwitch1.html

Famous Ghosts In American History

www.history.com/topics/halloween/haunted-historic-places

Chapter Eight

Rural Mysteries and the Bigger Picture

By Wm. Michael Mott

HAVING lived in many different locations in the USA and also overseas, I've seen a lot of strange things... And heard a lot of weird and anomalous first-person accounts of high strangeness. I've also heard more than my share of stories passed down from parents, grandparents, and even great-grandparents.

One constant theme I've found is that those who have had such experiences are often reluctant to talk about them outside of a very small circle of family and friends, and sometimes, they aren't willing to talk about them at all. Whether it's fear of ridicule, or of being ostracized by their church or community, they don't want to be stigmatized as "crazy", delusional or as a liar. Even worse, often people (particularly in the South) think that having a strange or anomalous experience reflects badly on them personally.

As a result, many either clam up about their experiences, or else they ask that their real names not be used in written accounts. But occasionally I receive first-person accounts from people who will, at the very least, allow me to share their stories or those of their immediate family members.

One state from which I've received some very interesting accounts is Mississippi. While many of these accounts seem at first glance to be more or less "standard" types of UFO and strange creature accounts, they actually vary in very distinctive ways which place them more in line with historical accounts of phenomena of a supernatural nature. Some are strangely reminiscent of Marian apparitions, angelic visitations, and demonic manifestations from the Middle Ages up through the present day.

America's Strange and Supernatural History

Jacques Vallee and John Keel have both pointed out the similarities between these more ancient phenomena and the manifestations of gods, goddesses and devils in the ancient world, and also of manifestations of UFOs, their occupants, and anomalous creatures and humanoids in more modern times. The reports I've received from Mississippi residents (and there are many) seem to be no different. Is there a message in these "visitations" or manifestations, or is simply, as Keel believed, the irrational (to humanity) activity of a deranged non-human intelligence?

Such events are usually interpreted through the lens of the historical time period in which they occur. In this short piece I will examine a few such cases, just from the state of Mississippi, that seem to fall within this category.

In the first case, a gentleman I know from long personal acquaintance sent me an account penned by his maternal grandmother. As is often the case in the South, he asked that I change the names or use initials in order to protect the family's privacy, and to avoid any stigma that his relatives might feel from the revelations. The incident took place in or near Ackerman, MS in 1940, and is recounted here:

In the year of our Lord, nineteen hundred and forty in the month of November, I saw the light. Our baby, C_____, was born in October of this year. We were so happy now to have two boys and a girl. Our family joy prevailed despite the fact of threatenings of an oncoming war.

To add to my happiness, D____ had gotten a logging job with C_____ M_____ and T_____ B_____ in the Panhandle Community of Choctaw County. This meant we would have a little extra cash for winter clothes and Christmas gifts. The depression of the 30's had been very unkind to us.

Usually it was dark when D____ got home from work. One night he came hurriedly through the door and said, "E____, come here I want to show you something. Come out in the yard, wait, and you will see." Then suddenly out in front of us appeared, in the dark of night, this dazzling grey light.

It dangled up-and-down and here-and-there in front of us. It never touched the ground. It looked very much like the light given off by a flashlight, with the color varying from light to grey. It darted from one place to another, changing shapes from the likeness of a huge bird, an airplane, a ball, then an oval shape. It covered a space of 10 to 20 feet. It seemed to appear near the location of people. What about the sky itself? I cannot remember if it was cloudy or clear; however, the light made no noise.

We soon went inside and busied ourselves with supper and other chores, not going back out to view this spectacular light. Then, D____ told me that C____ T____, a black man, began seeing this light between Ackerman and our house as they were driving home from work. They had stopped in the Bywy Community at Robinson's Store, encouraging those shopping to come out and see the light. Then suddenly while they were all outside in the back of the store, the light darted down–around and above M____ M____'s house. It then came over the house moving toward the store. It appeared right and then left–travelling quicker than the eye. However, it always seemed to appear in front of the person seeing it. One could not turn his head around and see it at his back. There might have been more than one light because it seemed to be appearing to many different people at the same time.

Others who saw the light were: R____ and G____ S_____ and Uncle A___ S_____s family. On this night, R____ and G____ were going from Mama's house to the General Moss house in Ackerman in their old Ford car. The light glowed in front of their car all above the way home. And then as they were going into the house, the light came down and hovered between them and the front door, just above the top of the door steps.

About this same time, my brother, J____ K., and a cousin, J. B. S_____, and some other boys had their guns out trying to shoot the light. They described it as two huge gray birds darting at each other.

The memory of this event has remained vivid throughout my life after this incident occurred. I am convinced that the light was supernatural. I wish, now, that I could have had the foresight to collect more data on the various sightings of the light; however, at the time, I did not seem to recognize its significance. But let me be assertive–I SAW THE LIGHT.

What are we to make of an account like this? The grandson stated that after this event, there was large round area in the yard where all the grass died, and nothing would ever grow there again... Yet no "flying saucer" was seen during this event. The woman was a very devout Christian and her account was apparently supported by a wide range of local people at the time (and I would wager that their descendants still talk about it today). It obviously affected her on a very deep, personal and perhaps even religious level. While it does share some characteristics with UFO events and Marian encounters, it is also similar to accounts from previous centuries regarding angelic visitations, fairy encounters, and prophetic events of a religious nature. Were the objects real and solid? Were they holograms of some sort, projections of the mad "super-intelligence" that Keel wrote about so often? Were they the creations and projections of the holographic "mech" of the subterranean "dero" or "tero" that Richard Shaver claimed to live beneath the surface of our own planet? Or were they, in fact, prophetic in some way of the coming war in Europe and the Pacific? After all, the symbols of both the United States and Germany were eagles...

We will probably never know.

Ten years later in 1950, around the month of April, another strange event took place some 70 miles to the south of Ackerman, on a rural farm near the town of Union, Mississippi. Union bears the distinction of being the only sizable town in the region to have escaped immolation at the command of William T. Sherman, as he made his march through the state (February 3–28, 1864) from Vicksburg to Meridian, burning and looting as he went. Union survived this near-genocidal event by virtue of its name, and Sherman spared it in a symbolic gesture of faux mercy.

In April of 1950, J_____ S_____ was a girl of eleven, and her sister P_____ was "seven or eight" years old. The girls were in the cornfield behind their house, helping their grandfather fertilize the seedling corn plants, when he called for them to stop what they were doing and to look at the sky. When they did so, they observed three "huge" cylindrical objects like "fat cigars", of a pale metallic hue, hovering over the fields and trees nearby. The objects were perfectly still in the afternoon sky.

The grandfather sent J_____ to run home and tell her mother to come look at this wonder. She did so, arriving out of breath at the simple homestead some two hundred yards away, and her mother rushed outside to take a look. As soon as she saw the stationary objects, she sent her oldest daughter back to fetch her younger sibling home, because she had an ominous feeling about the strange craft in the sky. J_____ did as she was told, and the grandfather joined them on the porch where the family watched the objects for at least thirty minutes. They felt the whole time like "they were being watched". Then, without warning, the objects accelerated from hovering silently to a blinding speed and shot away in the blink of an eye.

This was not the only experience that particular family had with unknown flying objects. Sometime in the early 1970s, the youngest son and his friends ended a camping trip abruptly in the middle of the night, when they were pursued through the woods by a huge glowing light the moved silently above them, and which hovered above them when they fell into a gulley on their mad dash out of the swamp.

Years later, he recounted these events to me, and stated that he and his friends had gone to "watch the lights coming and going from the swamp after dark", which apparently was a regular occurrence at the time. Needless to say, after being chased through the midnight forest by a very bright unidentified flying object, they ended this pastime permanently. To further complicate matters, in the late '70s a teenaged nephew told me how he had hidden in terror behind a rolled hay-bale at dusk, as a giant, hairy man-thing "about nine feet tall" stood in a ditch that crossed a nearby hayfield, scrutinizing the area as if sensing the presence of an observer.

As outlined by this writer in a previously published article ("Doorways: The Path Through A Dark Forest", Paranormal Magazine #64, Sept. 2012, pp. 32-33), the area in the general vicinity has experienced a number of "strange creature" and "entity" sightings. Many young campers and outdoorsmen have had similar experiences over the years, but are often reluctant to attach their names to them. As is typical for rural Mississippi, however, the percipients prefer to have their real names changed or omitted.

At 6:51 p.m. CST, in January 25th, 2014, I was contacted by a young man from a small rural community in this same area. He told me that he and his sister had been driving along a back-country road one evening, "heading to town", when his sister pointed out the window and yelped in terror. Slowing the car to a crawl, they watched as a group of "ugly, skinny creatures" cavorted and leapt about beneath a leafless tree in a field, some hundred yards away. The "creatures" suddenly noticed the car, and stood staring at the vehicle, whereupon the brother and sister took off for the town some seven or eight miles away. According to the teenage boy, they were further terrified to glimpse these same creatures, running impossibly fast, in the woods and fields alongside and behind them. Totally terrified by this time, they finally breathed a joint sigh of relief when they pulled into the little town and parked under the lights of the combination gas-station, convenience store and sandwich shop. Even then, they were scared to make the drive back home and lingered in town far longer than they had originally planned. The male witness described the creatures as "super skinny" and pale, and possibly hairless.

At first he agreed to speak with me in greater detail about this encounter or sighting; later he backed out, stating that his sister was worried that if he talked about the creatures they had seen, the "things" might get angry and "come after them". This is a common theme with experiencers in the region, and correlates with an interaction I had with a 16 year-old boy who, in 2011, told me that he was terrified of a "thing with a big white head" around seven or eight feet tall that wore a long black robe, and lived in a cave behind his house in the general area of rural Little Rock, Mississippi. He stated that this "thing" came into his yard at night and stood outside his window, and that he had seen it come and go from the cave, as had others. He also told me that he didn't want to talk about it anymore than he already had, because when he did tell others (particularly adults) about it, it would "get into his room and stand beside his bed staring at him, and he wouldn't be able to move", and that it would also "chase him in his dreams".

Games, Tricks or Guidance?

So what are we dealing with in all of these cases? Is there a common thread between them, other than their collective strangeness? In our "modern" society disdainful, fear-driven mockery masquerades as scientific-minded skepticism, and many would be quick to call these events hoaxes, "mistaken identity" cases of natural phenomena and creatures, "mass delusions" or "mass hallucinations" (the latter being an actual impossibility, since an hallucination can only appear in the mind of one percipient, and not to multiple witnesses simultaneously). But the witnesses themselves tell a very different story. Is there any proof? Nothing physically substantial beyond eyewitness testimony, which seems quite sufficient to send people to prison and even to the death chamber, when entered into evidence in a court of law.

Many or most of these accounts will no doubt be pigeon-holed into convenient categories, but if we look back through human history, we will find similar or identical events interpreted within the context of contemporary religious and folk-belief systems. The lady in Ackerman, Mississippi apparently had a vision as personally spiritual to her as Constantine did when he saw a giant crucifix in the sky above the Tiber river, or as the appearance of a radiant "lady" and "angel" were to Lucia, Francisco and Jacinta, in Portugal in 1916. Martin Luther was visited by an entity that he believed to be the actual devil-in-the-flesh, an apparition so real that Luther threw an ink-well at it; and the accounts of this type are almost beyond cataloging, so numerous are they in the human experience. The sheer number of such encounters belies simple explanation or dismissal. By now, Fortean scholars are well-acquainted with Keel's claims that the "Mothman" sightings were somehow a premonition of the collapse of the Silver Bridge, which resulted in the deaths of 46 people in the icy waters of the Ohio River, but this is not a singular event by any stretch of the imagination (and admittedly, if "Mothman" was a portent of disaster, it certainly spent a lot of spare time for months prior to the event, in frightening teenagers and lone travelers and allegedly stealing dogs for food and eating road kill as a nutritional supplement). Keel eventually postulated that there was no real "rhyme or reason" for these strange events, that in fact they seem nonsensical to us because they are, in fact, irrational and nonsensical, the product of a localized (to the vicinity of our planet) intelligence so alien to us as to appear irrational or even insane.

The bigger picture, however, does not seem to bear this out, at least not completely. If one views these events as preparatory, aimed at personal or even collective initiation, they then might fall into the context of a Buddhist ko-an, which is a statement of fact or a question which is fundamentally illogical, but which contains provocative concepts designed to provoke higher thinking in Zen practitioners. Since such events continue to baffle, confuse and mystify the most materialistic "scientific" thinkers (who more often or not, surrender in a fit of futility disguised as dismissal and denial, and reject as foolishness all such events, out of hand), we are also reminded of the Judeo-Christian viewpoint:

America's Strange and Supernatural History

"...God hath chosen the foolish things of the world to confound the wise; and God hath chosen the weak things of the world to confound the things which are mighty;" —1 Corinthians 1:27.

...Yet those same Scriptures also warn us about "false signs and wonders", designed by an enemy of humanity to mislead and confuse us all. In the event that the latter is the case (devils, "aliens", or ultraterrestials, all names being ultimately interchangeable and equally ambiguous), then such "wonders" are no more meaningful than the actions of the "preacher" who claims to be a healer as long as he has an auditorium filled with zealous fans, but who will not once walk through the cancer ward of a children's hospital, where child-like faith would surely be in abundance and his "gift" of healing would be most welcome. In such a scenario, these mysterious and frightening events would be designed to fascinate us, much as a shiny bauble fascinates an infant, and distract us from cleaning up after ourselves and improving our collective situation within a larger, everyday framework. They might also represent a form of sleight-of-hand that serves to distract us from very real activity going on nearby, much more opportunistic than we'd care to contemplate, activity which is perhaps also much more sinister in nature than we would ever permit ourselves to believe.

A Personal Puzzle

As an artist and photographer, I take many high-resolution pictures with my digital camera. I take quite a number of landscape and sky shots, because these often prove to come in handy for graphics and publishing projects. Dramatic lighting in particular is something that I strive to capture, so storm clouds, sunsets, twilight images and so on are often the subject of my spontaneous photo-shooting sessions.

On August 6th, 2013, I ventured out into the Mississippi twilight in an attempt to capture the color and contrast of a brooding day's end. During this jaunt I took a variety of photos in rapid sequence, as the sun was quickly sinking, having already set; facing the west, I took rapid shots in sequence to capture the sky in low-light. The digital camera was set on automatic, and the shots were about half a second apart. When I took the photos I noticed nothing anomalous or out of the ordinary in the environment.

America's Strange and Supernatural History

I didn't even look at all of the photos until December of 2013, when I noticed an anomaly in one frame. Honestly, I cannot explain this "artifact" in a digital photo. It's not as if there are negatives that can be damaged or affected by extraneous effects or influences. I waited nearly a year to share the image(s) with a select group of friends on Facebook, because I wanted to make sure that there was no error in the camera. Nothing like this has happened again, in the thousands of shots taken over the last year. The anomaly appears to be a genuine three-dimensional object. Since my background experience is heavy in image creation, image processing and computer graphics, I have found myself unable to come up with a logical explanation. For some perspective on my background, I have been a professional Art Director, Creator Director, Creative Services Manager, and so on, and over the years portfolios and tutorials of my digital design work have been featured in *IEEE Computer* magazine; *IEEE Computer Graphics and Applications* magazine; *Computer Graphics World* magazine (twice); and *Electronic Imaging* magazine (twice). I've also had work appear in *Computer Artist* magazine, and I co-wrote an article on the use of computer graphics and visualization in a campus and classroom environment (*Syllabus* magazine, March 1996, Vol. 9 #6—an issue for which I also did the cover art). There have been others as well.

Therefore, when I find a digital image artifact that I cannot explain or reproduce, then I have to scratch my shaven head in perplexity. I have shown the image(s) to others, including Lance Oliver, a field investigator for Texas MUFON, who believes it to be highly significant. It is not "computer graphics" and was most definitely not created in an image-editing program, which can be determined through a variety of means of interpolation and interpretation of the image data. Due to the low-light conditions, the image(s) lack the clarity and hyper-realism of digitally-generated imagery.

Whatever the anomaly is, it appears to be a large three-dimensional object with a distinctly cube-like or box-like shape. There are protrusions and flaps or flanges, and what appears to be a strut-like superstructure visible at one end. The object was probably one-quarter mile distant, so it is of significant size, perhaps as large as a tractor trailer container. The object is back-lit with the same ambient light which permeated the environment at the time, and the shadows correlate to the direction of the waning light source. Wisps of cloud obscure the edges.

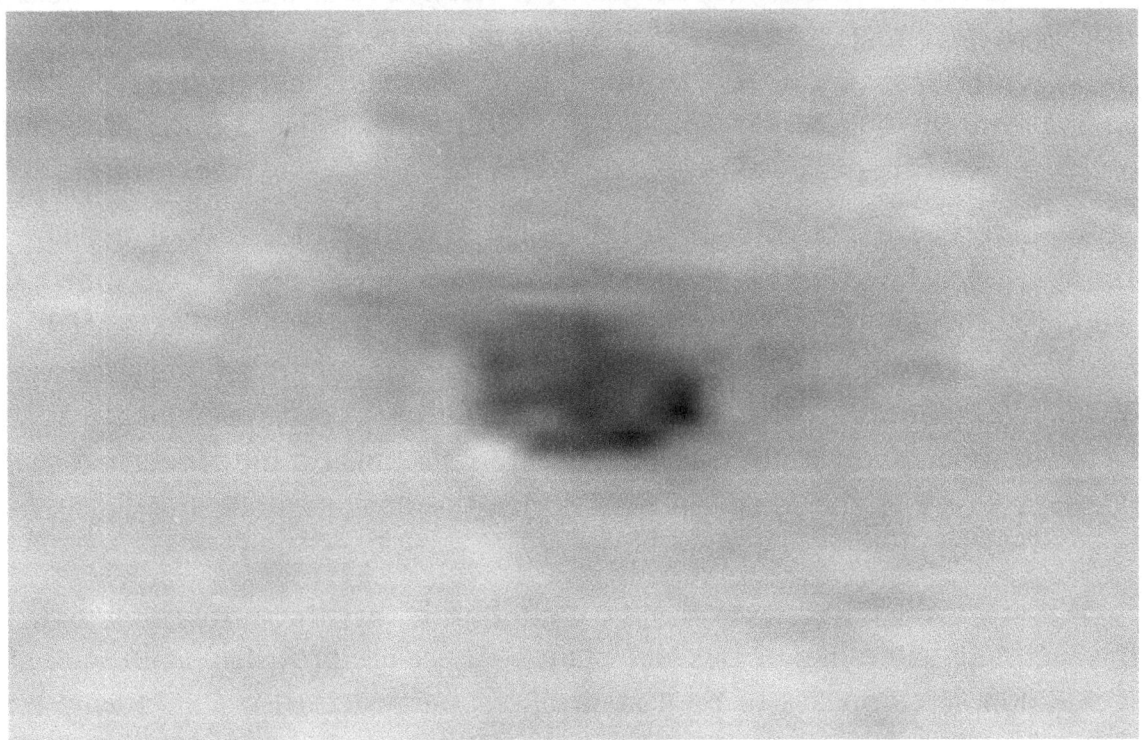

Whatever the anomaly is, it appears to be a large three-dimensional object with a distinctly cube-like or box-like shape. There are protrusions and flaps or flanges, and what appears to be a strut-like superstructure visible at one end.

What is this object? Why was it visible to the camera and not to the naked eye? Why does in appear in one frame and then vanish within one second, before the next? Since it did not appear to my naked eye, does it represent another level to the puzzle, i.e., a level which was not meant to be seen and described? It is not an intrusive experience by any description. It is an accident of mindless mechanical observation, that of the camera, and represents an objective piece of evidence of... something.

So what is it? As with the aerial apparitions seen in Ackerman, Mississippi in 1940, we will probably never know. The only thing to be ascertained is that it represents concrete proof for the presence of an unknown intelligence in our environment and our skies. I, for one, feel that the time for eye witnesses and those who have evidence of anomalous encounters and sightings to no longer remain silent, or to hide their identities out of some socially-ingrained, fear-of-being-ridiculed instinct or behavioral conditioning...to break out of that conditioning and step into the light of day.

Until we do this, nothing will change and we will continue wandering in the dark, groping for the tail of the elephant like the blind men in the fable, easily manipulated and misled. Forget "governmental disclosure", because more often than not, governments are just as befuddled as the rest of us. We have to continue with "personal disclosures". When the mass of humanity finally accepts and practices that, then the shadows—of doubt, fear, ignorance, superstition and conditioned obedience—will finally begin to be dispelled. We have been manipulated by these mysterious and shadowy forces, these "principalities and powers of the air," for far too long.

It's time to throw off the shackles and blinders and claim our freedom in every sense of the word.

The Footprints of the Damned

When writing about anomalous subjects, one has to be very careful to keep oneself out of the narrative as much as possible. Until my recent publication of a photo showing an unexplained aerial object, this has always been my policy as a Fortean writer and researcher, because one must remain as objective as possible in order for all data to be properly assessed.

America's Strange and Supernatural History

In his writings, the late John Keel related his own experiences, which were often encountered in his investigations, or as a result of them. Likewise, Brad Steiger has, over the years, shared personal investigative experiences, as well as some from his childhood. Yet both gentlemen remained highly objective in their investigations, research and analyses. The only times they brought personal experiences into their narratives were those times that strangeness affected them, or those close to them, directly.

When researching and investigating anomalous phenomena, a great deal of logical deduction comes into play. Patterns are assessed, eyewitness accounts are evaluated, and known facts within the scope of current scientific knowledge are brought to bear. Historical sources and accounts are also of great importance, as parallels to recent events or phenomena are often found within them. The type of information that often eludes investigators is "hard evidence"... I.e., a photo that cannot be explained as a hoax, inexplicable DNA evidence, or physical artifacts.

When it comes to the last-mentioned category, such artifacts have in fact been found, not once but many times. Manufactured objects like a candlestick and an iron hammer have been found encased in coal which came from deep strata having an age in the millions of years; and tiny, intricate metal objects resembling finely-tooled gears have been found. In South African pyrophylite mines, unexplained, precision-machined objects called Klerksdorp spheres have been found and recovered many times, from strata that is 3 billion years old. Skeptics attempt to explain the latter objects away as "calcareous concretions", by comparing the spheres to other objects found, but this is dishonest scientifically (equivalent to saying that bats and birds belong to the same family because both have wings and can fly, for instance) and intellectually. In short, it is a dismissal based in opinion and conjecture, and not in fact. A convenient equivalency or similarity is identified and then exploited in an opportunistic, eager fashion as an "explanation", when more often than not it is simply a thinly-veiled effort to debunk and discredit something that does not fit into the accepted, permitted and religious orthodoxy of modern scientific "thought".

In the stone bed of the Paluxy River, near Glen Rose, Texas, there are some very interesting footprints, fossilized in stone. One type of track present is that of a theropod dinosaur, three-toed on each foot, and fairly wide in configuration. The other set of tracks appear to be those of a bipedal humanoid of giant size, wearing footwear, which are placed roughly parallel to the dinosaur tracks. The rock containing these tracks was mud, back during the Mesozoic, a vast period of time which lasted from approximately 240 million years past, until the end of the Cretaceous period, some 66 million years ago.

Such pieces of "damned data", as Charles Fort termed them, do not fit into any "acceptable" school of "science". Therefore, they must be debunked, er...discredited, uhm...explained away as rapidly and with as much contemptuous disdain as possible. Their very existence is an upstart affront to the wardens of scientific fact, the gate-keepers of orthodoxy, the guardians of the hive, the high-priests of science themselves! With the Paluxy tracks this effort has resulted in explanations of them being nothing more than the "eroded" metatarsal dinosaur tracks of animals running on their heels and "carvings". Elaborate diagrams have been created to show "how" the very-wide dinosaur tracks eroded into comparatively narrow humanoid tracks.

And there you have it, case closed. Except for the data that the concerned and vexed paleontologists intentionally omit, ignore or don't mention... Such at the fact that the stride of the alleged tracks of a giant humanoid correspond to a humanoid stride, and look nothing like those of the loping, splayed stride of the nearby theropod tracks; or the fact that the line of supposedly "toes-eroded-away" tracks go on for quite some distance, yet never once is a verifiable, missing dinosaur "toe track" found that is connected to one of them. So either there were meat-eating carnivorous dinosaurs running around ancient Texas wearing tight-fitting sensible shoes, or apparently there was something, or someone, striding about with a foot structure and stride which would be that of a very, very large human being (or similar form). Here we have a procession of dinosaurs and giant, unknown bipeds, either walking side by side or in close chronology, or chronologically close enough to share the same muddy river bottom. Quite a procession indeed.

Or, to quote an earlier writer on these topics:

PROCESSION of the damned.

By the damned, I mean the excluded.

We shall have a procession of data that Science has excluded. -Charles Fort

America's Strange and Supernatural History

The power that has said to all these things that they are damned, is Dogmatic Science. - Charles Fort

Recently, while walking my dog on our rural property, I came across a rectangular-looking rock sticking out of the ground. With the help of my son I dug it up. It was the small end of a bigger stone, and the whole appears to be either sandstone or limestone. It is a very hard form of it, however. It was buried in the ground at about an 80 degree angle. It was facing an uphill direction on a gentle slope of terrain.

I took this weird find back to my house but it wasn't until the next day, when the light was "just right", that my girlfriend noticed that it "looked like a footprint".

Now we shall have something that is high up in the castes of the accursed...

- Charles Fort

The day after that I took some photos in late afternoon light, when the angle of illumination really brought out the details. I have since shown the photos to a podiatrist, who says that it is definitely a footprint of "some kind of animal". He said "The outline does have the shape of a rear foot of an animal. Not enough impression to make out details of the rear portion. Might be a toe walker as calcaneus bone is often elongated in dogs and cats for example and does not directly bear weight." A few days later, he contacted me again and stated the following: "I think a calcaneus (heel bone) is shown. That means whatever it was walked on the whole foot instead of metarsal heads and toes." In other words, it is definitely a humanoid footprint, one which is at least 30 million years old, and found in the New World. He also said: "The outline helped me a lot in analyzing. Enough to change my opinion of the print from toe walker to complete foot walker." Additionally, a renowned cryptozoologist and zoologist saw the photos and quickly said "Bear?" There is only one problem with this: If this is a chunk of stone from the Ciaiborne Group deposit, or the Tallahatta Group, then that would place it in the Eocene. There were no bears roaming the planet at that time, and few mammals of a size to make a print like this.

There was, however, a primordial, ancestral canine creature called an Amphicyonidae, or "bear dog". This nasty character roamed North America, Europe, Africa and Asia from the Middle Eocene until the Pleistocene Epoch, a period of over 44 million years. Could I have found a fossilized, prehistoric "bear dog" print? Well, only if bear dogs had opposing big toes, with four receding toes alongside them, much in the fashion of a human foot. Which, of course, they did not.

The fossil appears to represent a a shallow print, with mud or soil displacement to the sides, such as is left in very slippery mud. The other ("bottom") side is almost perfectly flat, apparently supporting the possibility of a cast-like fill where an imprint dried, then was filled in by more sediment which eventually became the fossilized cast.

Other opinions have been varied, and for the most part accept the fossil for what it appears to be. A bigfoot researcher stated that the print is similar to existing plaster casts of footprints left by "sasquatch" or "bigfoot," and seems to be "a very base form of them...a starting point ...maybe before evolving into the current foot."

A medical doctor and specialist in medical forensics took a look at the photos, and stated "it looks like you have yourself a (foot)print," and "Very interesting. I've not seen a fossilized one so you have something special." So we have input from two medical doctors (one a podiatrist, and one a specialist in forensics), a bigfoot researcher, and a cryptozoologist (and zoologist) who has examined many tracks in the field, and all four individuals see a track left by, at the very least, a foot.

This gives us a near-consensus on this anomalous object, at the very least, being a genuine fossilized footprint. But not so fast! I also contacted a professional paleontologist, and his assessment was not so glowing. In response to my email, he responded within an hour, and stated the following:

"To the untrained eye, something unfamiliar can look like ANYTHING, or whatever the eye is untrained to recognize. To the trained (professional) eye, there is considerably greater familiarity, thus fewer possibilities as to what could explain a given phenomenon (and thus fewer "mysteries" or "unknowns").

"True, the rock looks like a foot print (people show me rocks all the time that they say look like skulls, but aren't). There are actually a number of features that convince my trained eye that it is nothing more than a slab of sandstone with peculiarly parallel burrow fillings (on one end), probably produced by a burrowing decapod (e.g. ghost shrimp) on the seafloor. Not to

I have shown these photos to a podiatrist, who says that it is definitely a footprint of "some kind of animal." He said, "The outline does have the shape of a rear foot of an animal. I think a calcaneus (heel bone) is shown. That means whatever it was walked on the whole foot instead of metarsal heads and toes."

discount your podiatrist, but there are numerous things wrong with the footprint, if human (or "humanoid")...

- *The 'toe mounds' are wrong (e.g. they form more of a straight rather than a curved line).*
- *The 'inner arch' is convex and not concave.*
- *There is no outer arch.*
- *The 'ball' (heel) of the foot is much too subdued.*

"This is just a coincidental shape (or convergence of shapes). Coupled with the source, Eocene marine sediments often populated with the burrows of benthic decapods, I'd say you have only a conversation piece. However, if you were to show me just one more such "footprint," and in better shape than this one, then I might be willing to consider the possibility that...you now have two bizarrely shaped rocks."

I found this to be a very interesting response, in several regards. First: When I contacted the paleontologist, I made no mention of the terms "human" or "humanoid." None whatsoever. I just sent him a brief account of how I came to find the object, and some photos. So apparently he "saw" a humanoid footprint "with his trained eye", which apparently resembled one closely enough for him to subsequently make the comparison himself.

Second, the (seeming) print is extremely similar to some modern casts of bigfoot prints in overall structure (they tend to be "flat-footed," in most cases), including the observations he made about the "toe mounds" being in a straight line, the "inner arch" being convex, and the heel being "subdued." Considering that the strata the rock came from is probably between 35 and 46 million years old, and was near the surface for most of that time, it should be expected that some weathering would occur, particularly in an impression left as a shallow, "slipping" footprint ascending a muddy slope. A shallow footprint in very slippery mud would also, very likely, leave little to no impression from an outer arch, and the "heel would be subdued", with the toes digging into the slope of the hillside.

Third: the likelihood of ghost-shrimp sculpting the exact shape of a humanoid footprint, complete with big toe, smaller toes evenly distributed and perfectly parallel, and all properly placed and of proper relative size to one another, is about as likely as a hill of ants building a replica of the Eiffel Tower. His rapid expert description of this is to describe the toe imprints as "peculiarly parallel burrow fillings (on on end)." In other words, the parallel nature of these ridges was noted, but then summarily dismissed as being "peculiarly parallel." Having spent quite a bit of time in the woods, swamps and outdoors as a young man, particularly in search of isolated fishing spots, this author can attest to seeing "burrowings," tunnelings, and so on by tiny creatures, in muddy areas, on a regular basis, including inside the hoof-prints of cattle! I have even seen the mud-towers built by crawfish inside of cattle prints... and this fossil object has none of those features whatsoever. Additionally, I do not recall ever seeing perfectly-spaced and parallel "tunnels" by mud-burrowers...Ever. They meander, squiggle and loop below the surface, leaving weird raised patterns in the mud. His contention that the footprint-shape was created by the blind questings of sub-surface shrimp is not just absurd, but is comical. This out-of-hand dismissal is borne out by his closing statement:

However, if you were to show me just one more such "footprint," and in better shape than this one, then I might be willing to consider the possibility that...you now have two bizarrely shaped rocks.

In other words, and much like the paleontological evaluations of the Paluxy River tracks, if I were to find an entire series of fossilized footprints, they would not really be footprints... They would only be "bizarrely shaped rocks." Always. Nothing else is even remotely possible.

How "scientific."

It is a good thing that early humans did not count on the opinions of highly-specialized scientists when tracking game, or they would have starved to death and none of us would be here to ponder these matters.

In the topography of intellection, knowledge is ignorance surrounded by laughter. ~Charles Fort

But science is established preposterousness. ~Charles Fort

So now I have a fossilized something, a chunk of "damned data" in the Fortean sense, a "damned rock" in the literal sense. I suppose I will keep it, lest it go the way of so many other anomalous bones, skulls, skeletons and artifacts found in North America over the last 200 to 300 years, objects that were given over for temporary examination and safekeeping to various museums and "institutions," only to... disappear, to vanish into some hidden hell reserved specifically for such accursed and troublesome Lies of Nature. Will I ever get rid of this 30 to 40 million-year old object?

Probably not. As I said, I'll probably just keep the damned thing.

The God of the bees is the Hive. -Charles Fort

I will find out for myself. -Charles Fort

Chapter Nine

Are There Still Monsters?

THERE are monsters. Ask any child who has lain awake in the dark of night, certain that some unknown horror lurks in the shadows under their bed. Ask anyone who has walked through a dark forest, aware that inhuman eyes are following their every move. Ask anyone who has heard a strange noise where there should only be silence. They will tell you...there are monsters.

Perhaps there is a place deep within our brains that remembers a far off time when we huddled together in the cracks and crevices of rocks, listening for the black things of the night that hungered; always hungered.

There is a horror that exists inside us all. Oozing from the most primitive parts of the brain, this horror whispers to us in the night of unspeakable things lurking in the dark. From the beginning, humans have instinctively known that the shadows contain things not of this world. These denizens of the night – hairy monsters, wild men and other bizarre creatures – have haunted us in our dreams and apparently also in our reality. These creatures have been known by many different names, yet their descriptions remain eerily similar despite geographical or chronological distance.

In ancient Babylon there was the great Akkadian epic Gilgamesh that recounts the trials and triumphs of a legendary king by the same name. One of the many tasks Gilgamesh is charged with is fighting and defeating a hairy beast-man call Enkidu. Gilgamesh is successful at this and eventually the two become fast friends.

Modern anthropologists suggest that the similarity and dispersion of these tales may be a result of a "cultural memory" when mankind lived alongside other hominids. The Australian aborigines, when asked about their own versions of the wild man called a Yowie, state that the creature has existed as long as the "dreamtime," a far-off time that predates any written language or other forms of permanent record keeping.

Even in modern times, when we seem so sure of our knowledge and place in the world, strange creatures continue to intrude into our nice, safe lives where rational thought says they have no place. However, for those who became unwilling participants in the breakdown of their personal reality, the world, as they knew it, could never be looked at in the same way again.

Considering the growing human population and the spread of people from centralized locations into rural areas, you would not expect there to be much room left for denizens of the "dreamtime." Yet, if you were to ask anyone, anywhere, about local myths and legends concerning strange creatures, odds are that most would have a story or two to tell.

We like to think that things are different now, that we have tamed the things that used to hunt us in the night. It is comforting to think that our bright lights and big cities offer a refuge from those that would slake their thirst with our blood. However, are things really so different? Are we really as safe as we think we are?

Are there still monsters?

Blood is the Life

Over the years, strange attacks on animals and humans have been recorded and attributed to predators, other humans, and even supernatural creatures such as vampires. What makes these incidents similar is the general lack of blood found in the bodies. Primitive man believed that blood was sacred, the source of life in all creatures. When you lost your blood, you lost your life. So it made sense that the life force must be contained in blood.

The Old Testament is a good example of ancient beliefs regarding blood. Leviticus 17:14 states, that "the life of every living creature is its blood." The verse goes on to say that it is forbidden for anyone to eat blood because it is the source of all life.

Vampires and vampire-like creatures have been found in the folklore of every civilization, every culture, and every religion since the beginning of recorded time. In ancient Babylonia there was Lilitu, (in Hebrew Lilith or Adam's first wife in Talmudic lore); after her rejection of Adam's dominance, she becomes a demon that attacks infants and children in the night.

In India, tales of the Vetalas, ghoul-like beings that inhabit corpses, are found in old Sanskrit folklore. The Vetala is an undead creature, who, like the bat associated with the modern day vampire, is associated with hanging upside down on the trees found in cremation grounds and cemeteries.

The Chinese have the Ch'Iang (or Chiang-Shih), irrational creatures that are driven by bloodlust. They have difficulty walking because of the pain and stiffness of being dead so they hop instead. Some even will sexually assault their victims in addition to their bloodsucking.

The Malaysian Langsuitis is a woman who wears a gown, has long nails and long jet black hair. This vampire has a hole the back of her neck which she uses to suck the blood from children.

The Scotts tell of the Baobham sith, which takes the form of groups of beautiful girls who lure their victims into the woods and marshes to drain victims of blood.

The Jersey Devil

In the United States, the granddaddy of spooky creatures has to be the Jersey Devil. This weird beastie of the New Jersey Pinelands has haunted New Jersey and the surrounding areas for over 260 years. The Jersey Devil, sometimes also referred to as the Leeds Devil, is considered by most scholars to be a legendary creature. Nevertheless, some estimate as many as 2,000 people have claimed encounters with the Devil over the centuries.

A lot of what we now know about the Jersey Devil is thanks to the diligent research of writer Dave Juliano who managed to track down numerous, never reported, encounters with the Devil. Juliano is now convinced that there is evidence to support the existence of an animal or supernatural being known as the Jersey Devil.

One of the most popular legends on the origin of the Jersey Devil says that a Mrs. Shrouds of Leeds Point, NJ wished that if she ever had another child, it would be a devil. Her next child was born misshapen and deformed. She sheltered it in the house, so the curious couldn't see him. On a stormy night, the child flapped its arms, which turned into wings, and escaped out the chimney and was never seen by the family again.

Another story says that the Devil's mother was a young woman from Leeds Point who fell in love with a British soldier during the Revolutionary War. The other people of Leeds Point cursed her, since the child was born of an act of treason.

In another legend placing the birth of the Devil in Leeds Point, the creature was said to be punishment by God upon the people of the town for their mistreatment of a minister.

Another story placed the birth in Estelville, NJ. Mrs. Leeds, of Estelville, finding out she was pregnant with her 13th child, shouted, "I hope it's a devil." She got her wish. The child was born with horns, a tail, wings, and a horse-like head. The creature visited Mrs. Leeds every day. She stood at her door and told it to leave. After awhile, the creature got the hint and never returned.

Still others say that Mother Leeds of Burlington, NJ was a supposed witch. One night in 1735, she gave birth to the Devil's child, who changed into a horrible winged creature and flew out the chimney after beating everyone present at the birth.

There are other variations of the story, but a common fact binds most of them together, the use of the name Leeds, whether as the birthplace or the mother's name. Atlantic County historian Alfred Heston says that a Daniel Leeds came to Leeds Point in 1699, and the Shrouds also lived in the town. Prof. Fred MacFadden of Coppin College in Baltimore says that a "devil" was mentioned in Burlington records from approximately 1735. All these facts seem to suggest that there is some basis in fact for the Devil legend.

The Jersey Devil was known for its so-called "chimney raids" where it would enter a house through the chimney terrorizing the inhabitants. It would allegedly tear up furniture, chase people and pets, and kidnap children by dragging them up the chimney. Its less violent activities included tangling clotheslines, rustling bushes, hovering over lone travelers, and casting strange shadows.

The creature was described as being about four feet tall, with a large, hideous head shaped like a horse and eyes that glowed red in the dark. It has yellow, pointed teeth, two horns protruding from its forehead and leathery wings spanning two feet, enabling the monster to fly. It is nocturnal with a yellow glow and the stench of fire and brimstone. Its mournful cry was said to cause death to all who heard it.

In the 1830s and 1840's, the Jersey Devil was reported in Virginia. Among its victims were mutilated livestock, dogs, geese, cats, and ducks. It allegedly attempted to grab children as well.

The most incredible flurry activity regarding the Devil did not happen until 1909 when literally thousands of encounters with the beast were reported. Articles printed in the now defunct **Philadelphia Record** chronicled the Devil's exploits. During the week of January 16th to the 23rd, the Jersey Devil reached a crescendo of popularity while managing to terrorize the entire population of the Delaware Valley. So great was the attention paid to the creature, it received national news coverage.

The first sighting of this "flap" came early on the morning of the 16th. That is when Zack Cozzens saw it by the side of the road as he was driving through Woodbury. "I first heard a hissing sound," said Cozzens, "Then, something white flew across the street. I saw two spots of phosphorous--the eyes of the beast...It was as fast as an auto."

On the other side of the Delaware River, in Bristol, Pennsylvania, liquor store owner John McOwen heard a scratching sound, and looked out the window to see something like a gigantic bird. Later on that night, James Sackville, a patrolman, saw the creature flying and screaming. About the same time, the postmaster, E.W. Minster, was awakened by a sharp scream, and saw a flying monster with a long neck and a horse-like head. The next morning, the Devil's hoof prints were found in the snow.

America's Strange and Supernatural History

Back in New Jersey, in the city of Burlington, the Lowdens woke up to find their trash half-eaten and mysterious hoof prints all around. Many of Burlington's yards contained these strange marks. Similar tracks--going up trees, over walls and rooftops, and disappearing in the middle of a field, were also found in Columbus, Hedding, Kinhora and Rancocas. Dogs brought in to follow the trail seemed oddly reluctant to do so.

Very early Wednesday morning (at approximately 2:30AM), Mr. & Mrs. Nelson Evans, residents of Gloucester, were awakened by an odd noise. Looking out their window, they observed a creature that could only have been the Jersey Devil.

"It was about three feet and a half high, with a head like a collie dog and a face like a horse," the couple agreed. "It had a long neck, wings about two feet long, and its back legs were like those of a crane, and it had horse's hooves. It walked on its back legs and held up two short front legs with paws on them. It didn't use the front legs at all while we were watching."

Mrs. Evans gathered up enough courage to unlatch the window. "I managed to open the window and say, 'Shoo', and it turned around and barked at me, and flew away."

A Burlington police officer and Rev. John Pursell of Pemberton both saw the Devil. Rev. Pursell said that the creature was like nothing he had ever seen. The inexplicable hoof prints were found near Haddonfield and Riverside; the Devil was seen flying about near Collingswood. At the Mount Carmel Cemetery in Moorestown, John Smith saw the flying monster, as did George Snyder of the same town.

The next day, the Devil was seen flying above a trolley car near Clementon. In Trenton, E.P. Weeden heard wings flapping and found more inexplicable hoof prints, which were also found at the arsenal in Trenton. Trolley cars in Trenton and New Brunswick were supplied with armed conductors in case of a Devil attack, and churches in Pitman and many other New Jersey communities were filled with people. Farmers on both the Pennsylvania and New Jersey sides of the Delaware found their chickens mysteriously killed.

In Camden, a Mrs. Sorbinski heard a strange noise, and looked outside to see the Devil standing there, its paws gripping her dog's back. She hit the creature

America's Strange and Supernatural History

The Jersey Devil

with a broom and it dropped her dog and flew off. The police, hearing her screams, managed to fire upon the creature near Kaigan Hill.

The next morning, one of Camden's policemen, Louis Strehr, said that he saw the Jersey Devil drinking from a horse trough. In Mt. Ephraim, the school was closed due to lack of attendance, due to fear of the Devil, as were factories in Gloucester and Hainesport. Later on that day, both Blackwood policeman Merchant and Jacob Henderson of Salem saw the Devil.

The reports soon began to die off and the Devil disappeared just as quickly as it had arrived. As time went on, the Devil flap of 1909 was largely forgotten by the outside world. However, in New Jersey, the Devil remained alive in the hearts of local residents who knew that it would return again someday.

Years later, in 1934, Iola Gabriel, of Egg Harbor Township, had a frightening experience in 1934. Gabriel, 70, who grew up in Galloway Township, was a carefree second-grader playing in the Pomona Elementary School yard when she saw a hideous, devil-like creature.
"It's no laughing matter," Gabriel said. "He stood there on the road and looked at us."

Gabriel's devil description was different. She said the fiend stood at least 6 feet tall to her young eyes. "He was red with horns," she said. However, before she could take a long look, her entire class rushed inside the building to tell their teachers.

"I can picture him now," Gabriel said. "I've seen him."

It was not until 1951, that there would be another outburst of Devil sightings. As reported in The Philadelphia Record, a ten-year-old boy sighted a creature "with blood dripping from its face" outside his window. With that, the Jersey Devil was back in vogue once again.

Within days of this initial report, there were more, even stranger, encounters. In separate instances, Ronald James, Mrs. Elmer Clegy, and Mrs. William Weiser filed reports of hearing unearthly screams in the woods. This time around when the creature was seen it was described as being over seven feet tall in one account, or resembling an average sized caveman in another. Many of the sightings describe the creature as resembling a large kangaroo, except with a much larger head and fierce disposition. Reports swamped the local police who were not amused with the growing situation.

In order to try and stop the wild rumors, the police began hanging signs across highways that read, "The Jersey Devil is a Hoax." Not to be swayed, many residents took to the wood with weapons in hand with intentions of killing the Devil. Fearing that several armed civilians running around with guns could develop into a dangerous situation, the police arrested several would-be Devil hunters on sight. Civil authorities quickly dismissed any accounts of the Devil as hysteria.

Once again the sightings dropped down to a trickle as the Devil once again vanished. However, as long-time residents know, the Devil never stays away for long.

In 1966, Steven Silkotch of Burlington County blamed the deaths of 31 ducks, three geese, four cats, and two German Shepherd dogs on the antics of the Devil. That same year, Ray Todd and some friends saw a strange, faceless, scaly creature with black hair moving across a field near Morristown, New Jersey.

Cate Bishop, an Ocean City homemaker in her 30s, clearly remembers an autumn night in 1973 when she came face-to-face with the Jersey Devil. Bishop and two girlfriends were walking a moonlit trail in Mays Landing on their way to a house party. They were late, so they decided to take a shortcut through the brush, she recalled.

"We heard something crashing around in the woods and then this little creature between 3-4 feet tall sprang out of the woods into a clearing," Bishop said. "To me it looked like a goat with dark fur, but jumped on its hind legs only. It had small horns like a young goat and little tiny wings on its back," she added.

The three girls, then all about 15 years old, bolted in the other direction and headed for paved streets.

"As we would run past houses that had dogs, we would hear the dogs barking and then quiet again," Bishop said. "After we were a good distance past the houses, the dogs would start barking again."

Bishop swears the Jersey Devil chased them to their friend's house that night. "I clearly saw it," she said. "Later, we talked about it and tried to convince ourselves that we hadn't seen it, but I guess I was the only one who believed."

Also in 1966, the devil was spotted by a young couple who were parked at an old quarry near Edison. As reported on the website Rutgers Rarities (www.rutgersrarities.com/Phenomena32-JerseyDevil.html), Janet and Frank M. were parked in their car in the lowest portion of the quarry on September 9, when they suddenly heard a "very loud, galloping sound." The couple saw a "large horse-like creature that glowed with a green transparent light fly down and land by the couple's parked car. It was so close that both could hear its loud, heavy panting/snorting noises.

Frank and Janet both screamed, and then Frank promptly stepped on the gas and drove as fast as he could out of the quarry.

"The scariest thing about this creature was that I could see right through it," Janet recalled. "It was right at the side car window, I could see the cliff right through its body, and I remember being amazed that I could see the cliff ledge and sky so clearly through the creature's body."

Frank later described the creature as being around the size of a horse, but the strange green light it projected spread as wide and high as the side of a house.

After racing out of the quarry, the couple noticed that the creature had vanished. They circled the area, but it had disappeared as quickly as it had appeared.

Jerseyite Joe Springer recalled years later how a man heard the Devil's screams in the Barrens in 1974. In 1981, the Devil returned to Lake Atsion, and was seen this time. And in 1987, a German Shepherd dog was found lying 25 feet away from its chain. It was torn apart and partially consumed. All around its body were strange tracks.

The years 1999 and 2000 saw a huge uptick of Devil reports all across New Jersey and even into Philadelphia and New York. Every year there are new Devil sightings and the strange phenomenon shows no sign of going away anytime soon.

Tales of the Jersey Devil are still remembered today and it is doubtful they will ever be forgotten. In fact, most people in the Pine Barrens area cherish the tales as their own unique legend. To them, it doesn't matter if the Jersey Devil is real or not, because late at night, when the wind whistles eerily through the trees, you know the Jersey Devil is out, creeping on the edge of our dreams.

America's Strange and Supernatural History

Mysterious Attacks and Mutilations

Because of these early beliefs, man has always felt a superstitious horror when dealing with attacks that involve the loss of blood. Throughout history, there have been numerous reports of strange attacks and mutilations that seem to go beyond normal animal predators.

The strange, dark creature that skulks in the night is a universal fear that seems to occasionally leave the world of nightmares and cross over into reality. There are striking similarities between the historical Jersey Devil and modern reports of a creature known throughout the America's as the Chupacabra. Eyewitness descriptions of both beasts are strangely similar.

The Jersey Devil was often described as around four to five feet tall, having a large head with dark or glowing eyes, two short front arms with paws that looked more like human hands with long, sharp claws and bat-like wings that the animals can use to fly.

Descriptions of the Chupacabra almost exactly match descriptions of the Jersey Devil. And both creatures share a fondness of mutilating livestock and draining the blood of their victims. It would seem that the Jersey Devil has family down south.

Actually, the Jersey Devil seems to have kin all over the planet. A quick tour through old newspapers and journals shows a pattern of vampire-like activity that continues even today.

Those who have been unlucky enough to have bumped into the Chupacabra generally report that the creature stands about four or five feet tall, is grayish in color with spikes on the top of its head. It has short pudgy forelegs, or arms, that end in claws and large powerful hind legs. The Chupacabra has huge bright red eyes that glow, long fangs, and an odd long slimy pointy tongue that continually glides in and out of its mouth. This thing exhibits intelligent behavior and possesses the ability to evade detection and capture.

The creature is also described as having wings and, in one account, "flew at two human subjects who fled for their lives." The creature reportedly "hops around like a kangaroo and exudes such a pungent sulfur-like stench that one close encounter left an individual coughing for days.

America's Strange and Supernatural History

As in past cases, attempts to track down the Chupacabras have met with failure. If history is any indication, the Chupacabras will never be caught, and the strange events will remain a mystery. It is as if the mystery mutilators appear out of thin air, do their damage, and then, disappear into the night.

Killer Kangaroo's And Devil Monkeys

One such mysterious creature that seemed to appear out of nowhere was the notorious "Killer Kangaroo" of South Pittsburg, Tennessee. In mid-January of 1934, something described as looking like a giant kangaroo terrorized rural Marion County, along the Tennessee, Alabama border.

According to the local newspaper, the Reverend W.J. Hancock saw the animal and said it was "as fast as lightning" as it ran and leapt across a field. This beast was reported to have killed and partially devoured geese, ducks, and several large dogs. One witness named Frank Cobb claimed the kangaroo attacked and ate a German Shepherd dog, leaving only its head and shoulders behind. A tracking party followed the kangaroo's prints to a mountainside cave, where the trail ran out. The creature disappeared and was never found.

In southwest Virginia, Paulette Boyd told researcher Chad Arment about an incident that happened to her parents in 1959 involving a "pseudo-kangaroo" that has been named by other researchers as "devil monkeys."

Boyd said her parents were out driving early one morning around 4:00AM when they rounded a curve in the road where there was a high embankment on the right side. The couple noticed a movement in the headlights on the embankment.

"My Dad thought that it might be a deer, and slowed the car for my mother to get a better look," said Boyd. "Suddenly, a 'creature' sprung from the embankment to the road, headed directly for the front window of the car. It looked as if it would crash right through the window and into the front seat. Instead, with a twist of its body, and a spin of its front arms, it changed course, and came to land beside the car on the passenger side. When my mother turned to look, its face was pressed against the passenger window, only inches away from her."

America's Strange and Supernatural History

The description of this creature is as follows: Light, taffy colored hair, with a white blaze down its neck and underbelly. It stood on two large, well muscled back legs, and had shorter front legs or arms. No tail was visible.

"When it landed beside the car, my father hit the gas and sped up—the creature kept up with the car for a short while, but then fell behind—but never stopped chasing the vehicle, grasping for the car with its front paws. When they later examined the car, three long scratches were found on the passenger side, from the front door to the rear, all the way into the bright under-metal. They vow (and I believed them) that this was no bear, or dog, or even an escaped kangaroo (as someone once suggested), but something completely unknown and unexplainable." (*North American BioFortean Review* Volume II, Number 1, 2000)

It is interesting to note that a creature described as a "Screaming Kangaroo" was reportedly seen all over the western United States in the 1950's. Local newspaper reports from Utah, Arizona, Nevada, and New Mexico describe these animals as being at least 150 pounds, with large hind legs, stubby arms, and sharp teeth. When cornered, they would scream a piercing scream. Some people claimed that the creature resembled a dog, a kangaroo, and a pterodactyl with large reptilian or bat-like wings.

Perhaps the bloodthirsty kangaroo continued to move southward because in 1975, Puerto Rico was invaded by the so-called "Moca Vampire," an entity whose activities began in the town of Moca's Barrio Rocha, where it killed a number of animals in a grisly fashion never before seen. Fifteen cows, three goats, two geese and a pig were found dead with strange puncture marks on their bodies, indicating that some sharp object – natural or artificial – had been inserted into them.

Autopsy reports showed that the blood had been drained from the animals, and local police officers were mystified as how a wild predator could have scaled the fences surrounding the dead animals' pens. After killing more than ninety animals in a two week period, the vampire then went after larger prey on March 25, 1975. When Juan Muñiz was returning home to Moca's Barrio Pulido, he was attacked by a "horrible creature covered in feathers."

During the 1970's, Waukesha County, Wisconsin, experienced a phantom kangaroo infestation. Various people saw them, including deputy sheriffs and school bus drivers, all of whom were familiar with the local wildlife. On April 24, 1978, two men managed to take a polaroid photograph of one of the phantom kangaroos near Highway SS and Highway M.

America's Strange and Supernatural History

The laborer threw rocks at the creature to frighten it away, but it flew at him, scratching his face and neck. An armed group of locals sought to find the strange being, but no trace was found.

The vampire continued to kill on and off for the next several months before finally tapering off. Like the Chupacabras killings twenty years later, the majority of the Moca Vampire's attacks occurred at night or in the early pre-dawn hours. Those cases in which eyewitnesses managed to see the perpetrator usually described it as a weird bird or as a kangaroo-like creature.

Unexplained Livestock Deaths

The mutilation of cattle seems to involve a different set of circumstances then past vampire-like attacks on livestock. While cattle mutilations almost always involve the complete draining of blood, physical mutilation of the flesh is so apparent that seasoned ranchers are shocked by the unusual nature of the deaths. No one really knows when the first unusual cattle mutilations began.

Records show that during the summer of 1963, a series of mysterious livestock attacks occurred in Haskell County, Texas. In a typical case, an Angus bull was found with its throat slashed along with a saucer-sized wound in its stomach. The attacks were attributed to a wild beast of some sort, a "vanishing varmint" as the ranchers took to calling it. As the attacks continued through the Haskell County area, the unknown attacker assumed mythic proportions and a new name was created, "The Haskell Rascal."

The July 23, 1964 edition of the *Denton Record-Chronicle* reports, "Some folks in this tiny West Texas town say the critter is seven feet tall, four feet across arid growls. They claim it shuffles along in the night, or rattles in the brush, or keeps out of sight just over the rise. It looks, they say, like a hulking gorilla."

The article continues... "Charley Gant, a rancher in the area, said he saw it Saturday and Sunday night, and unloaded a pistol at it without luck. 'If Charlie Gant says he saw it, you can count on it,' a neighbor declared. Another supposed incident with the critter involved a woman and her young son walking near a pond. The boy, and then the mother, saw the critter. 'It turned around, growled and began throwing rocks before fleeing. My boy turned white as a sheet,' the mother said."

America's Strange and Supernatural History

Whatever the Haskell Rascal was, it was never caught and the attacks slowly stopped. Throughout the following decade though, there would be similar reports of unusual attacks and mutilations on livestock throughout the U.S.

In 1973 a plague of cattle mutilations swept across the country alongside a huge UFO flap, with many sightings taking place in the same areas that strange cattle deaths were taking place. In November of 1974, rumors began to connect the sighting of UFOs with mutilated cows that were being found in large numbers in various Minnesota counties. Dozens of UFOs were reported in Minnesota and dozens of cattle were found dead and mutilated. Although the sightings and mutilations were never correlated, many felt that the number of sightings was added proof that the UFOs were somehow involved.

Throughout the 1970s and 80s there was an unprecedented onslaught of strange livestock deaths that left ranchers and law enforcement officials baffled. Even though mutilations have been reported less frequently, due in part to an increased reluctance to report mutilations on the part of ranchers and farmers, the odd killings have continued into the 21st century. In the United States alone, over ten thousand animals have reportedly died under unusual circumstances.

Because of the strange nature of the killings, wild stories and rumors have surfaced over the years in an attempt to explain what is really going on. Chief among these are stories that aliens are harvesting cattle at night for their evil purposes. The extraterrestrials' preoccupation with cattle is apparently due to the fact that the ET's absorb nutrients through the skin. The blood that they acquire from the cattle is mixed with hydrogen peroxide, which kills the foreign bacteria in the mixture, and is "painted" on their skin, allowing absorption of the required nutrients. Supposedly human blood is preferred by the aliens, but cattle blood can be altered to serve the same purpose.

There is no hard evidence that these rumors are anything other than "urban legends" (or in these cases "rural legends"). The only differences between the old vampire stories and the modern mutilation reports are the proposed identity of the attackers. Cultural conditioning can play an important role in how such mysterious attacks are understood. If a society believes in supernatural entities that thirsts for the blood of the living, then any mysterious deaths where blood is noticeably absent would be attributed to a vampire.

However, in the modern age of science, supernatural creatures have been regulated to the realm of fairy tales and superstition. So when any unusual deaths occur that involve the loss of blood, the attackers are no longer seen as undead vampires, but instead blame is laid at the feet of beings from another planet. The only real truth is that we have no idea who, or what is responsible.

Red Eyes Glowing in the Dark

The dark things that go bump in the night apparently can come in all sorts of different shapes and sizes. Commonly, they are reported to be just a large, dark form, often with glowing red eyes. Author John Keel in his book **Strange Creatures from Time and Space** speculates that these things could be masses of energy without form or substance. Many witnesses say the eyes were strangely hypnotic and seem almost to be a focal point in the dark mass.

Perhaps these creatures have no real form and draw substance from the minds of those who see them. Social expectations, childhood fears, even archetypical imagery could play an important role in their ultimate appearance. This could also explain why, despite geographical location and intensive manhunts, these creatures seem to appear and disappear with impunity.

Like the Pine Barrens in New Jersey, it is not unusual for certain areas to have an extended history of strange events. Dedicated researchers when investigating anomalous events such as UFOs, often find a long history of unreported sightings of strange creature, animal mutilations and even ghostly activity in a specific area. In fact, it is extremely rare that any of these strange happenings occur by themselves. These clusters of weird phenomena over a certain region are known as Window Areas and generally have a long history of unexplained events.

There are possibly thousands of Window Areas scattered all across the planet. These are the places where madness dwells, where our ancient nightmares take on the cloak of reality, if only for a brief time. Do our fears make them real? Do our minds give them form where first there were only glowing eyes in the shadows? Is it blood that allows them to maintain life a little longer before being called back into the chaos of oblivion?

America's Strange and Supernatural History

The dark things that go bump in the night apparently can come in all sorts of different shapes and sizes. Commonly, they are reported to be just a large, dark form, often with glowing red eyes. Many witnesses say the eyes were strangely hypnotic and seem almost to be a focal point in the dark mass. Perhaps these creatures have no real form and draw substance from the minds of those who see them.

America's Strange and Supernatural History

We now have at our disposal the toys of science to research and document the strange places where fantasy and reality collide. Will these devices prove once and for all that our world is far stranger then we could ever imagine? Or will the truth remain forever elusive, safe and secure in the dark places that make up the dreamtime?

So as you try to sleep tonight, wondering what that noise was in your closet, or what strange thing is moving in the shadows just beyond the headstones in the cemetery, remember that we are not that far removed from our distant ancestors whose blood and flesh nourished unseen horrors. For even safely behind our locks and security cameras, we still cannot hide from the monsters.

America's Strange and Supernatural History

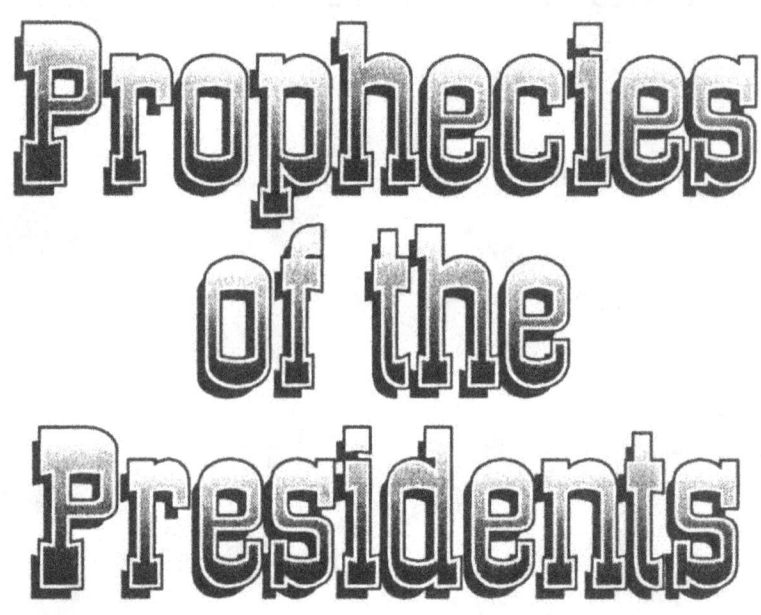

Prophecies of the Presidents

THE SPIRITUAL DESTINY OF AMERICA REVEALED

BY
TIMOTHY GREEN BECKLEY
&
ARTHUR CROCKETT

INNER LIGHT PUBLICATIONS

Contents

Introduction 172
Chapter One: The United States in Prophecy 176
**Chapter Two: The Mystical Origin of
the Great Seal of the United States** 182
Chapter Three: Our Psychic Presidents 194
**Chapter Four: Our Martyred Presidents—
Visions Of Doom And Death** 206
Chapter Five: A Colossus Shall Fall 216
Chapter Six: The Sibylline Prophecy 222
**Chapter Seven: The Polar Shift
and America's Destiny** 224
**Chapter Eight: America—The
Reincarnation of Atlantis** 236
**Chapter Nine: Is America Receiving
Guidance From Heaven?** 244
Chapter Ten: America's Great Curses 246
**Chapter Eleven: America's Coming Revolution—
Trouble From Within Not From Russia** 256
**Chapter Twelve: Space Visitors
Watch Over America** 262
**Chapter Thirteen: The Secret Government—
Who's Really In Control?** 283
**Bonus Section -
Psychic Predictions For The Future Of The United States** 295

The Great Seal of the United States, front and back view.

Introduction: America's Destiny in the New Age

Those who are familiar with the spiritual principles this country was founded upon, realize that America has an important role to play in the New Age: an age of reason and enlightenment which is soon to engulf the entire planet we live on.

Nothing in history happens just "by chance," and so God had in mind for us a unique place in the world—He wanted a country that would help lead mankind in the direction of freedom, love and perfect balance for all of mankind.

There is every reason to believe that many of our founding fathers were reincarnated philosophers from Greece and Rome (and perhaps other planets) who originally lived in the time of Atlantis, and had re-entered physical shells in order to help reshape the history of the planet for centuries to come. Their main objective was to steer humans on the proper course and to see that this great nation got off on the right footing.

History, itself, tells us that our early leaders were spiritually motivated and knew exactly what their mission was to be. They instinctively knew they had a connection with the .Supreme Being and realized fully well they were to be an intricate part of the passing away of the "old order" and were to assist with the formation of the "New World Order" as prescribed by universal plan.

It was certainly not pure "coincidence" that the likes of

Washington, Jefferson, Paine and Franklin emerged when they did to help lay the foundation for what shortly was to become the thirteen colonies. It was more than "luck" that the Bill of Rights and the Constitution would stand for generations as the inspiration for free men everywhere.

As we shall see, many of our founding fathers knew they had a special purpose for being here and lived their lives accordingly. They did not hesitate in the face of prison sentences, the firing squad, or any other adversity that was continually placed in their way. There is every reason to believe that many of these statesmen were psychic themselves, "tuned in" to higher power and they even went so far as to belong to secret occult orders or lodges. Many of our presidents, legislators and early military leaders were given at birth a sixth sense that enabled them to see the future and to become aware of obstacles that would hinder their chosen course. Washington, Lincoln and other chiefs of state were men of great vision and history shows that they often depended on an inner sense of knowing to pull them and the country through particularly tough times. They did not sneer at things unseen and unknown, but utilized them to all our advantage without personal benefit, whenever the opportunity arose. They, along with men the likes of Roosevelt and Patton, were quick to call upon the "invisible kingdom" for support and guidance when their own earthly energies were perhaps a bit too depleted to serve them well.

After a serious study of the factors at our disposal, it becomes altogether obvious that the Heavenly Host has smiled upon this country since the days of the American Revolution, and has inspired much of the heroics we can be so proud of. And, while at times, it may seem like we have been abandoned — that we have lost our spiritual qualities — the truth is that such greatness only lies dormant, ready to burst forth and glorify once again the nation that the sun always shines upon.

As we leave behind the materialistic age and enter a new period of prosperity for the human race, once again it will be America who will lead the way with its sense of fair play and freedom and justice for all. Since the end of World War II, we have seen in our skies strange signs and wonders which the Bible even tells us will appear before the End of Time. Common sense alerts us to the fact that in the aftermath of the atomic bomb being dropped on Japan, there must have been cosmic repercussions that were felt throughout our solar system.

Space visitors in craft we have come to call UFOs or flying saucers have been with us throughout history and are probably even responsible for a great deal of the phenomena described in the Bible, as well as being behind the miracle at Fatima. Friendly space brothers under the guidance and protection of the Almighty have shared with our leaders knowledge and spiritual insights which have enabled the United States to take its lofty position in the earthly community of nations. There is every reason to believe that the majority of our presidents have experienced close encounters during their terms in office and properly realized the significance of these Heavenly messengers who come to earth with peace in their heart. It would seem, that it is only the power of the military-industrial complex (which Eisenhower warned against) which prevents this sensational news from reaching the public and from fulfilling the prophecy that in days to come the world will be a better place to live in.

As you read **PROPHECY OF THE PRESIDENTS,** be prepared for cosmic revelations to unfold before you. For the first time, you may truly realize the significance of being an American, and what part our country will play in the months and years ahead. We can only hope and pray that our elected officials will follow the inner light that will guide us all to cosmic perfection and into an age that will herald peace for all time.

Timothy Green Beckley
& Arthur Crockett

Prophecies of the Presidents

Chapter One: The United States in Prophecy

The dream that was to become America began in a vision seen by our first president.

According to various esoteric sources, the United States was meant to play an important role in the spiritual growth of this planet. From the very beginning our founding fathers seem to have been divinely inspired, and it is as if some invisible—but powerful—hand helped unite this country and guided our leaders through a series of very difficult crises.

George Washington, Benjamin Franklin and Thomas Jefferson, all seem to have had a direct link with providence and realized that they were placed here especially to help lay the groundwork for our fabulous nation. During the Revolutionary War even when it looked like the British would be victorious, Washington never gave up because he inwardly knew that the turmoil before him would soon perish. In fact, later in his life, Washington wrote a letter to the governor of Connecticut in which he stated that it was "almost possible to trace the finger of Divine Providence through those dark and mysterious days which led the colonists to assemble in convention, thereby laying the foundation and prosperity, when we had too much reason to fear that misery and confusion were coming too rapidly upon us."

A Belief in Supernatural Forces

A look into history shows that neither Washington, Franklin or Jefferson tried to play down their strong individual belief in supernatural forces, and the omnipresent power of a superior being.

Researcher Corine Heline points out that a series of Ben Franklin's debates with the pro-vaccinationists took place in "a coffee house frequented largely by unconventional foreign travelers and soldiers of fortune. Here Franklin discovered a young medical student who was interested in esoteric subjects and so he acquired his intimate companionship. Together they practiced various old alchemical formulas, rites and ceremonials."

We also know that Benjamin Franklin accepted the theory of reincarnation. His epitaph, which he wrote before his passing reads as follows: "The body of Benjamin Franklin, is like the cover of an old book, its contents torn out and stripped of its lettering and gilding, lies here, food for worms, yet the work itself shall not be lost for it will appear once more in a new and more beautiful edition corrected and amended by the author."

Not that much is known about Thomas Jefferson's metaphysical thoughts, though a magazine published more than a century ago tells us he was an astrologer. We also know that his ideas about religion were considered to be highly controversial. He often told friends that he did not feel that many of those who professed to be following the teachings of the Lord were really doing so. In fact, federalist leaders tried to pin the label of atheist on Jefferson, but this term certainly couldn't apply since he went to the trouble to author a book titled "The Life and Morals of Jesus of Nazareth," of which Jefferson said: "A more beautiful or precious morsel of ethics I have never seen; it is a document in proof that I am a real Christian, that is to say, disciple of the doctrines of Jesus." It would be interesting to see how Jefferson would react to today's attempt to do away with the separation of church and state, an ideal our forefathers promoted heavily since they believed very strongly in freedom of religion which allowed for many independent beliefs, and not just those necessarily put forward by the large, organized churches.

George Washington's Vision

It was, in fact, George Washington who seemingly led the way for this country to accept the theory that our country was formed under divine providence. During the American Revolution, it was Washington who had a vision which laid before his eyes the future of the thirteen colonies, later to become the United States.

As you may remember from your school days, the darkest period during the American Revolution occurred in 1777. The winter that year was horrendous. General George Washington had suffered some severe reverses and his rag-tag army, locked in at Valley Forge, was slowly starving and freezing to death.

Washington was often seen with tears in his eyes. He felt helpless against the frightful weather and the superior forces which drove him back to the desolate spot in Pennsylvania. It was his daily habit to go into a thicket, out of sight of his troops, and drop to his knees in prayer. He asked again and again for aid and comfort from God. His prayers went to the Divine Providence with the hope that He would bring the suffering troops through these dark days of tribulation.

The General and the Beautiful Lady

One day Washington gave strict orders that he was not to be disturbed in his headquarters. He had an important dispatch to prepare and he wanted no interruptions. While he worked he felt disturbed. He looked up and was startled to see a lovely young woman standing before him. She was by far the most beautiful creature he had ever seen, yet she did violate his privacy and he asked her why she had come in.

Washington asked that question four times, but received no reply. He felt strange sensations passing through him. He wanted to rise, as any gentleman would, but felt riveted to his chair. And all during this time he was unable to tear his gaze away from her.

As he stared at her, the air in the room appeared to glow. He said later that he felt as though he may be dying; that the sensation within him could have been akin to a near death experience.

The Woman Spoke

Washington's gaze was fixed on this woman. She then raised her arm to the east and said, "Son of the Republic, look and learn." Washington reported later, "I looked and beheld a heavy white vapor rising, at some distance, fold upon fold. This gradually dissipated and I looked upon a strange scene. Before me lay spread out in one vast plain all the countries of the world — Europe, Asia, Africa and America. I saw rolling and tossing between Europe and America, the billows of the Atlantic Ocean and between America and Asia lay the Pacific."

At that point Washington saw a dark, shadowy entity that looked like an angel. It was suspended in mid-air between America and Europe. The angel dipped water out of the Atlantic ocean and sprinkled it on America. He did this with his right hand. With his left hand he sprinkled water on the European countries.

As soon as that was done, a cloud rose from those countries and traveled across the ocean to envelop America. There were sharp flashes of lightning. Washington heard the moans of people and realized that the sounds were coming from America. The angel repeated the action, sprinkling America and Europe with water. The great cloud was then drawn back to the ocean, where it dissolved.

A Strange Warning

Washington said: "I cast my eyes upon America and beheld villages, towns and cities springing up one after another until the whole land, from the Atlantic to the Pacific, was dotted with them. (Remember, this was when America consisted of only 13 colonies and thoughts were not of expansion, but of survival). Again I heard the voice say, 'Son of the Republic, the end of the century cometh. Look and learn.'

"And with this the dark, shadowy figure turned its face southward, and from Africa an ill-omened spectre approached our land.

"It flitted slowly over every town and city of the land. The inhabitants presently set themselves in battle array against each other. As I continued to look I saw a bright angel, on whose brow rested a crown of light on which was traced the word 'Union,' place an American flag between the divided nation, and say, 'Remember, ye are brethren.' Instantly the inhabitants, casting from them their weapons, became friends once more, and united around the National Standard."

Obviously, Washington's vision showed him that one day his country would be embroiled in a great civil War.

Washington's Most Frightening Vision

The dark, shadowy angel put a trumpet to his mouth and blew three distinct blasts. That was followed by his again sprinkling Europe, Asia and Africa with water from the Atlantic.

Washington said: "Then my eyes beheld a fearful scene: from each of these countries arose a thick black cloud, and throughout this mass gleamed a bright red light, by which I saw hordes of armed men, who, moving with the cloud, marched by land and sailed by sea to America; which country was enveloped in the volume of cloud.

"And I saw dimly these vast armies devastate the whole country and burn the villages, towns and cities that I beheld springing up.

"As my ears listened to the thundering of the cannon, the clashing of swords, and the shouts and cries of millions in mortal combat, I again heard the mysterious voice say, 'Son of the Republic, look and learn.' As the voice ceased, the shadowy figure of the angel for the last time dipped water from the ocean and sprinkled it upon America. Instantly the dark cloud rolled back, together with the armies it had brought, leaving the inhabitants of the land victorious."

Interpretation

Apparently, Washington saw an invasion of the United States by forces from Europe, Asia and Africa. In Revelations 9:13-16 it is mentioned that a horde of 200,000,000 men will be in combat. This could be the vision seen by Washington.

Washington's Third Vision

"Once more I beheld villages, towns and cities springing up where I had seen them before; while the bright angel, planting the azure standard he had brought in the midst of them, cried in a loud voice, 'While the stars remain and the heavens send down dew upon the earth, so long shall the Union last.' And taking from her brow the crown on which was blazoned the word 'Union, she placed it upon the standard while people kneeling down said Amen."

The Three Perils

General Washington said that the whole scene began to fade, and he saw nothing now except the curling vapor that he had witnessed during the beginning of the visions. Then that disappeared and he was now where he was at the beginning — in the presence of the lovely visitor.

She said to him, "Son of the Republic, what you have seen is thus interpreted. Three great perils will come upon the Republic. The most fearful is the third, but the whole world united shall not prevail against her. Let every child of the Republic learn to live for God, His land, and the Union."

The woman disappeared.

The three perils have been interpreted as the American Revolution and the War of 1812 as the first peril, the Civil War as the second, and a possible invasion of the United States as the third. Though this has not yet occurred, there are those who believe we may be headed in that direction!

Chapter Two: The Mystical Origin of The Great Seal of the United States

Have you ever looked closely at a one-dollar bill? Please do. You will see both sides of the Great Seal of the United States. Have you ever wondered about it? Do you know that one of the most puzzling mysteries connected with the growth of our country is associated with the Great Seal?

History tells us that the Continental Congress on July 4, 1776 asked Thomas Jefferson, Benjamin Franklin and John Adams to put their heads together and arrange a seal for the United States of America. At that time there were only 13 states.

The task was more difficult than these three men had supposed. Their own designs were not suitable. Designs that were submitted to them by others also failed to produce the desired result.

The deadline approached and no one had come up with a satisfactory seal...

Thomas Jefferson's Strange Meeting

Jefferson, Franklin and Adams were exhausted. They'd spent the entire day poring over designs that fell short. It was late at night now and Thomas Jefferson told the others that he needed some fresh air. He excused himself and took a walk in his garden.

In the darkness he saw a man approach him. The stranger was covered from head to foot in a long black cloak. Jefferson could not even see the man's face. This visitor told Jefferson that he knew what the three great statesmen were trying to do and that he had a design which would be appropriate and meaningful.

Jefferson listened while the man described what he had in mind. The plans were perfect! They were exactly what was needed. Jefferson hurried back into the room to tell the other two what he had heard. He rushed away from the stranger so quickly that he forgot to thank him.

Moments later, when the excitement was over, the three men went into the garden to see if they could find the strange man. They couldn't. He was gone.

So it is that the three founding fathers and all of the other patriots of the day never knew who really designed the Great Seal of the United States.

The mystery is one which will probably never be solved, though some theorize that this man may have been a space being, an angel or an alchemist with a secret society which had gotten its start in Europe centuries before and has tried to inspire mankind for good ever since.

What The Stranger Proposed

The man in the long cloak suggested to Jefferson exactly what you see today on one-dollar bills. This Great Seal is also applied to about 3,000 documents annually, including presidential proclamations, ratifications of treaties, commissions of cabinet members and ambassadors, and a great many other federal documents. On most of these official papers, only one side (the front) of the Great Seal is shown. Only on the dollar bill are both sides shown.

The obverse, or front side, shows an eagle. The reverse side shows a pyramid. The front side shows a circle above the head of the eagle, and in it are thirteen "pieces argent." The eagle's breast is covered with a shield with thirteen stripes. The right talon holds an olive branch with thirteen leaves. The left talon holds thirteen arrows. On a ribbon around the eagle's neck are the Latin words "E Pluribus Unum," which means "out of many one," or "one out of many," meaning one union of many states.

On the reverse side you can see an unfinished Egyptian pyramid. The capstone above it is surrounded by light. It is not yet in place atop the pyramid. In it you can see an eye, which is symbolic of the all-seeing eye of God. The Latin words above the eye, "Annuit Coptis," means "God has prospered our beginnings." The Roman numerals seen at the pyramid's base are "1776."

Below the pyramid are the Latin words "Novis Ordo Seclorum." There are actually three translations: "A New Order of the Ages," or "A Mighty Order of the Ages Lives Anew," or "An Ancient Order is Born Again."

Who Was The Stranger Who Gave Us The Seal?

No one knows, but we do have a strong clue. To dig it out we must turn to the Old Testament. There you will find that the Israelites wandering in the desert to find the Promised Land came upon a mountain. It was no ordinary mountain, but a rock and marble fortress. There are mammoth palaces carved into the beautiful marble. In the Old Testament it was called Seal. Today this place has been renamed Petra. The Israelites did not know who did the magnificent work; nor do we.

However, the second chapter of Deuteronomy reveals the first time the Israelites saw Petra. The Bible also tells us of the last time they will see it. In the book of Revelations, Chapter 12, we learn of a pregnant woman, an Israeli, who is in labor to bring forth a child, which is symbolic of the church. The chapter reads, in part, "...and the dragon stood before the woman which was ready to be delivered, for to devour her child as soon as it was born. And she brought forth a man child, who was to rule all nations with a rod of iron: and her child was caught up unto God, and to His throne. And the woman fled into the wilderness, where she hath a place prepared of God, that they should feed her there a thousand two hundred and threescore days...And to the woman were given two wings of a great eagle, that she might fly into the wilderness, into her place, where she is nourished for a time, and times, and a half time, from the face of the serpent."

Petra and The Eagle

Two rose-red marble obelisks stand sentinel in Petra. They were probably built by Hadad, who was held captive in Egypt as a child and was returned to Petra as a young man. Eventually, the Arabs made Petra their capital. It was a rich caravan city for one thousand years. The Romans built two roads to Petra to tap its wealth.

But for the next one thousand years it was lost to the world. Petra was abandoned and forgotten. And it was not re-discovered until the early 1800s. Since then it has become a tourist attraction. Most people look at it and then forget it.

They also look at the giant eagle carved in marble, yet they don't see its resemblance to the eagle on the American dollar bill.

Petra and Two Eagles

According to the Scriptures, at the time of the great battle of Armageddon, and at the beginning of the terrible Tribulation, God will take the Jews left in Palestine and keep them safely until the trouble is over. He will take them on the wings of two eagles.

Now these eagles will have to be very large because He has deemed that 144,000 people will be saved from the holocaust. Did He really mean eagles, or do they symbolize two giant carriers—space ships perhaps?

The Eagle, Jefferson's Stranger and The Great Seal

The eagle that one can see at Petra is huge and was carved into the side of a rock cliff. The detail is rather intricate. Strangely enough, this eagle is poised exactly the way it is on our dollar bill!

There are no other portraits, statues, or renditions of eagles that were done in exactly the same way!

The mystery is clear now, but the solution is not. Thomas Jefferson undoubtedly was visited by some spiritual being who knew all about the revelation concerning Petra. There appears to be no other way to explain it. There is no record to show that Jefferson ever made a trip to this ancient desert fortress. Such a trip in the 1770s would have taken months, and historians are able to account for Jefferson and his daily routine for almost all of his adult life.

Importance of The Number

There are many mystical meanings placed on the Great Seal and since it was introduced numerous attempts have been made to crack the symbolism and find a secret code that may exist within the various figures on the seal.

Writer C.W. Deans, for example, says he has found a wonderful series of what he says are mystical uses of the number thirteen which can be applied to a special Anglo-Saxon and Israel interpretation of the Great Seal in accordance with Biblical prophecy.

"Besides the usually recognized series of thirteens in the stars and stripes, the arrows and leaves and berries, and the thirteen letters in E Pluribus Unum and Annuit Coeptis and thirteen rows of stones in the pyramid, there are other signs showing that God inspired the design of the marvelous seal."

Deans suggests that the reader look at the following examples:

"The stars in the cloud of glory above the spreading eagle wings, as Israel is borne upon the eagle's wings of God's parables in the Bible, are in a special arrangement resembling the seal of Solomon or the Shield of David, all of which have 12 letters. It is most surprising that the 13 stars also have 13 letters in them. Surely even this series of 13's indicates that the God of Israel planned, and designed, and inspired the setting down of this symbol in Israel."

Dean wants us to believe that this numerological "coincidence" is not a coincidence at all, but a way of God to tell us that the United States is to be the new Jerusalem, or the nucleus of the Kingdom of God on earth, as predicted in the Bible.

Doesn't it seem likely that if this were the case, God would send all His "messengers"—use all His powers—to guide and protect us? As this book will try to document, there is a good possibility that He has sent His legions of angelic beings and His Heavenly Hosts (spiritually advanced space beings) to keep tabs on our activities and to try and see that they follow His divine plan for us as closely as possible.

Ye Are All Brethren

The greatest living authority on the Great Seal is a Maryland man named Dr. Robert Hieronimus. The bearded artist and scholar has for several years been attempting to arouse interest in the seal, its creation, and the meaning of its images.

On June 20, 1982, Dr. Hieronimus delivered a speech at Independence Hall in Philadelphia, Pa., on the occasion of the Great Seal's bicentennial. He has been particularly influential in trying to get an official die of the reverse side of the Great Seal (bearing an eye in a triangle and pyramid) cast by the government. This reverse side is only seen on the back of the dollar bill, while the obverse side (dominated by the bald eagle) was struck many years ago by proclamation of the United States Congress. There are those that place a negative connotation on why this has not long ago been done. Generally, there is a feeling that those who do not "follow the path" of light, but are in league with the "dark side" want to keep this symbol from official use because it at least on a subconscious level represents a powerful talisman for good which could very well send only positive vibrations, that might enhance the psychic health of the entire planet. It is more or less symbolic of the phrase, "Ye Are All Brethren," which represents America's stance on freedom to the rest of the world.

Much of the thinking offered by Dr. Hieronimus has even been printed in the Congressional Record. In the edition of April 28, 1983, Dr. Hieronimus offered this spiritual message as to the importance of both sides of the Great Seal:

From The Congressional Record

"In 1825, 1841, 1877, 1885 and 1903 dies were cut for the Obverse of the Great Seal, but the Reverse, with the pyramid and the eye in the triangle, was repeatedly neglected! To this day only half of the United States' Great Seal has been used in its official capacity as defined by the Continental Congress in 1782. Is there some important meaning in this fact?

"The Obverse Seal depicts a nation capable of continual rebirth—the eagle is symbolically related to the phoenix. We are strong courageous defenders of the justice (arrows), generous and humanistic (olive branch). The cluster of stars above the eagle (which was referred to as a 'Crown of Glory') symbolizes the spiritual unity of all, or common purpose of the states. America's destiny is to maintain the principles carried in the eagle's beak. E Pluribus Unum—Out of Many One.' The Obverse Seal thus represents our outer image—what we stand for in the world.

"It is the Reverse side of the Great Seal which delineates the significance and values of America's inner strength and accord. The pyramid is symbolic for the strength and duration of matter, the physical nation. Suspended above it is the "All Seeing Eye of Providence" representing inner direction or spiritual guidance. The radiant eye illuminates and completes the unfinished apex of the pyramid. Annuit Coeptis, 'He favors our undertaking,' communicates the union of spirit and matter, a perceived blessing upon Novus Ordo Seclorum, America, 'the New order of the Ages.'

"Throughout the world the pyramid, or mountain, symbolizes a place of initiation where one is introduced to the process of self-reliance. Each stone (individual) contributes to the stability of each layer (state). The interdependent, yet self-governing layers (states),, comprise the whole (nation). The pyramid's solidarity depends on the integrity and method of organizations used to manifest the principles which guide its construction. The Reverse Seal symbolizes America's inner self."

The Eye in The Triangle

In his own personal writings on the subject of the Great Seal, Dr. Robert Hieronimus has gone a bit further in his linking the seal to various metaphysical teachings. Understandably enough, he has often had to play down this approach when trying to get his ideas across to the Congressmen, Senators and even to Presidents, whom he has been corresponding with on the subject for many years.

The "eye in the triangle" on the Great Seal's reverse side is also of particular importance in mystical thought.

"The components of the eye in the triangle also have occult significance. The triangle has been used by the Rosicrucians as the basis of a law which they refer to as the "Law of the Triangle." In short, if something exists (a thesis), its opposite must also exist (antithesis), and it is the merging of the opposites that forms the synthesis, and the final leg of the triangle. The Rosicrucian Order lists a series of triangles to illustrate the law of the triangle found in nature, for example, solids, liquids, and gases; spirit, life, and matter; stability, mobility, and rhythm; inertia, energy, and law; mineral, vegetable, and animal; time, space, and measure; past, present, and future; duration, distance, and measure, etc.

"It is also curious to note that nearly all religions possess trinities, trimurdils, or triads. For example, Christianity: Father, Son, and Holy Spirit; Judaism (Cabala): Kether, Chochma, and Binah; Egyptian: Osiris, Isis, and Horus; Hindu: Braham, Vishnu, and Shiva; etc. Buckminster Fuller's ideas concerning the importance of the triangle in the structure of his domes, because of their strength, are a remarkable illustration of how science and religion sometimes share common laws. It is the belief of some occultists that the reason for the triangle's importance to man is the etheric nature of our present solar system, being constructed out of triangles and wedge-shaped structures."

Dr. Hieronimus points out that the eye itself also represents a great tradition in metaphysical and spiritual law. "To the ancients," he notes, "the eye was the window of the soul. The sense of sight was, and still is, considered to be the most excellent of the five senses because it does not depend on contact with or close proximity to an object. The single eye carries with it special significance because it refers to the third eye, or spiritual eye, which allows one to glimpse and move into higher states of consciousness." This "third eye," states the scholar, has been known by many names. "It has been referred to as the inner light, intuitive power, illumination, the philosopher's stone and clairvoyance."

The Atlantis Connection

Not yet finished with his discourse on the Great Seal and the "eye" in particular, Dr. Hieronimus contends that this eye is "probably the most obvious symbol, and perhaps is the signature, of the secret societies," so often written about in classic metaphysical literature.

Says Hieronimus on this very subject: "Starting with Egypt, some go as far back as Atlantis, as the eye of Osiris, the single eye has its origin in the symbol of the sun. The triangle, in a sense, can be linked to a prism through which the light of the sun passes, resulting in the colors of the spectrum (rainbow). The rainbow acts as a bridge, at least in symbol, to higher consciousness. By placing the pyramid below the eye of Providence, as in the final design of the reverse of the Great Seal, we are saying, in effect, that the pyramid is at the receiving end of the bridge, and through its use as a chamber of initiation, man can be re-united with the Divine. It has been noted also, that without the eye in the triangle, the pyramid remains unfinished, while the capstone itself is a complete pyramid. It is therefore the assigned job of America to link the eye in the triangle with the pyramid. Until this is done, the work of America remains unfinished.

A Biblical Tradition and Possible Outer Space Link

In his research on the Great Seal, Dr. Hieronimus has come across many writers who have professed to understand the deep-rooted significance of this divinely inspired talisman. In his book *The Two Great Seals Of America—History And Interpretation*, he mentions the work of Charles Totten, who was convinced that a relationship existed between the scroll in the eagle's mouth on the Great Seal, and the "book" which the Lord talks about in Revelations. Totten writes: "The book sealed with its seven seals that 'no man nor creature could open save He in Whom all men are one' was light itself, so that thereon no man could look until the seal was broken... In its higher sense, it is this book whose unsealed roll the eagle ever regarded as the bearer of the scriptures."

Hieronimus cleverly points out that the phrase, "He in whom all men are one," is quite close to the actual interpretation of E Pluribus Unum which is the literal basis of America's "Melting Pot" philosophy, and which expresses a belief in synthesis, and the unity of mankind. To the mystic, America plays a very important part in the scheme of evolution of life on this planet. To prove this out, the dedicated researcher quotes from the work of Frederick H. Werth, whom he sees as best expressing this belief. "America's mission in this majestic scheme of evolution," says Werth, "is that of amalgamating the contribution of all ages into a culture so wide and so deep, that the full play of man's innate divinity will be assured. To this high purpose, America must dedicate her liberty."

In conclusion, Hieronimus brings in what may be yet additional proof that angels and outer space beings are part of the overall scheme of things as far as our country's spiritual growth is concerned.

"The phrase one becomes many, or 'many become the one,' is very familiar to those who are students of theosophy, for it is used in reference to Beings who are Teachers of man, and other life forms on all planets, and solar systems. The phrase 'one becomes many' is used when the consciousness of one of these exalted beings is transmitted to lesser beings. One could reverse the process by relating that the lesser beings are overshadowed by the consciousness of the one, who is sometimes referred to as the 'Silent Watcher.' One Rosicrucian Society uses the phrase 'The one and the many' or the 'One becomes many' as their fourth aphorism: 'That all beings are in truth but expressions of the One Being—centers of consciousness, form, and activity within itself—is a fundamental tenet of all occult and esoteric teachings.'"

Americans have every reason to be proud of their heritage, but they should realize that every race and ethnic group must by divine rule—play an important part in the eventual outcome of world history. God wants us to know that every American is truly "unique," but that we must all work hand in hand if we are to lift ourselves to a higher vibration and see the formation of the New

Jerusalem on earth. Indeed, God has sent His angels and His Heavenly Hosts to guide us, but we must learn to heed their advice and avoid listening to the "messengers of deception" who would try to turn our heads against providence.

As we shall see in proceeding chapters, there has often been an organized attempt by forces working behind the scenes, to dispel our overall development as a country with spiritual goals, and to hinder and ridicule—and even assassinate—anyone who would genuinely try to bring peace and freedom to our shores and eventually to the rest of the world.

Author's Note: Readers interested in learning more about Dr. Robert Hieronimus' theories concerning the Great Seal are invited to write for a list of available papers and publications (he can be reached at 3 Woodland Court, Lutherville, Md. 21093). Some of the material in this chapter was taken from Dr. Hieronimus' book, *The Two Great Seals of America* and is copyrighted by him.

THE WHITE HOUSE
WASHINGTON

December 3, 1976

Dear Mr. Hieronimus:

This brief note is to thank you personally for the valuable assistance you provided my staff in connection with the Bicentennial. I understand they found your historical research particularly helpful.

I also want to take this opportunity to compliment you on <u>The Two Great Seals of America.</u> In its explanation of the symbols of our heritage, this work is indeed an appropriate publication for our anniversary year.

Again, thank you for your cooperation and contribution to our national celebration.

Sincerely,

Jerry Ford

Mr. Robert Hieronimus
2405 Ruscombe Lane
Baltimore, Maryland 21209

Chapter Three: Our Psychic Presidents

Many of our trusted statesmen as well as their appointees have been gifted with a sixth sense that has enabled them to judge the right moves to make in moments of extreme crisis. Manly P. Hall, one of America's foremost metaphysical writers, mentions in his book, *Story of Astrology*, an authority named John Hazelrigg, who says that a good number of the signers of the Declaration of Independence were well versed in the mystical sciences.

This above statement is warranted, Hazelrigg notes by, confirmation to be found "by annotations in the margins of the astrological books in the Thomas Jefferson Library, now in the Library of Congress; Franklin was a self-confessed votary, confirmed by his scientific delving and his *Poor Richard's Almanac;* and one cannot read Thomas Paine's *Age of Reason* without being convinced of his conversancy with the principles of astro-science and its philosophy; other signers could be included in this numeration."

President Theodore Roosevelt, we are told, kept his astrological chart mounted on a chess board and was said to consult it during crucial moments in his presidency. During the Franco-Prussian War the Germans consulted an astrologer named Raphael to find out when the planetary configurations were at the right points for starting their offensives. Raphael was probably right, because the Germans rewarded him after the war. Mussolini had his own astrologer in one Signor Rosconi, who told the

Duce that he would annex territory in the next conflict, which is probably why he invaded Ethiopia.

Furthermore, Count Hamon (better known as Cheiro, one of the greatest astrologers of all time) stated that many well-known figures were true believers, among them Admiral Dewey, General Nelson A. Miles, and President Grover Cleveland.

But this data is pretty light weight when compared with the following historical facts...facts which show that many of our elected representatives, heroic military bigwigs and Chiefs of State knew of the future and possessed a highly accurate gift of prophecy.

Prophecies Of The Presidents (Franklin D. Roosevelt)

Franklin Roosevelt was a firm believer that dreams were prophetic. He knew that his own were, and that one in particular was responsible for the saving of many lives.

He awoke one night from a sound sleep. For some reason he didn't quite understand, he was deeply worried. The dream he'd just had disturbed him. He saw a terrible accident take place at the airport in Washington, D.C.

Before he went back to sleep that night he placed a call to the airport authorities and asked them to check out the facilities. Because he was the President, the order was carried out right away. The investigation showed up a dangerous situation on the runway. It could have been responsible for a terrible disaster.

Because of FDR's dream, a new and safer airport was built.

FDR's Premonition Of His Death In Office

It is an established fact that when emotions are highly keyed, one may find that he has heightened perception. This must have been the case with President Roosevelt, who was known to open his Bible whenever he was beset by a personal problem. He would usually glance at the pages until he found a verse that stood out from the rest. He would accept this as his answer.

The day he was to take his oath of office for the third time was a cold and windy one. Just as he was about to place his hand on the open Bible, a breeze flipped the pages. He read the verse now open to him. It was II Corinthians, 13:1-3, and it said:

"This is the third time I am coming to you. In the mouth of two or three witnesses shall every word be established. I told you before, and foretell you, as if I were present...if I come again, I will not spare."

President Roosevelt told the incident to his friend, Louis Howe, and said that while he read the words they seemed to brighten on the page. He told Howe that he knew now that he would not survive a fourth term in office.

President George Washington Appeared In A Vision, Made Prophecy

At one tragic point during the Civil War the Union forces were shattered. President Lincoln called on General George B. McClellan to take command and somehow restore order.

General McClellan responded immediately, and spent a long day at his desk laying the groundwork for the rehabilitation of the northern armies. Late that night he dozed off at the desk, but was suddenly awake again, and noticed that the whole room was filled with a radiant light.

He then heard a voice, and slowly the face of George Washington materialized. Washington's first words were a warning that Confederate troops were on their way to capture the nation's capital.

General McClellan felt at the time that the knowledge he received from George Washington was supernatural. Because he followed the first President's advice, he was able to stop the northern invasion by the Confederacy at Antietam in September, 1862.

General McClellan's Account

The general remembered that the voice of Washington was amazingly clear. He said:

"General McClellan, do you sleep at your post? Rouse you, or ere it can be prevented, the foe will be in Washington! You have been betrayed, and had God willed it otherwise, ere the sun of tomorrow had set, the Confederate flag would have waved above the Capital and your own grave. But note what you see. Your time is short."

The general said that while Washington spoke he saw a living map which showed all of the troop positions. He took up a pencil and copied down everything he saw—and what he saw were the enemy troops marching toward Washington. Actually, the troops were not marching, but they were the plans the Confederates had devised for the future!

When Washington was assured that General McClellan

understood the military situation, he then talked to the general about the 20th century, when other perils would befall the nation.

Washington's Prophetic Words

"General McClellan, while yet in the flesh, I beheld the birth of the American Republic. It was indeed a hard and bloody one, but God's blessing was upon the nation, and, therefore, through this, her first great struggle for existence...He sustained her, and with His mighty hand, He brought her out triumphantly.

"A century has not passed since then, and yet the child Republic has taken her position of peer with nations whose pages of history extend for ages into the past. She has, since those dark days, by the favor of God, greatly prospered. And now, by the very reason of that prosperity, has she been brought to her second great struggle.

"This is by far the most perilous ordeal she has to endure, passing as she is from childhood to open maturity, she is called on to accomplish that vast result, Self-Conquest; to learn that important lesson—self-control, self-rule, that in the future will place her in the van of power and civilization.

"It is here that all the nations have hitherto failed, and she, too—the Republic of the earth, had not God willed otherwise—would by tomorrow's sunset have been a heap of stones, cast up over the final grave of human liberty. But her cries have come up out of the borders like sweet incense into heaven. She shall be saved! Then, shall peace be upon her, and prosperity shall fill her with joy.

"But her mission will not be finished, for ere another century shall have gone by, the oppressors of the whole earth, hating and envying her exaltation, shall join themselves together and raise up their hands against her.

"But if she be found worthy of her calling, they shall be truly discomfited, and then will be ended her third and last struggle for existence.

"Henceforth, shall the Republic go on, increasing in goodness and power until her borders shall end only in the remotest corners of the earth, and the whole earth shall, beneath her shadowy wings, become a Universal Republic!"

Strange Marks on McClellan's Map

When the vision faded, the general went to his map and noticed all the markings and symbols on it showing how the Confederate Army planned to move on Washington. He wrote later:

"Our beloved, glorious Washington shall rest...until perhaps the end of the Prophetic Century approaches, that is to bring the Republic to a third and final struggle when he may once more...become a Messenger of Succor and Peace from the Great Ruler, who has all nations in his keeping..."

Washington's Prophecy on America

Lucy Brown was one of the better-known mediums of the 19th century. In 1881 she allegedly contacted the spirit of George Washington, who predicted fascist dictatorship and its threat to America's destiny. Miss Brown recorded the President's words, which follow:

"Clouds in the horizon are looming up to overcast the future of America; becoming very dense, dark and foreboding ill, will burst in an unexpected moment upon the heads of her people.

"The mutterings of discontent, engendered by a sort of incipient, despotic rule, mild, perhaps at present in its hold over the masses, and swelling into vaster proportions and power, is breeding discontent and inharmonies in the ranks of all classes of minds who labor diligently for a subsistence and gain a small and inadequate pittance of their hourly needs and daily bread.

"The widespread and desolating schemes of the robbers of the people of their rightful inheritance to life, land, home and pursuit of happiness, cannot, does not, go unnoticed by the hosts of spirits who occupy positions above the mortal sphere, where with cultivated and penetrative vision, we discern the secret workings of men's minds and motives, which are out-wrought in every variety of consequences.

"The happiness of the individual depends upon the uses he

makes of the opportunities given him to choose and improve.

"So may it be said of a nation or a government.

"If, for instance, a national government may choose to treat arbitrarily any portion of its people, considering not their merits and needs, and ignores their inherent rights, it infringes its own right to tranquillity, peace and prosperity, to that extent, that dissatisfaction and disintegration within its own domain are engendered and the consequence issue is disruption and open rebellion.

"Then follow the crises of war, and all its attendant evils. It is thought by some to be the great revolutionary means of developing better conditions.

"John Adams, an associate spirit, has said, 'War is the hub of civilization, the periphery of which is spiritualization of the moral and emotional nature of the masses.' So it will be upon the earth a brooding over the American continent at present, a brighter sphere which, when the portending clouds and elements have expended their forces, will come forth purified from the dross of selfishness and corruption that now pollutes society and nations."

President Thomas Jefferson's Prophecy

"If the American people ever allow banks to control the issue of currency, first by inflation, and then by deflation, the banks and corporations that will grow up around them will deprive the people of all their property until their children will wake up homeless on the continent their fathers conquered."

President James Madison's Prophecy

"We are free today, substantially, but the day will come when our republic will come to impossibility because its wealth will be concentrated in the hands of a few. When that day comes, then we must rely upon the wisdom of the best elements in the country to readjust the laws of the nation to the changed conditions."

President Abraham Lincoln's Prophecy

"I see in the future a crisis approaching that unnerves me

and causes me to tremble for the safety of my country. As a result of war, corporations have been enthroned and an era of corruption in high places will follow. The money power will endeavor to prolong its reign by working on the prejudices of the people until all the wealth is aggregated into a few hands and the republic is destroyed."

Woodrow Wilson's Prophecy

"The masters of the government of the United States are the combined capitalists and manufacturers of the United States.

"The government of the United States at present is a foster child of the special interests. It is not allowed to have a will of its own.

"The government, which was designed for the people, has gotten into the hands of bosses and their employers, the special interests. An invisible empire has been set up above the forms of democracy.

"America is not a place of which it can be said, as it used to be, that a man may choose his own calling and pursue it as far as his abilities enable him to pursue it.

"American industry is not free as it once was free; American enterprise is not free.

"We have restricted credit, we have restricted opportunity, we have controlled development, and we have come to be one of the worst ruled, one of the most completely controlled and dominated governments in the civilized world—no longer a government by free opinion, no longer a government by conviction and the vote of the majority, but a government by the opinion and duress of small groups of dominant men."

Spirit Of William Penn Made Prophecy, Chastised A President Here.

William Penn was born in 1644, was an English Quaker who advocated religious tolerance and was the founder of Pennsylvania. He was vitally interested in the colonization of America. The Quaker also planned the city of Philadelphia. Penn died in 1718, satisfied that America would one day be the land of the future.

It is not known if Penn was reached by a medium during the 18th century. During the 19th century, in 1881 to be exact, Penn's spirit did return through a medium and made some startling observations and prophecies.

His words were recorded during the seance and are repeated.

Penn Speaks

"I, William Penn, come this morning in accordance with a previous arrangement with my co-laborers, to make known some things of interest to the people, and finding the opportunity favorable for our reception, we will now say: many changes are occurring and will take place which no human effort or power from the spiritual world can avert.

"We therefore desire that our mediums should place themselves in receptive conditions to the intelligence of the superior Spirit realm, so that they may better endure the trial of modern times.

"In regard to affairs of national import, there will be much dissatisfaction, which will result in the disintegration and disruption of imperial governments in the Old World.

"There will be much bloodshed, which cannot compensate in any degree for wrongs, however light or great.

"In looking over our own beloved country, we see elements at work that will culminate in subjecting the masses to the few 'bondholders and Shylocks' that compose the monied oligarchy of America, and will render obsolete the stars and freedom in our land."

Penn's Warning

"The people have no idea how deeply laid are the plans to control and subject the masses to despotism of the money power.

"Like a vast network are the corporations of the East and West, laying their schemes to entrap and confine to certain limitations the people that form the integral parts of the Republic.

"Charles Sumner is now striving to influence some members

at the Capital to thwart the designs and counteract the plottings of the telegraph companies, who would control all the wires, even the submarine. And there will be a long and strong fight ere the United States Government will manage them as it does the postal department, which would be more in harmony with the people's needs.

"Another reform is very much needed, that is now being overlooked by the general populace, because they do not apprehend the dangers before them.

"The tendency of the present administration (Rutherford B. Hayes was president in 1881) is pointed directly to the usurpation of the peoples' rights, religiously, politically, socially and financially.

"As an evidence of the truth we utter, take notice that within two years a monetary panic (Penn was off by one year; the panic occurred in 1884), such as has not occurred, will follow as the direct result of the peculiarly intriguing manipulation of United States bonds, Moines and properties.

"An unwise policy was instituted by a few monied men, who have held in their hands the reins of government ever since Abraham Lincoln came to live with us."

Penn Says Our Liberties Are Eroding

"The barriers to the future liberties of the people are gaining strength and thickness every day. We would speak in tones that should reach every heart of the sons and daughters of toil, and quicken them to deliberate and intense thought, to vigorous and systematic action.

"A yoke more weighty than the Egyptian gods placed upon the neck of serfdom is theirs to wear, if they heed not the voices of the air, earth and sky, and seek to resist the encroachment of the enemies of liberty."

Penn's Proposal

"One thing more. There is now a bill before the Spiritual Congress, and it will soon be presented to the people of the

United States, so formed in justice and equality, that there can be no way of escaping its binding power to protect all men, women and children in their inherent right to life, liberty and the pursuit of happiness, and to insure this possibility each individual shall have the lawful right to just so much land as he, she or they, as a family need for their own comfort, happiness, pleasure and home. No more, no less.

"The land, like the air and water, belongs to God and the universe. No man, nor combination of men, collectively or severally, have any right to more than they need and can judiciously make use of, than they have to the patent and sole right to bottle water, or confine the air in a casket, and thus deprive the citizen and laborer of the elements which build up and maintain not only the individual life, but the very foundation upon which national prosperity exists.

Penn Predicts Crash

"So we make no treaties with sordid selfishness. Nor can we tolerate longer the iron arm or golden rod that goads people on to servile bondage and squalid want. And you need not be surprised to hear of immense failures in commercial ranks. Merchants, stockbrokers, railroad magnates and other consolidated companies, as well as individual enterprises, will by some fearful means, become prostrated and utterly fail financially.

"A crash is coming. It is inevitable; and the millionaire of today will be the pitiable mendicant of tomorrow. They have built an immense structure upon a false base, and like the sands of the restless sea, it will be washed beneath them. Goodbye,—WILLIAM PENN. Ten o'clock a.m., March 13, 1881."

Obviously, Penn knew what he was talking about. He accurately predicted the Crash of 1929, when millionaires lost their fortunes overnight, with many of them becoming charges of the state.

Prophecies of the Presidents

Chapter Four:
Our Martyred Presidents—Visions Of Doom And Death

In at least several instances, the President of the United States realized in advance that he was not going to live out his duly appointed term in office. Prophecies of personal doom including successful assassination attempts are peppered throughout the history of the occupants of the White House and those who have been close to the presidents have also had such premonitions, either their families or close staff members.

Four Presidents died by the hands of assassins—Lincoln, Garfield, McKinley and Kennedy. Two of them predicted their own deaths, Lincoln and Garfield. (Kennedy's strange obsession with death will be noted later.)

The man originally appointed to kill Lincoln was given a brand-new rifle equipped with a telescopic sight. He was a Confederate sharpshooter. But he showed up drunk for the job and plans had to be put off.

Lincoln and Kennedy were killed on Friday. Both were elected to Congress in a year ending in 47. Both were elected President in a year ending in 60. (All presidents who took office in years ending with zero have died while serving as Chief Executive—with the lone exception of Ronald Reagan, who did survive an assassination attempt early in his term.)

Both Lincoln and Kennedy saw military service, Lincoln in the Black Hawk War and Kennedy in World War II. Both were over six feet tall. Both were champions of civil rights. Both were shot in the back of the head and both were with their wives at the time. The alleged assassins of Lincoln and Kennedy were shot to death before they could be brought to trial. Both Presidents lost children through death. Both were avid readers of the Bible, often quoting from the New and Old Testament. Kennedy's secretary's name was Evelyn Lincoln, who was always concerned for his safety. Lincoln's safety, while he was in New York, was handled by the superintendent of police, whose name was Kennedy. Lincoln's successor was a man named Johnson, who was born in 1808. Kennedy's successor was a man named Johnson, who was born in 1908.

James Garfield's Premonitions

The 20th President of the United States, James Garfield, was convinced that he would die young and often said as much to his friends. His reason was that his father had died young, so he expected to follow suit. He was 49 when he was assassinated.

The frightening premonition came to him two days before he was shot. He called for Robert Lincoln, the son of the late president, and sat him down for more than an hour, questioning the young man on all of the details of his father's death.

Garfield's killer was an addled lawyer named Charles Guiteau. He thought that if he killed the president the party would be reunited and the Republicans would be so pleased that they would give him a government job.

Guiteau went to Washington after borrowing thirty dollars. He followed the president into Christian Church on Vermont Avenue and sat two pews behind him. He aborted that attempt because he was afraid of killing innocent people.

His next try came on June 18, 1881, when he followed the President and Mrs. Garfield into a railway station but again decided not to shoot because Mrs. Garfield was ill and would not be strong enough to stand seeing her husband killed.

Finally, on July 2, 1881, Guiteau caught the President during an unguarded moment at the Baltimore and Potomac railway station in Washington. He fired two shots at close range.

The bullets did not hit vital organs, but they did carry infection. Bungling doctors probed for those bullets for weeks, but could not get them out. Desperate now, they went to see Alexander Graham Bell, the inventor of the telephone, and asked him to devise an instrument that would emit an audible click when it was brought near metal. Bell put together a device that worked beautifully for many years and was replaced only when X-rays were invented.

Bell told the doctors that when they used the device they had to be sure that no metal was near the patient. They did not heed his warning. They used the electrical probe on Garfield but it didn't work.

What the medics failed to consider was that the president was lying on a bed with a metal frame and metal springs! He died on September 19, 1881.

Lincoln's Strange Dream

On April 11, 1865, four days before his assassination, Abraham Lincoln spent the evening with his wife, Mary Todd, Col. Ward H. Lamon, who was a lawyer and Lincoln's aide, and two other guests. The conversation turned to dreams, and Lincoln said, "I had one the other night which has haunted me ever since." He was urged to report on it, and he did so, but with an air of sadness.

"About ten days ago I retired very late," Lincoln began. "I had been up waiting for important dispatches from the front. I could not have been long in bed when I fell into slumber, for I was weary. I soon began to dream. There seemed to be a deathlike stillness about me. Then I heard subdued sobs, as if a number of people were weeping. I thought I left my bed and wandered downstairs. There the silence was broken by some pitiful sobbing, but the mourners were invisible. I went from room to room; no living person was in sight, but the same mournful sounds of distress met me as I passed along. It was light in all the rooms; every object was familiar to me; but where were all the people who were grieving as if their hearts would break? I was puzzled and alarmed. What could be the meaning of all this? Determined to find out the cause of a state of things so mysterious and shocking, I kept on until I arrived at the East Room, which I entered. There I met with a sickening surprise. Before me was a catafalque, on which rested a corpse wrapped in funeral vestments. Around it were stationed soldiers who were acting as guards; and there was a throng of people, some gazing mournfully upon the corpse, whose face was covered, others weeping pitifully. 'Who is dead in the White House?' I demanded of one of the soldiers. 'The President,' was his answer; 'he was killed by an assassin.' Then came a loud burst of grief from the crowd, which woke me from my dream. I slept no more that night; and although it was only a dream, I have been strangely annoyed by it ever since."

Mary Todd Predicts Lincoln's Death in Office

Shortly before he was elected president, Lincoln had a vision. He was tired after a long day of speech-making and lay down to rest. He then caught a glimpse of his face in a mirror. As he stared at it he saw a double image of himself. The second image was pale, like a dead man's face. A few days later the same vision came to him, only this time he talked about it with his wife, Mary Todd.

Mary's interpretation was that her husband would be elected to two terms as president, but that he would die during his second term.

Lincoln's Prophecy On The Day He Was Shot

On April 14, 1865, Lincoln was shot. Earlier that day he had been so troubled by a dream that he mentioned it to his cabinet. He told the group that in his dream he had seen himself sailing in an indescribable vessel and moving rapidly toward an indistinct shore.

John F. Kennedy's Strange Home Movie

Ralph G. Martin reports in his book, *A Hero For Our Time*, published by Macmillan, that President Kennedy made a home movie depicting his assassination. The film was made on September 21, 1963, two months before he was shot to death.

The photographer who shot the movie said that Kennedy wrote the script and did the filming on a weekend in Newport, Rhode Island. Photographer Robert L. Knudsen said, "He just called me over one day and said they wanted to have some fun and shoot a movie."

According to the book, a man with binoculars watched the president as he got off the *Honey Fitz*, the Kennedy yacht, and walked down the gangplank. Following the script, Kennedy suddenly clutched his chest and fell flat on the ground. Behind him coming down the gangplank were Countess Crespi and her small son. Both stepped over the president's body as though he wasn't there, and continued on out of range of the camera.

Jacqueline Kennedy was right behind the countess. She, too, stepped over her husband's body. Behind her there was Red Fay, the Under Secretary of the Navy and Kennedy's PT boat buddy. Fay stumbled and fell directly on Kennedy. As he did so, a geyser of red came out of the President's mouth and soiled his sport shirt.

The scene was shot several times. The photographer has not revealed what had become of the film. It is not in the archives of the John F. Kennedy library in Boston, according to Mary Lee Quinn, an audio-visual curator.

The photographer said, "There were about four other couples there. They thought it would be kind of fun to do it. There was a little dialogue, but I'm not about to repeat it. It was done in confidence, and even though he's dead, it's still in confidence."

Photographer Knudsen said that when Kennedy was killed in Dallas on November 22, 1963, he remembered the home movie. "I wondered if it was a premonition he had, or a quirk of fate."

JFK Was Preoccupied With Death

Martin's book reveals the fact that Kennedy gave lots of thought to death. After he returned from his trips he would always say, "Thank God I wasn't killed today."

The president was forever asking friends how they would like to die. Finally, one of them asked him, and he said, "Airplane." When asked why, he said: "It's quick."

Kennedy's Premonitions

Pierre Salinger, JFK's press secretary, said that the president had a premonition a few days before going to Dallas. He said to Salinger, "Somehow, I wish I didn't have to go to Dallas. I guess it is because there is so much to be done here." He had a feeling that he should not go to that city. There was no such feeling about going to Florida, or, for that matter, to any other city in Texas.

Kennedy made a remark to a group of Secret Service men in Hyannisport just before leaving for Dallas: "I wonder if they will shoot me in church. If they do, they'll have to get you fellows first!"

Noted Persons Who Predicted JFK's Death

A short time before his death, famed novelist Taylor Caldwell wrote an article about the danger of a presidential assassination at the hands of a subversive group.

Famed seer Jeanne Dixon of Washington, D.C. was interviewed by author Jess Stearn and predicted Kennedy's death. As time drew near, she tried desperately to warn him.

Evangelist Billy Graham had a disturbing dream about President Kennedy on the day before he was shot. He said he tried to reach Kennedy by phone to warn him not to go to Dallas.

Gilbert Holloway, prominent metaphysical lecturer, had written a note of warning to JFK, requesting that he stay away from Dallas.

A Dying Boy's Dream

Ricky McDowell was eight years old and dying of leukemia. He was at Doctor's Hospital in Columbus, Ohio. The boy fell into a coma that lasted for 48 hours. When he came around he told his mother that he had a dream in which President Kennedy had died.

Ricky reported this dream at 7:00 a.m., November 22, 1963, about six hours before the president was killed.

JFK Listens To Man Who Saw A Vision

Sidney Lansing was driving his car through a rainstorm in Norfolk, Virginia, when he had a vision showing President Kennedy being assassinated on a public street in front of thousands of witnesses.

Lansing went to Washington and patrolled the sidewalk in front of the White House. He carried a sign which detailed the frightening vision. The man kept his vigil for days.

On several occasions Kennedy passed the man in his car and waved to him. The FBI eventually had the man hospitalized for observation and questioning. While Lansing was still in the hospital, President Kennedy came to see him. The two talked at length about the vision, and in the end, JFK told Lansing that he was grateful for his concern and interest.

A Clairvoyant's Incredible Vision Of Kennedy's Death

A Los Angeles clairvoyant and psychic, Helen Greenwood, had the most vivid and detailed vision of the assassination of all. In a dream she saw President Kennedy in Dallas riding in an open car. The dream occurred a few months before the president made the trip.

Helen Greenwood saw in her vision the crowded streets and the cheering throng. She could feel the excitement of the day. She then saw a rifle being aimed at the president from a high window above the street. She heard the shots. She saw the president grab for his throat, then sink to the floor of the car, his red hair covered with blood.

Mrs. Greenwood was so frightened by her dream that she tried immediately to contact the FBI. She succeeded, but no one believed her. She then switched her attention to the Los Angeles office of Governor Brown. She telephoned the office daily. The only one who was impressed with the story was a secretary named Mrs. Nova Corey, yet nothing was done about it.

In desperation, the woman contacted Reverend Maurice Dawkins of the Independent Church of Christ. Rev. Dawkins was a delegate from Los Angeles to the White House Conference of Religious Leaders.

The September 1963 issue of the *National Examiner* printed the letter written by Rev. Dawkins to Mrs. Greenwood. He wrote:

"I recall so clearly your warnings to me and your urging me to deliver a message to the White House to the President or his brother...that the Kennedys must not be permitted to go South.

"On May 18th (1963) following my 24 hours vigil at the Lincoln Memorial, I spoke to Pierre Salinger about the dangers involved and delivered your message of warning. At the White House Conference of Religious Leaders in June, I spoke of it again to the president and his brother in general terms, but not as emphatically as you had instructed me. In August, prior to the church bombing in Birmingham, and again in September, you urged the sending of warning telegrams to Senators Kuchel and Engle, and to Robert Kennedy, to give protection to the Kennedys, and let Vice President Johnson make any trips to the South that had to be made.

"I now know the tremendous significance of your saying we must pray for President Kennedy—that he will not die as Lincoln died. I thought of this when I referred to President Kennedy in the Hollywood Palladium in June 1963 as 'The New Lincoln.'"

After the assassination, Rev. Dawkins said to Mrs. Greenwood: "Perhaps, Helen, this has been God's way of using a good man as an instrument; a sacrifice that will save all mankind."

Noted Psychic Sees JFK Dead Before 1964

One of the most outstanding psychics in 1963 was James Gordon, 28. He had been tested for several years at the University of Chicago, which declared that Gordon had an 85 degree accuracy. In February of that year he sat with a group which discussed many topics. One of them was Kennedy. Gordon was asked if he thought JFK would be re-elected in 1964. Gordon's answer was that there were many parallels between Kennedy and Lincoln, and that Kennedy could meet the same fate as Lincoln late in 1963.

Was JFK Reincarnation Of Former VP?

There are many who believe that President Kennedy was John C. Calhoun in his last reincarnation. Calhoun was born in 1782 and died in 1850. He was from South Carolina and was Vice President under John Quincy Adams and Andrew Jackson.

JFK's Shocking Speech

In June 1963 the civil rights riots and violence were at their peak. James Reston in the New York Times reported that Kennedy made a speech to representatives of both sides of the civil rights issue. After he talked about the problems facing both factions, he drew a slip of paper from his pocket. On the paper was the famous Shakespearean speech of Blanche of Castile from King.

He read the words with deep emotion and the audience was astonished. These were the words:

The sun's o'er cast with blood: Fair day, Adieu!
Which is the side that I must go withal?
I am with both. Each army hath a hand;
And, in their rage, I having hold of both;
They whirl asunder...and dismember me.

Vision At JFK's Funeral

One of the president's closest friends, who has psychic tendencies, prayed at his funeral. She suddenly felt that she was having an out-of-body experience...another dimension of time. The woman said later that she had a greatly heightened sense of perception.

In her altered state she saw a huge ship in the Potomac River. On the starboard side she saw two men standing close together. One was old and slightly taller than the younger one. The older man had his arm across the shoulders of the other.

Both wore expressions of infinite peace. The woman saw clearly that one man was Abraham Lincoln and the other was John F Kennedy.

The woman felt that they were on the Ship of State, and that the older man was turning the helm over to the younger.

Kennedy's Favorite Precognitive Poem

JFK enjoyed reading Alan Seeger's poem, "I Have a Rendezvous with Death." He loved Tennyson's "Holy Grail" and "Idylls of the King." The latter told the story of the Knights of the Round Table. To Kennedy, the White House was Camelot.

Jacqueline revealed that her husband's prayer was that when death came, it should come in a moment. One stanza of Seeger's poem reads:

I have a rendezvous with death .
It may be he shall take my hand
And lead me into his dark land .
And I to my pledged word am true,
I shall not fail that rendezvous.

The question is, are all these precognitive dreams and visions of assassination attempts pure "coincidence," or I have our leaders been given advance warning by some Heavenly Host-so that they can get their own personal affairs, as well as the affairs of the country, in order? The spiritually aware realize that nothing happens by "chance" in God's universe, and that there is a purpose and a reason for every event even if we do not understand it at the moment.

Chapter Five:
A Colossus Shall Fall

Author's Note: This Chapter is authored by the New Age teacher, FRATER VIII, who says that sudden and startling CHANGES are due among all the people on earth and on the earth itself in the next couple of decades. They are in the active process of materializing among the people and on the earth NOW.

• • •

Approximately every 2,000 years, we move from one Grand Sign of the Zodiac to another. These Grand Signs overlap each other by approximately one-tenth of a sign—200 years. Thus, the Sign of Pisces is overlapped forward on Aquarius and Aquarius is overlapped backwards on the old and ailing Grand Sign of Pisces. In the year 2000 A.D., this overlapping period is said to be equal and Aquarius will have the upper hand immediately.

This period of 200 years when the Grand Signs fight each other is called a "Cusp." About the turn of the present century, 1900, Aquarius began to enter this "cusp period." However, it was a very minor influence and did not cause poor, old Pisces any concern.

It was not until World War I, in 1914, that the old order of Pisces began to "take notice," and, in 1917, when General Alemby took Jerusalem without firing a shot, there was a definite indication that Aquarius had gained much power. Of course, the old Piscean Forces were not beaten by any means, as you will note by recalling the greatest war ever fought—World War II.

In 1960 it was just 60 years since Pisces began to wane—he has done a lot of "warning" in that length of time, but not nearly as much as he is going to do between now and the end of this present century—2000 A.D. In the same length of time, our Aquarius has passed through "babyhood" and is now a "husky Youth," a young man who will in the future subdue every opponent.

By 2000 A.D., the fight between the two Grand Signs will be over...excepting for a little "mopping up," which will be completed by 2100 A.D. This is said to be a "Century of Grace" to give the recalcitrant souls who cannot adjust themselves to the MILLENNIAL ORDER an opportunity to make the transition.

We must not feel there is nothing good in Pisces. Actually, there is much good. This positive good will remain and it will be carried into the NEW SEVENTH MILLENNIUM—the "Thousand Years of Peace."

However, all that which is deeply negative in the Piscean Regime will have to be rooted out and eliminated before the end of this present Century. That is where you and I fit into the colossal "weeding-out" picture. We are literally weighted down with old Piscean misconceptions that will be our undoing in the remote and in the near future if we do not rid ourselves of these negative Piscean influences.

Never has there been a century in all of history where the positive stood out from the negative with such clearness. Never has there been a century where so many coming events have been revealed to the peoples of the earth as in this present Century. This marvelous information is "coming in" from many sources and, for you, it will minimize, to a very great extent, the cataclysms which will play havoc with most of the world.

Most of the prophets of old had something to say about our particular time—the last part of this century. But in every prophecy there were two groups of people—the wise and the foolish virgins. The Wise virgins were the people who not only heard of coming events, but set about immediately to cope with them: How, they learned, to turn a negative event into a positive one. The Foolish Virgins were the ones who, listening to the report of coming events with considerable interest, did not do a single thing concerning the matter.

More recent prophets, both men and women, have told of things that would "shortly come to pass" in their particular time and of things that would come to pass at the "end of the age"—*in our particular time.*

Nostradamus predicted, in 1549, the events of the 20th Century—our time. We haven't the space to go into all of these prophecies. He was said to have prophesied concerning Mussolini and what manner of death he was to meet. He also said: "the barren shores of the Holy Land will bloom forth with a new, shining city by 1950." This, of course, meant Tel Aviv. Nostradamus, a Jew, became a devout Roman Catholic, but he never entirely "deserted his people," the Jews.

In a prophecy of Nostradamus concerning the United States, we read: "The financial citadel of the nation whose holiday is Thursday (Thanksgiving) will be moved to a central area, and leave ruin against the sky." This, of course, would be New York City—probably not too far in the future.

Another Nostradamus prophecy reads:

"Garden of the world, near the New City,
"In the way of the man-made mountains,
"Shall be seized on and plunged into a ferment,
"Being forced to drink sulphurous poisoned waters."

This, too, could be New York City, and in the near future. For the "man-made mountains" are no doubt "skyscrapers," and the Garden could be a resort or "playground" near the city which would be covered by a tidal wave of waters mysteriously poisoned. Whether the "poisoning" would be made-made or due to underwater volcanic activity (such as might happen if ancient lands were to arise in that vicinity) is a matter of conjecture.

It is interesting to note that while Michael Nostradamus was writing his "quatrains" in France, Mother Shipton was writing four-line prophetic verse in England. She was not too well educated, but that didn't make any difference to her. If the meter wasn't always correct, she avowed that what she said was, which

PROPHECIES OF THE PRESIDENTS

later proved to be true.

Recently, here in California, through a Seeress named Teska, ten more versus of Mother Shipton saw the light of day. They are interesting as they pertain to our time.

The last line of her first verse is very interesting. It reads in this way:

"A Colossus 'neath the waves shall fall."

Then she goes on in the second "quatrain," which reads:

"Shores will change, while mountains tumble,

"Mighty sounds in sky will rumble.

"All this comes when time stands still,

"When Cassiopeia climbs the hill."

Let us start with the last line of the second verse first: "When Cassiopeia climbs the hill."

Cassiopeia is a constellation of five stars in the northern hemisphere forming an irregular "W." Cassiopeia was "climbing the hill" on the —ascendant— until May, 1959, when she reached her zenith. For a moment, "time stands still" at the zenith, but now, Cassiopeia is in "retrograde" and during her retrogression, "mighty sounds in sky will rumble." This could have a double meaning. We think of "sky noise" as thunder and lightning and that could be true in a very great way when the elements get to working against each other. Also, man-made noises—super jet planes, atomic and other bombs—will probably be in the future colossal alongside our present planes and atom bombs.

"Shores will change, while mountains tumble" is a very interesting line. This seems to tie in with the first line—"A Colossus 'neath the waves shall fall."

Actually, at the present time, there is but one "Colossus" in the world, and that colossus is known as the Statue of Liberty in New York Harbor. When the "shores change," and "mountains tumble," I am quite confident that the raging flood coming in from the Atlantic Ocean will topple the "Grand Old Lady of Liberty" off her quite solid foundation.

Of course, this will cause the flooding of the entire eastern seaboard. Edgar Cayce, in one of his psychic readings, when asked the question: "Will there be any changes in the earth's surface in North America? If so, what sections will be affected and how?" replied:

"All over the country we will find many physical changes of a minor or a greater degree. The greater changes, as we will find in America will be the North Atlantic Seaboard—WATCH NEW YORK!" (311–8; Ms 7: April 9, 1932.)

Also, he prophesied while in a trance state: "Poseida will be among the first portions of Atlantis to rise again." Cassiopeia will be retrograding heavily at that time and there is nothing like a great constellation to wreak havoc on a planet so small as the earth.

What will cause the heavy flooding of certain parts of the earth? In the *Saturday Evening Post,* a number of years ago, there was an excellent article that answered this question perfectly. It explained, in the fewest possible words, that the flooding is caused by the slippage of the "skin" of the earth being pulled around on the earth itself by the South Pole—which will then be in a warm latitude—and the ice and snow will melt very rapidly, causing all oceans to rise. Also, the slippage of the earth's crust, which only extends down less than 50 miles, will slip faster than the waters can adjust themselves to the new land position and will, quite naturally, flood vast areas for a short time, until the waters have an opportunity to recede to their former position.

As the slippage in the Americas has always been from North to South, and in Africa, Europe and Asia, from South to North, there will be a great deal of flooding of North, South and Central America. Only the entire surface of the earth slips around.

This is easily possible because down in every direction (below 50 miles) the earth's crust or "skin" rests on molten liquid lava. the earth's surface can slip around to another position without, in any way, changing the position of the globe as to its orbit and its position in relation to the sun.

Colossal changes are coming and we cannot do anything about it; but the speed with which they come—that is a matter about which we can do something very vital.

We read in the Old testament about a man named Jonah. The Lord wanted him to go to a certain city—Ninevah—and preach. But Jonah didn't want to go and he fled in the opposite direction. The Lord, however, made the going so hard for poor Jonah that he was willing to come back to Ninevah and preach as he had never preached before. On account of the wickedness of the city, Jonah had just 40 days to try to save it. He did such a good job of preaching and converted so many of the wicked that the entire city was spared.

And so, we, with our vast amount of knowledge (still unused) can, if we do the right thing, slow down the coming catastrophes, and…will be able to adjust ourselves to the situation and the situation to ourselves no matter how fierce and foreboding they may seem at the time.

Chapter Six:
The Sibylline Prophecy

From the famous "Sibylline Oracles" of the Greeks, comes the marvelous Sibylline Prophecy. It foretells the coming of genuine World Peace, and the Reign of Justice for all men.

"The KINGDOM of god shall come upon all good men; for the Earth, which is the produce of all things, shall yield to men the best, and infinite fruits. And the Cities shall be full of good men, and the fields shall be fruitful, and there shall be NO WAR upon the earth, nor tumult, nor shall the earth groan as by an earthquake. No wars, no drought, nor famine, nor hail to waste the fruits…for there shall be NO MORE WARS.

"NO WARS, no drought, nor famine, nor hail to waste the fruits; but there shall be great Peace in all the earth, and one King shall live in friendship with the other to the end of the Age.

"And the Immortal, who lives in the heavens adorned with stars, shall give a common law to all men in all of the earth, and instruct miserable men that things must be done; for he is the only God, and there is no other. And he shall burn the great strength of men by Fire.

"Then he shall raise a Kingdom forever over all men when he hath given a Holy Law to the Righteous, to all whom he promised to open the earth; and the world of the blessed, and all joys, and an immortal mind, and eternal cheerfulness. Out of every country they shall bring Frankincense, and gifts to the houses of the Great God, and there shall be no other house to be enquired for by the generations of men that are to come, but the faithful Man who God has given to be worshiped, for mortals call him the Son of the Great God.

"And all the paths of the fields, and rough shores, and high mountains, and the raging waves of the sea, shall be easily passed or sailed through in those Days; for all Peace shall happen to the Good, through all their land, the Prophets of the Great God shall take away all slaughter...for they are the judges of mortals...and the righteous Kings. And there shall be just riches for men, for the Government of the Great God shall be just Judgment."

NOTE: The above paragraphs are taken from Book III, Pages 80–2, of *The Sibylline Oracles* by Sir John Floyoer. The additional paragraphs, which now follow the above, are translated from the Greek "Sibyllae," book XIV, and appear in the Conclusion:

"NOW NO LONGER shall gold and silver be full of guile, nor shall there by possessing of land nor toilsome slavery; but one love and one ordering of life in kindness of soul. All things shall be common and light equal in the lives of men."

"Vice shall leave the earth and be sunk in the divine ocean. Then this is the Summer of mortal men nigh at hand. Strong necessity will be laid upon the world that these things be accomplished. No wayfarer meeting another will then say: 'The race of mortal men, though now they perish, shall some day have rest.'"

"And then a holy people shall wield the scepter of the whole world through all the ages, along with their mighty offspring."

Chapter Seven: The Polar Shift and America's Destiny

Does America have a prominent place in the future destiny of this planet? Riley Crabb, longtime director of the Borderland Sciences Research Associates (now retired to Australia), believes it does. "Time and again when one delves into the literature having to do with today's crisis in world affairs, one finds references to the leadership planned for America *after* the cataclysms are over.

"It is my purpose in this work to make use of various sources, old and new, in referring to the cataclysmic activity which is presently upon us and to emphasize as much as possible the positive aspects of the change. I believe all of you here are searching for truth, for answers to some of these great problems; you want assurance that it is possible to survive and thus to share in the building of the New Age. I do.

"I am sure many of you are familiar with the work the Borderland Sciences Research Associates. I have been a member since 1951 A

Mark and Irene Probert

large part of their work has been the dissemination of information received through the mediumship of the late Mark Probert, of San Diego, California.

The controlling group of individuals who use Mark's body for communicating with us here in the three-dimensional world call themselves the Inner Circle. I'd like to quote from one of the seances of the earlier days. It was held in San Diego on March 3, 1949. A control who identifies himself as Kay Ting, of Chinese origin, is speaking.

"There will come a time when your civilization will be as greatly advanced as the East in the study of life—what you call metaphysics. Man is ever striving to find his way home, home to one-ness with the Father. When that time comes for you Americans you will then have the most advanced civilization on earth. In all the past history of man never has there been a time such as there will be when this comes to your country. Why? Because you are so far advanced in your material science, which was something that was very much neglected in my time on earth.

"That is why they went down, India and China—almost all of the East, they neglected the material, concerning themselves only with the spiritual and mental. This is so always; if man neglects the physical he loses the mental. It is impossible to talk of either one alone. Man is a holy trinity of physical, mental and spiritual…"

Kay Ting

It is true that we have over-emphasized the material here in the West, but that was necessary and is necessary. As Kay Ting put it, "It is better that you understand the world you are in, in all of its parts; then you can go ahead with the spiritual."

Importance of Planetary Rhythms

One of the important studies of the planet we are on is the earth itself, its cycles, its rhythms. Some of the planetary rhythms are comparatively short and easily observed: night and day and the four seasons, spring, summer, fall and winter. The longer ones, however, are more difficult to observe: the emergence and submergence of land masses from the ocean, glacial periods, the shifting of the poles; these seem to be governed by cycles or waves of energy which are thousands of years from peak to peak. One civilization may come and pass away entirely on the rising swell of some cosmic wave. Its inhabitants, under this mighty, subjective and positive influence, may thus create a culture whose bounty is the envy of mankind. Another civilization, born on the downward slope, may create nothing but misery for itself, and all around it! In each case only the disinterested observer standing outside the civilization would be aware of the difference, and the cause.

There are many indications that we are in the midst of a changeover from a negative to a positive period in the long, long history of this planet. You can find them in science, in astrology, in philosophy and in religion.

In speaking of this mighty change it might be well to keep in mind the difference between cataclysm and catastrophe. Cataclysm is Nature at work. The breaking up of ice in the northern rivers in the spring is a good example of this. Who could or would stop that from taking place? It becomes catastrophe, however, when an ice-jam in the river threatens a man-made bridge, and destroys it. One or two may be hurt; a few more are inconvenienced; to the rest of us it's just an item in the morning paper.

Cataclysm is always going on sometime, somewhere on the face of the globe as the earth goes on about its daily business. Catastrophe, too, is always with us as some human beings get caught up in these things. The only advice I can give is to keep yourself in tune with Nature, with the mighty Consciousness which lies behind all manifested life, so that you are always in the right place at the right time.

As the Space Visitor, Des'ka, told Doris LaVesque a couple of years ago: "Catastrophe can be avoided by Christ-like thinking, and will be averted for those who think Christ-like."

The Polar Flip

One form of cataclysm which has aroused considerable scientific interest of late is the so-called Polar Flip. More correctly this should be tabled "the movement of the earth's crust into and out of the polar regions".

Space Visitors have told their contactees that they are here to observe a crisis of planetary significance. A shifting of new lands into the North and South Polar regions would indeed assume celestial importance. The Antarctic continent would find itself in a temperate climate, and a new equatorial bulge might bring new lands to the surface in the Atlantic and Pacific oceans.

This subject is discussed at length in a book issued some years ago by professors Charles H. Hapgood and James H. Campbell. The title of the book is *The Earth's Shifting Crust.* In it they review at length the various theories put forth by science to explain the so-called glacial periods. In it they propound their own theory that a glacial period on any continent indicates the time when that continent was in one or the other of the Polar Zones!

Every continent—North America, Africa, Europe, Asia—shows evidence of having been encased in ice at some time or other. Yet entrenched doctrine maintains that the poles have always been in their present location. This in spite of the fact that fossil remains of domesticated animals have been found in Siberian islands in the Arctic ocean—among the bones of mastodons and other prehistoric monsters. Also in these regions can be found the remains of tropical plants!

The growing accumulation of evidence of this kind, against entrenched doctrine, has kept the polar shift controversy alive. In school years ago you and I learned that the poles have been in the same locations for millions of years. This accounted for the gradual accumulation of ice on the Antarctic continent and on Greenland. Researches of Navy scientists at the South Pole in 1957 revealed that the South Polar ice cap is of comparatively recent growth. Through radio-carbon and ionium testing of the age of the ice it was found that the 10,000 foot plateau at the pole is only about 10,000 years old!

Now, geologists are pretty well agreed that it was about that long, 10,000 years, that the North American glacier melted away. Comparing these two facts, Hapgood and Campbell came to the conclusion that the shifting of the earth's crust was the cause of these simultaneous events. The North American continent moved away from the North Polar Zone; the Antarctic continent moved into the South Polar zone at the same time.

Hapgood says that the simplest and most obvious theory for explaining any ice age is that the area concerned was at one or the other of the poles during the period of glaciation. Previous to the last polar shift the North Pole was in the Hudson Bay region. A glance at the world map shows that the land mass lay to the southward of the pole. Thus the off-center thrust of the weight of ice was southward of the pole. When the billions of tons of ice finally overbalanced the centrifugal force of the earth's spin, it pulled or tipped the earth's crust southward, on our Western side of the world, over two thousand miles, setting up new locations of the North and South Poles where they now are.

To simplify our understanding of this problem we'll have to assume arbitrarily that the angular relationship of the earth's axis to the sun will remain unchanged during the shift we are discussing here. I believe the polarity of the earth's magnetic field may be reversed at the time of a flip. In fact this may be the invisible, solar trigger which sets off the physical movement! How this may be accomplished will be discussed later. But I believe the axis and the magnetic field maintain their tilt, 22° away from parallel to the sun. This latter condition sustains the seasonal rhythms so necessary to the evolution of the second and third Kingdoms here on earth, vegetable and animal, and of our own Fourth Kingdom, the human.

The Sidewise Heave of the Mass of Ice

Since the North Polar area at the present time is ice-covered ocean, the responsibility for the next polar movement is on the vast pile of ice at the South Pole. A glance at the copy of Hapgood's diagram shows "what an enormous sidewise heave results from the eccentricity of the geographical center of the ice cap". The center of the ice cap is 12° off the center of rotation. The direction of the thrust is along 96° East Longitude. When and IF the break comes it will pull the southern part of South America into the South Polar region. At the other end of the earth, Siberia will move into the North Polar region and America will move further southward into the tropics. If the move is anything like the one which occurred some eleven thousand years ago, it will put Southern California within 5° of the equator!

General McClellan's Dream

To return to our main theme, let us now skip back in time to November 1861. It was well over a hundred years ago that General George B. McClellan was made Commander in Chief of the Union Armies by President Lincoln. The Nation's capital was threatened by Confederate forces when McClellan took over. One night in his quarters, as he was going over maps in preparation of his campaign, he fell asleep or into trance.

A thunderous voice awoke him, to look at a living map of the entire Eastern part of the United States. It showed the positions and planned movements of the enemy, all set up as countermeasures to his own plans. Jesuit agents in Washington, "commandos" of Lincoln's mortal enemy, Pope Pius IX, had stolen his battle plans. Quickly, McClellan transferred the data from the living map to his own maps on the table. Curious as to the identity of the Visitor who had invaded his privacy in quarters, McClellan finally looked up. He was confronted by the glorified face and figure of George Washington.

"General McClellan, while yet in the flesh I beheld the birth of the American Republic. It was indeed a hard and bloody one but God's blessing was upon the nation."

After this reminder of the Nation's founding the bewildered McClellan was told how America "has been brought to her second great struggle...for the most perilous she has to endure; passing as she is from childhood to opening maturity."

The war to preserve the Union, Washington said, would force the nation to learn self-control, self-rule that would place her in the van of civilization. Then came his reference to the third and last great crisis of this nation, the prophecy so poignant with meaning for us today.

"But her mission will not then be finished. For ere *another century* shall have gone by, the oppressors of the whole earth, hating and envying her exaltation, shall join themselves together and raise up their hands against her. But if America still be found worthy of her high calling they shall surely be discomfitted, and then will be ended her *third* and *last* great struggle for existence. Thenceforth shall the Republic go on, increasing in power and goodness until her borders shall end only in the remotest corners of the whole earth, and the earth shall beneath her shadowing wing become a Universal Republic. Let America in her prosperity, however, remember the Lord her God, her trust always in Him, and she shall never be discomfitted."

According to Hanly Hall this story first appeared in the Portland, Maine *Evening Courier* of March 2, 1862 in General McClellan's own words. Mr, Hall made it the subject of a chapter in his timely book, *The Secret Destiny of America.*

The Issue Is Still In Doubt

"Over a full century has gone by since that momentous night in November 1861 and America is in the midst of a great crisis. As we read the scare headlines in our daily newspapers some of us might think the issue is still in doubt. Down deep inside we know better," or so says Mr. Crabb, the former head of BSRA.

"The forces of Light will win out on this plane. I believe they had won out on the Inner Planes. It is my belief that the forces of evil tried to precipitate this planetary crisis back in the late 1940s with the atom bomb experiment program. I believe it was their intent to catch the swell of the cosmic movement in such a way that when the polar movement came it would shatter the planet into bits and pieces, as apparently happened to the planet Maidek, of the fifth orbit, ages ago.

"Millions of the egos or souls of the inhabitants of Maldek are in incarnation here on the earth, to face the Judgment Day again, and to face the temptation to misuse atomic power and blow up their planetary schoolroom again. What prevented the Korean war from spreading on into a worldwide atomic conflict in the early 1950s? 1 believe it was the heartfelt prayers for peace and goodwill of men and women of goodwill all over the world, in every race and nation. They brought in the cosmic intervention. I don't believe any one individual on earth could have saved us.

"I don't believe we can prevent what our military men call grass fire wars from starling. World War III, if you want to call it that, will probably start somewhere around the perimeter of China. It will cost us plenty in men, material and money. But I believe with Phylos and other prophets that Nature will take up quickly, so quickly in the wake of such a conflict that our war-making potential will very quickly be neutralized. "Earth changes will take place in the very middle of the conflict."

"That last phrase is from an interesting four pages of prophecy I found in the files of material at Borderland Sciences Research Associates headquarters in San Diego when I took over as director. The prophet—or should I say the medium—through whom the visions came, is C.H. Kramer of Chicago, Illinois. These statements were made way back in 1946. He was sure the cataclysmic activity would begin in four years, by 1950, and the Korean conflict could have been the start of it all; but Someone intervened, on behalf of those mortals who want a newer, better way of life; so many more years have gone by; nevertheless some of the things he said are interesting enough to bear repeating as a semi-close to this discussion.

The Mother Country of the Sixth Race

Kramer supports the Washington prophecy with this observation: "At the start of a new cycle there is always a Mother Nation—a nation that serves to lay the foundation for the new civilization. America will be the Mother Country of the Sixth Race. Many people from other lands will come to the United States, when signs reveal the doom of their homeland. They will branch out later to new lands."

He predicts that America will be a vast land when the cataclysmic changes are over, gaining much new land from the receding seas. "The seas surrounding this continent will sweep over the coastal regions, then recede for some distance beyond the old shores. New lands will rise from the seas not far from the new coastline."

The above prediction reminds me of a question from the audience when I gave this talk at Santa Ana, California many years ago.

"Do you think Southern California will go under the ocean as some have prophesied?" a lady asked me.

"Of course not," I replied.

"Why not?"

"Because I live here, Ma'am!" (Laughter from the audience.)

"Though this country will survive," continued Kramer, "most of its people will not survive the change. Neither will there be many people left in the lands that remain...Everything will crumble under the trembling earth...The passing of the old world will see this planet in darkness for three days and nights, accompanied by a violent shaking."

Now here's a detail about the actual change which I haven't seen anywhere else. I pass it on for what it may be worth.

"People may be on safe ground," Kramer said, "*but they will not remain conscious through the earth change.* As they hug the shaking earth they will fall into an unconscious sleep which will last for the duration of the change. When the survivors regain consciousness, *they will not remember the former world.* This blankness regarding the past will last for some time."

Here, you see, is an indication of how complete the change will be. Those chosen to survive to father and mother the new race, will have the past blotted out completely for some time.

They will literally have to build new personalities, new emotional and thinking patterns, based on the higher principles of the New Age! Truly when Jehovah says, "I will build a new heaven and a new earth," he means it.

"Memory of the past will gradually return to the people," Kramer prophecies, "yet they will not be the same people, in mind. Their minds will be changed, as changed as the world...

When the change takes place on this planet, changes will also be occurring on other planets. There will be a new sun and moon. The new sun and moon will be much brighter."

The Rotten Timber Must Go

You and I know that you cannot build a new building on the crumbling foundations of the old—and expect it to stand! The outworn, outmoded social and economic institutions of our day will not be dragged over into the New Age. As would be expected, Kramer takes a swipe at them, too, saying, "The old dogmas and their useless rites, confessionals and saviors will perish with the old world. There will be no religious beliefs in the new world, but there will be the code of Right Thinking, which will reward the race with peace and contentment."

He gave other details of the change which time and space won't allow here, but I like the way he ended the discourse, "Farewell to a delusioned, disintegrated humanity. Farewell to the bigotry, the ignorance which held man in bondage so long. Welcome to a new era, an era of peace and brotherhood, an era where man shall live in the Light of Reality."

Times of crisis are times of opportunity for the forward-looking, but they are times of tragedy for those who cling to the past. Inspiring as some aspects of the subject may be, there are other aspects which are extremely heavy and depressing regardless of how they are handled. I could scarcely have pushed through it in the way I have if I weren't sure that others, like me, are engaged in the search for Truth, whatever that truth is, wherever that search might lead. I sincerely hope that the ideas presented here may help you to see some semblance of order and purpose behind the chaos which daily confronts us. It looks as though conditions will continue to be chaotic for the unchanged of heart. For those whose lives are established on a firm, spiritual foundation there should be nothing to fear, or such fears as do arise should be washed away by the Light of that Spirit which passeth understanding.

The Time of Decision

In searching about for a way with which to close this message, I found it in George Van Tassel's *Proceedings*, a telethought message received by him from Contamarra, from Arcturus:

"Since we have arrived near your solar system, we greet you there on Salon Shan. We recently tried to contact you from our system, recognized by your people in the skies as Arcturus. We are known in the Confederation as the 'Sons of Adonai'. We have come on a volunteer mission, to do service to the people of your planet.

"Our craft is sitting here in space, outside your Solar Vortex. This craft will carry close to twenty-five million people; and we have just discharged thirty-eight thousand of our smaller ships from it. It is difficult for minds such as yours, that function by the brain, to comprehend the magnitude of our operations throughout the universe. We never do things on a small scale. We only serve to our greatest capacity as servants and instruments of a greater capacity.

"You have always had the right to choose, since your birth and in all generations of your humanity. You have not chosen wisely; because under your social and economic systems, and under your religious administrations, you have been subject to custom and to class distinction.

"So we have come. You will be awakened in great numbers, not to a service, not to any great knowledge. You will be awakened to a choice. Great multitudes of you will suddenly discover that there are two ways to go, and you will have to make a decision. If you decide to become servants in the Light of an Everlasting Love then you will be guided. Some of you will be directed, following a strong inspiration that will change with each moment. This we have came to do for you and with you. We can only influence and direct those who make the choice to serve humanity in every possible way.

"We do not especially like this assignment. It should never be, that any people should have to be directed and guided to bring about their own survival!

"In addressing you at center 'C', as we understand your point has been designated, each one of you this night has either made a choice or is about to make one. To those whom we see have made a choice, we pledge to you in the Living Light that we shall not at any time lead you or direct you in any way detrimental or injurious to your individual person.

"In this service to your people, in this great crisis of your system and your planet, we understand the failure of your civilization. We have come to help you. We shall move in with protection, with power, with Light and Truth, and surround and guide everyone who makes the choice rightly.

"Those who do make the choice in complete faith in the Everlasting Light shall not be touched by anyone who would harm them. No jail shall hold them. Their blood shall not flow from wound of foe. When we pledge our assistance in the Light of Understanding we stand on our oath.

"So, from the system of our sun, Arcturus, we the 'Sons of Adonai' are in your skies. We are watching individuals; we are awaiting your decisions.

"I leave you by extending the love of our people.

"I am Contamarra."

Chapter Eight: America—The Reincarnation of Atlantis

When we think of the lost continent of Atlantis, most often times we probably see with our "inner eye" images of tall, Roman or greek-like pillars jutting out from futuristic landscapes. Our mind wanders and we glimpse an era of fabulous technology in which science has conquered all hardships and eliminated all diseases. We picture skyscrapers made of crystal, we see saucer-

Noted researcher Brad Steiger poses before bust of one of the great Pharaohs of Egypt who may have been in contact with space beings.

shaped vehicles floating above the glittering streets and byways, and we find a mighty race of people, just and courageous. A race that has adapted to the environment of Earth, as well as having learned how to make long journeys to the planets in this solar system and beyond.

This is not to say that this "land beyond known lands" hasn't had its moments of difficulty and despair, when thankless leaders tried to undermine the greatness of this civilization and turn its from one radiating the wholeness of being, to one that embraced darkness.

After decades of struggle and war, a super-civilization has emerged from out of the ashes of an all-out battle for the minds and bodies of humankind. Suddenly, there is a rumbling in the ground and mighty quakes rock the continent, threatening to split it in half and send the empire toppling into the sea, sending a millennium of harmony that has never flourished before or since on our planet.

Wouldn't you think that the leaders of Atlantis would want to do something to keep their dream alive, to preserve and pass their wisdom and knowledge down from one era to the next?

According to astute researcher and renowned author, Brad Steiger, there is now sufficient evidence that scientifically proves that our civilization is NOT the first to have existed upon this planet; that other cultures have flourished from time to time, and that doubtlessly the most powerful was what we have come to call Atlantis.

"Traditionally, Atlantis was a continent in the Atlantic Ocean," says Steiger. "Shaken by a series of violent cataclysms, it sank below the surface of the waters—where, logically, glaciers and weather could not get at it."

Writing in his most recent contribution to metaphysical and New Age literature, Steiger in *Overlords of Atlantis & The Great Pyramid* (Inner Light Publications) notes that "mankind appears to have regretted this loss very deeply, as several years ago a public opinion poll found that the people in the United States would rank the discovery of Atlantis as great a news story as the Second Coming of Christ."

From his extensive research and on-the-spot investigations in various remote corners of the globe, Steiger justifiably concludes that "civilization on Earth has been cyclical and that there have been highly evolved human or hominid cultures before our present epoch. Atlantis may be but a symbol of man's racial memory of that time before our own. Within man's collective unconscious may lie half-hidden and almost forgotten memories of a time when man-creatures lived in god-like splendor while Homo sapiens groveled in awe of his magnificent predecessors."

In his book on Atlantis, Steiger—whose previous works have sold a total of over 15 million copies worldwide—does a respectable job of defining the time and those dimly remembered god-men, pointing out example after example where today's archeologists have deliberately ignored proof positive that humankind has not always been ignorant, and that the age of science and technology existed thousands of years ago, and did not begin in the century in which we now find ourselves living.

"Less than four decades ago," notes Steiger, "it was generally believed that if man did exist in America over 5,000 years ago, he was nothing more than a primitive hunter. Then, Dr. Paul Sears of Yale University dug up some maize pollen grains from about 240 feet below the surface of the dried lake bed on which Mexico City is built. Maize is the most highly developed agricultural plant in the world, so highly developed that scientists have never been able to trace its original ancestors. According to radio carbon testing, the pollen grains form the Mexican lake bed are at least 25,000 years old."

Likewise, Steiger goes on, "reports of a dawn man 15 to 20 millions of years old found in an Italian coal mine were released in the mid-1950s. Dr. Helmutt de Terra of Columbia University told journalists in Rome that a section of jawbone, along with the bones of the feet and hands of Oreopithecus, had been found. "Java and Peking men go back a mere 300,000 years," the Phoenix-based lecturer and scholar quickly points out, "so how can science account for these findings, unless perhaps an alien form of hominid life came to Earth at the dawn of creation and lived here, perhaps seeding the planet with beings that flourished, ending up as life as we now know it."

Division of the Sexes

In *Overlords of Atlantis*, Steiger gingerly attempts to trace in great detail the build-up of Atlantis, as well as its ultimate destruction into the sea.

Delving into the abundance of channeled material derived from the Edgar Cayce readings, Steiger formulated a vision of a fantastic world of uneclipsed scientific technology caught in a primeval struggle between the forces of good and evil. He tackles the question of the development of the various races and even offers an explanation for the division of the sexes.

"According to Cayce (who is widely known as the 'Sleeping Prophet of Virginia Beach,' who gave over 25,000 readings during his life) the soul is androgynous—that is, it incorporates both the male and female principles. It was in Atlantis, therefore, if Cayce is correct, that sex came into being, due to the separation of these two principles. The combination of projection into animal forms and the arrival of sex produced some strange bedfellows. The offspring of these unions were frequently grotesque mixtures of human and animal traits. There were great differences of opinion concerning the nature of these 'things' as they were called. The 'things' remained a central issue throughout the history of Atlantis, dividing the two rival groups that soon developed."

The Death Ray

The Atlanteans also apparently took a liking to convenience inventions—devices that would lighten their work load. One of these devices, Steiger reveals in *Overlords of Atlantis*, was the so-called Death Ray or "super-cosmic ray."

The greatest advancements of Atlantis, however, seem to have been in the field of transportation. "At least this field is dealt most heavily upon in Cayce's readings. Page after page of his life readings describes the marvelous way in which people could fly through the air in types of craft. Furthermore, Cayce hinted at a type of travel that went beyond machines, rendering them unnecessary. His suggestion that the Atlanteans could travel through elements other than air, and could also transmit thoughts through the ether, present innumerable possibilities of outer and inner space communications, as well as interdimensional travel."

In researching what Cayce and others have had to say, Steiger seems convinced that the Atlanteans had also harnessed the power of crystals, something that New Agers are just beginning to understand and on a limited basis trying to duplicate themselves. In a shocking statement, Brad offers a theory—based on scripture—that Noah's Ark was actually powered by an Atlantean crystal, and that the great Biblical figure "may have been a surviving Atlantean piloting his mercy ship by means of one of these power crystals."

Preserving The Atlantean Records

With the imminence of the coming disaster that would topple Atlantis there was feverish activity among record-keepers to preserve the wisdom that was theirs. "Repeatedly, a client of Cayce's was told that he had been connected with the preserving of the records, and that his work of that lifetime would soon be discovered in modern times.

"There were three principal caches of Atlantean historical records. One set of records was allegedly left in a temple in the Yucatan, which can still be seen; one set resides in the Hall of Records, a small pyramid in Egypt as yet undiscovered—publicly at least—but which is prophesied to be found before the end of the century; and the third set sunk with Atlantis.

"This third set of records, however, was reportedly contained in the Poseidian temple of Iltar, and this temple is to rise intact, the records preserved."

It is the rising of this temple that Cayce indicates would herald the eventual complete re-emergence of Atlantis. "There is recent archaeological evidence," Steiger goes on, "in support of such an occurrence, offered by the discovery of an ancient sunken 'temple' off the coast of Bimini in the Caribbean Sea. It was in this area that Cayce had placed the temple of Iltar."

The Great Cheops Pyramid

Backing up his own conclusions that the Great Pyramid was more than just a tomb, Steiger again calls upon Cayce and thinkers like the late theorist, Otto Binder. Every student from the third grade on knows about the vast complexity of this monument, a true wonder of the world. Its size and construction boggles even the keenest minds of today. The Great Cheops Pyramid covers 13 acres and is 481 feet high and 756 feet wide at each side of its square base.

Steiger quotes journals and text to prove that the master wizards of Atlantis left their home before it disappeared and wandered to other parts of the world in an attempt to carry on their heritage. Some journeyed to South America, some to North America and perhaps the wisest of all ventured into Egypt, convarying messages to Moses and the Pharaohs.

Utilizing their mastery over the elements, they helped to construct the Great Pyramid, housing within its stone walls such information that has yet to be revealed to the spiritually dead world. Instead of utilizing tens of thousands of block toting slaves to hoist the solid granite stones into place, the early Egyptians used levitation devices, and in addition called upon the assistance of friendly space beings to assist in their chosen task.

Steiger predicts that as humankind evolves spiritually, more and more of this hidden data will be disclosed. A great deal of information will be revealed sometime before the turn of the century, when Atlantis will rise from the depths of the ocean and we will be re-united with the survivors of the continent, some of whom have subsequently set up operations in secret locations both underground beneath the mountain ranges of Tibet, and on nearby planets.

"Many years ago," says Steiger, "I began to send out questionnaires to individuals who had read my books and thought somehow they might have an important mission as part of the New Age we are now being swept up in. Many of them turned out to have the same characteristics, and I concluded that they might be 'star people' reincarnated here on Earth at this time to serve a humane purpose." But, Brad was puzzled to find out that many of these felt more allied with Atlantis than they did with the stars.

"Edgar Cayce told us years ago that the vast majority of Americans had experienced past lives on the continent of Atlantis," Steiger professes in *Overlords of Atlantis & The Great Pyramid.* "In my own research—in addition to what many past life readings reveal—it seems that many of those who are alive today feel that they have somehow—through some unexplained means—been reborn at this time in history to put forth the advanced knowledge that was so widely taught by the Overlords of this once-proud lost land. We could," says Steiger, "actually conclude that America herself is actually the reincarnation of Atlantis. In the United States, we have been given an opportunity to develop our civilization to the point of the same crucial decision encountered by the Atlanteans: power for the good of Earth and her people, or power for evil.

"The Law of Cause and Effect may seem unnecessarily harsh to some, but to those who trust it, it is the law of compassion. According to the precepts of reincarnation and karma, if a man—or a nation—errs and strays from the path, he is not condemned for all eternity. All is not staked on one throw of the dice."

Atlantis Reborn

"If such is the case, and America truly is Atlantis reincarnated, then it is evident that we are fast approaching the crucial hour of decision. All the necessary cards have been dealt; we have split the atom; we have confused the natural evolution of our planet with pollutants; we have cracked the DNA code and can duplicate it in our laboratories; we have developed weapons of destruction so powerful that one thimble-full of bacteria can destroy all life forms on Earth; and anti-ballistic missile silos—with government support—are defacing the landscape.

"We are truly being confronted by the other side of the two-faced results of technological advances. The one side promises knowledge gained to aid mankind, to end disease, to increase crops, to promote production of labor-saving devices. The other side leers at the destructiveness made possible by the same knowledge.

"The final choice made by Atlantis, even if allegory, if not reality, is overwhelmingly evident by its totally complete destruction. The choice we as citizens of the United States will have to make may one day make itself known by the same cataclysmic changes that took place on Atlantis!"

A Philadelphia medium, Evelyn Hellings, says ghost of Revolutionary War hero speaks frequently to her.

Chapter Nine: Is America Receiving Guidance From Heaven?

You know those Revolutionary War heroes we have heard so much about? Well, they might still be with us. In Philadelphia, the ghost of Nathaniel Greene appeared, commenting on America's future.

A 55-year-old Philadelphia woman, with an established reputation for being incredibly psychic, says she has had repeated contact with the ghost of a long-dead Revolutionary War hero who—during his life—was second in command to General George Washington.

Evelyn Hellings maintains her initial encounter with Major General Nathaniel Green took place in the summer of 1971, while she was going through some dusty books at the New York Historical Society Library. "I was doing extensive research for an article on little-known Revolutionary War battles. A young man, one of the librarian, brought over to the table at which I was seated a number of really old and yellowing volumes. They were so worn by age, that I was reluctant to touch them.

"I opened one volume, and on the page I had accidentally turned to was a portrait of Nathaniel Green. Without any advance warning, the air around me became exceedingly cold, as if I were in an ice box. Suddenly I was engulfed by a deadly silence, and I became completely unaware of my surroundings. It was as if I had been placed in an isolation booth, away from everyone else."

It was at this point that Evelyn claims she felt "someone" touch her. "A hand came to rest on my left shoulder. I could feel the imprint of every finger—they were hot, like burning fire. Somehow I *knew*—I guess you might say I sensed—that the spirit of Nathaniel Green was right there beside me."

Mrs. Hellings insists that a voice spoke to her in a clear and distinct manner. "I turned around and saw no one, but I could feel the weight of 'his' hand on my body. Then, out of nowhere, I heard someone speaking.

"Nathaniel Greene spoke with conviction, and at the same time it was like a tremble, as though he sighed. He told me that to bury a man does not mean he is dead. Death, he explained, is but a transient state—'the soul does not expire, but is suspended like iridescent cobwebs on the images of time!' These were his precise words."

Asked what message the Revolutionary General—who died at the age of 44 from sun-stroke—wished to convey, Evelyn Hellings says his greeting was both heart-warming and sad. "He said we—the United States—must go back before we can go ahead. Nathaniel observed that we as a people have forgotten so much, and that there is so much we have to learn. He told me there's too much greed. Everything is greed and money. People do not care for one another, there is too much prejudice and there's too much hatred. He said he has returned because he feels he is needed—he's returning to give advice."

After what seemed like an eternity, but was only a matter of five or six minutes, the voice faded and the impression of a hand on Evelyn's shoulder disappeared. "I was shaken but not overly disturbed, having been familiar with such manifestations previously." Mrs. Hellings revealed that she had encountered spirits before, at some 20 haunted houses in various states. "People are always calling me in to find out who is haunting their dwelling. I guess these things just attach themselves to me."

Looking back, and shaking her head to make certain it was not a dream, the Philadelphia sensitive says the temperature of the library returned to normal and the activity of those around her began once again. "Things were just like they had previously been, although I know my life had been drastically changed."

After the events of that summer day, Evelyn says she began to do extensive research on Nathaniel Greene, and discovered two astonishing things: "I found that General Greene, who passed away in 1782, was himself very psychic. He retreated at several battles on the advice of spirits, but always won these skirmishes in the long run. Furthermore, I discovered he was an ancestor of mine—that we were directly related on my mother's side."

So began the first of many meetings. "He always appears much the same way. I've never seen him physically—only sensed his presence and felt his warm hand on my person. He told me that at times the founders of our country are so close that we could just about reach out and touch them. It's just like the fourth dimension, Nathaniel Greene explained. For example, they can be doing things, but we can't see them. It's as if someone were inside a house but with their blinds down. They are there, but from our position outside they seem invisible. Nathaniel Greene has repeatedly informed me that our nation's forefathers, including Washington himself, are standing nearby to offer us aid and protection at this critical period in our history."

An interesting sidelight is that Evelyn comes from a lone line of psychics. "My Grandmother Eva was a medium. Her talents were phenomenal, and I'm told they were even made available to authorities assigned to the Lindbergh kidnapping case. A private detective hired by the family went so far as to call upon my grandmother for assistance. Great Grandfather Jonathan heard voices. Grandpa was a professional gambler, until one day a spirit spoke to him and he became converted, lecturing widely on the evils of gambling. He wrote a great deal on the topic, and to this day, one of his books, *The Reformed Gambler*, is considered a classic."

Evelyn Hellings has used her psychic gifts in many areas. Her clientele, all who agree that she possesses amazing abilities, include Dagmar Gadowsky, silent screen star, actress Claudia McNeal, gospel singer Louise Williams, and record executive

Kenneth Gamble.

"Nathaniel Greene was a great American," Evelyn concludes. "He saw beauty in every living thing. Writing poetry was one of his pastimes—unheard of for such a man, high in the military. Not only was he second in command, but he considered the first President of our land a dear friend, going so far as to name his children Martha and George, in honor of the President and the First Lady. I'm certain that his interest in this nation lives on and has survived the grave!"

Chapter Ten: America's Great Curses

Over the decades since the founding of our great nation, many powerful curses have been placed upon our leaders.

There is an old legend which we have no reason to doubt, which says that Chief Tippecanoe, who fought long and hard and was finally defeated by Zachary—"Old Rough and Ready"—Taylor (the 12th President), placed a curse on the white man's nation as he went to his death. Supposedly the curse of Tippecanoe ties in directly with the strange cycle of presidential deaths which takes place every twenty years. It is said that before he was killed, Chief Tippecanoe uttered harsh, condemning, words to Zachary Taylor, proclaiming with his last breath that future leaders would not live to see their terms in office completed.

In more recent years we have had to combat other curses, including one put on America by the ruthless "Poppa Doc" the mad dictator of Haiti who practiced a sinister form of voodoo keeping his own people enslaved through the powers of his occult-oriented secret military police.

Furthermore, it is not generally realized that the Ayatollah, the religious zealot who rules Iran with an iron fist, long ago made a pact with demonic forces to overthrow the United States. "He's an agent of the devil himself," says his former friend, Abolhassan Bani-Sadr, who insists that Khomeini was once an angel, but became possessed by negativity once he came to power.

As we shall now see from the following true stories, it is necessary for our nation's leaders to be well versed in metaphysics and in the use of talismans such as the Great Seal, in order to effectively combat the evil they have often had to do battle with. Naturally, it is difficult to explain such circumstances to the public, but history does often fill in gaps which are left open to avoid possible hysteria.

The Seeress of the Capital

Jeanne Dixon of Washington, D.C. has no peer when it comes to predicting future political events. Heads of state have called on her for counsel. Celebrities in nearly all fields have consulted her. The seeress has never commercialized her gift; she and her husband operate a successful real estate agency in the capital.

When we talk about Jeanne Dixon, we need the space of an entire book. Here, we can only touch on the highlights of an amazing career.

Her abilities were well known during World War II, and it was in late 1944 that President Franklin D. Roosevelt summoned her to the White House. He wanted to know how much time he had left to complete his mission. Miss Dixon told him that because of his failing health he did not have more than six months. She was right. FDR died in April 1945.

The President then wanted to know about the country's future relationships with Russia. The seeress told him that relations with Russia would deteriorate for the next 25 years, but would then strengthen when the United States and the Union of Soviet Socialist Republics would form an alliance against Red China.

The term "Red China" was baffling to Roosevelt. In 1944 China was under the thumb of Japan, except for a few provinces controlled by Chiang Kai-shek. Mao Tse Tung, chief of the Red partisans, was all but unheard of in those days. No one at that time thought that China would become a communist nation.

Nevertheless, Jeanne Dixon told FDR that Red China and Africa would become great problems for the world in the future.

On another occasion she was at a reception in Washington in 1945. She stated flatly that on June 2, 1947, India would be divided. Colonel Nawabjaba Sher Ali, the Military Attache, was skeptical. Still, it happened, and on the day Jeanne Dixon predicted.

Miss Dixon was also present at a party in Washington honoring Winston Churchill. The hosts were Lord and Lady Halifax. The year was 1945 and Churchill was up for re-election. Jeanne Dixon suggested to him that he delay the election because there was a strong possibility that he would be defeated. The Prime Minister replied, "England will never let me down." The country did. He was defeated by Prime Minister Atlee.

The seeress predicted that the United Nations Secretary General Dag Hammarskjold would die in a plane accident in Africa. In the middle of 1947 she said that Mahatma Gandhi would be assassinated within six months. It happened on January 30, 1948.

Dixon's Attempts To Save JFK's Life

As far back as 1952 and 1956, Jeanne Dixon predicted that a future president would be a young, tall, blue-eyed man with thick brown hair. This is an accurate description of John F. Kennedy, elected President in 1960.

Three months before Kennedy was assassinated, Dixon made a surprise visit to Kay Halle, a woman who knew the president personally. Dixon said she had a message for him and that it had to reach him soon. The message was that Kennedy was not to travel to the south, that such a trip would be fatal to him. Halle refused to relay the message.

We can't lay blame on Kay Halle because it is not likely that Kennedy would have heeded the warning. His character would not have allowed it. We also know that John Kennedy ordered the plexiglass bubble removed from his car.

Jeanne Dixon next went to the FBI and the CIA. Neither agency would take her seriously, their argument being that they dealt with facts, not premonitions. So the seeress was stymied. There were three days left and there was nothing she could do. Kennedy went to Dallas and was killed.

Dixon's Predictions on Russia

Space travel in 1953 was consigned to comic books. But in that year, May 14, Jeanne Dixon was on an NBC-TV program broadcasting from Washington, D.C., and it was then that she predicted that a silver ball sent up into space by Russia would be seen on the ground by nearly the whole world. In 1957, Russia's Sputnik I was launched.

On that same TV program on another date in 1953, Jeanne Dixon predicted that Malenkov would be replaced in two years by a man with an oval-shaped head, wavy gray hair, a little goatee and greenish eyes. This was a description of Marshal Bulganin, and he took over from Malenkov in exactly two years.

A New Leader Emerges

Mis Dixon believes that a new spiritual leader will rise up to lay the foundation of an era of peace. He was born on February 5, 1962, at a time of the rare conjunction of seven planets, the first of its kind in four hundred years.

According to Jeanne Dixon, this child was born in the Middle East and is a descendant of Queen Nefertiti and the Pharaoh Amenhotep, who established the cult of One God centuries before Biblical monotheism.

The great reformer will combine all religions and ideologies into one doctrine which will revolutionize the world. War will end once and for all. The revolutionary leader will spread his teachings from the early eighties and by 1999 his power will reach all the people on earth.

Is Jeanne Dixon talking about the Second Coming?

Lyndon Baines Johnson and the "Sudden Death Lodge"

This story happened when Lyndon Johnson was vice president of the United States. The date was July 15, 1961. He visited the U.S. Embassy in Karachi, and as soon as he arrived a weird event took place.

An attache found himself locked in the conference room. He banged on the door until he was heard by someone on the outside, who collected the keys and tried to open the door. For some strange reason, the keys didn't work. The door would not unlock. Finally, it had to be broken down.

Johnson was curious. It didn't seem possible to him that a key made for the lock on the door failed to open it. He pressed for answers until somebody finally told him the story.

The Curse

The citizens of Karachi, Pakistan were well aware of the problem behind the locked-in diplomat. When LBJ insisted on knowing the real reason, he was told that the four-story embassy building on Victoria Road stood on a plot of land that had been vacant since 1925. Buildings grew all around this plot—restaurants, big hotels and shopping centers. No one thought to build on the plot until the Americans came along, saw it and decided to put the embassy there.

Older residents knew it was folly to do such a thing. The Pakistanis knew that there was a 100-year curse on the land and that it should be left alone.

LBJ Hears a Weird Tale

The curse was first revealed in a book by Percival Christopher Wren, *Dew and Mildew*. Wren was an inspector of schools in Karachi at the turn of the century.

According to the author, a Muslim saint was buried in this plot of ground and a fakir, or pious mendicant, took it upon himself to look after the tomb. Word came to the fakir one day that a rich Parsi merchant named Sohrabji Rustomij Potwallah had bought the land and intended to build a large bungalow on it. The fakir went to the merchant and asked him not to defile the saint's tomb. It was a waste of time. The man's pleas were ignored.

The fakir then cursed the merchant and his family. He cursed the unbuilt bungalow and all who would ever live or serve in it.

As if to add dramatic emphasis to the curses, the fakir dropped dead.

LBJ Listens to a Starting Story

The merchant defied the curses and started to build his

palatial bungalow over the tomb. That was a mistake. Workmen unearthed a nest of cobras while digging the foundation. One man was bitten. He died on the spot. Later, another man fell from a scaffolding and died. The watchman's son was killed when he overturned a cauldron of boiling pitch. The watchman himself died when he was hit on the head by a falling brick.

The merchant, Rustomij, got his house built, but the curse continued. One evening he saw his little nephew playing on the banister of the new house. He shouted to the boy to get down. Instead, the boy became startled and lost his balance. The merchant ran to catch the falling boy, but in doing so he tripped and fell, crushing the boy to death and killing himself at the same time.

The house was inherited by the merchant's son, Dorabji. He died soon after from blood poisoning contracted from a cut on his hand by a rusty nail in one of the window frames.

The house then went to the merchant's grandson, Hormasji. He was so shaken up by the series of death associated with the house that he committed suicide.

Eventually, the house was tenanted by an Englishman and his wife—a Mr. and Mrs. Reild. Reild went insane after five weeks in the house. He cut his wife's throat and committed suicide.

The house became known as the "Sudden Death Lodge."

The Curse Continues— Earth and Air, Fire and Water

The next tenants to move into the bungalow were four British subalterns who laughed off the curse. Each of them, however, had the same dream. He saw a fakir standing next to four open graves and screaming, "Earth and air, fire and water!"

Later, one of the officers fell into a deep pit and was buried alive by workmen making a new parade ground. Earth claimed the first victim.

Another of the four subalterns took up flying and became one of the first pilots to be killed in a monoplane. Air took him. The third officer was burned to death when a kerosene lantern tipped over and set fire to a small hut he was in at the time. Fire claimed him.

The fourth officer was so thoroughly frightened by the curse that he did everything he could to avoid being consumed by water. He stopped swimming. He seldom bathed, and he drank only water that was tepid. But the curse was too strong. An old-style marble soda-water bottle exploded in his face and killed him.

U.S. Embassy Built on Haunted Ground

Over the years, the "Sudden Death Lodge" claimed several more victims. Finally, no one wanted to live in it. In 1925, after the place had deteriorated, it was torn down. The plot remained empty until the Americans bought it in 1955. The architect selected to design the new embassy, Richard J. Neutra, heard about the curse and decided to play it safe. He talked to theologians on the best way to "appease" the soul of the Muslim saint.

Two years later, September 9, 1957, the embassy's foundation stone was laid. The ceremony was unusual, at least for Americans. For the first time in an official American function, a Muslim and a Christian sat on the rostrum with the other VIPS. They were there to bless the ground before the stone was laid.

Neutra went even further. He designed the building so that the structure was not on top of the saint's grave, but around it. The space was left vacant.

LBJ Was A Believer

The vice president listened to the whole story and did not pooh-pooh it. Instead, he asked: "Is the curse still active? Is the embassy haunted? What can we do about it?"

Those questions were answered by the Pakistan government. It changed its capital from Karachi to Rawalpindi. The embassy building became a consulate and a new embassy was built in Rawalpindi.

At the time, LBJ said, "Well, that's one way to handle the situation."

And what about the curse? No one knows for sure, but it may still be working.

American Indian Spirit guides often channel their messages through mediums referring to the future of America, helping to guide and direct our actions.

Chapter Eleven: America's Coming Revolution—Trouble From Within Not From Russia

Libby Collins is a psychic who has produced amazing information while in a trance-like state. Not long ago she underwent hypnosis in an effort to break the cigarette habit. While she was under, her hypno-therapist noticed that she began talking in a voice other than her own. It was a man's voice and it mentioned facts and events that had happened two centuries earlier.

The hypnotist recognized from what was being said by the voice controlling Libby's vocal chords that the speaker was Alexander Hamilton, the famed Revolutionary War figure.

Hamilton's Prophecy

Libby Collins was in a hypnotic trance for about twenty minutes. During that time, in the hypnotist's presence, the voice of Alexander Hamilton spoke. He said:

"America remains a great nation. But there will—by necessity—be many changes in its form of government in the years ahead. Men who have chosen personal gain over the welfare of the people have caused our country to suffer mightily. Some have already been removed from high office. Others are due to follow."

Interestingly, Hamilton made this prediction long before the

Abscam indictments.

The hypnotist asked Hamilton where he was speaking from. The reply: "I reside in a place which is altogether more peaceful than your physical world. There is no war here, no sickness, no poverty, no want." Hamilton added that he spoke now because he felt that if America did not return to its proper path there would be troubled times ahead.

"There will be a river of blood," he said. "Tears of anguish will flood the land. There will be terrible fighting on the soil of Europe. Many brave men, many courageous people, will die needlessly. There will be much killing. Senseless slaughter."

Hamilton's Warning

"There are certain individuals who seek to render the Constitution useless. Don't let them do so! They will try to silence the voices of dissension. They will attempt to abolish freedom of speech. They will put America in a vulnerable position where she can be attacked. In the eyes of the world we will appear to be the ones at fault, and in a sense we will be, for the leaders of this once proud land will push us to the point of no return."

Hamilton Reveals Conspiracy

"Unbeknownst to you, conspirators are attempting to drain America of its gold. As Mr. Washington's Secretary of the Treasury, I have kept a personal vigil on a progressively worsening situation that has been taking place behind your backs. Little by little, the gold bars stored in your Fort Knox are being moved out of the country, until finally there will be no gold there at all. At least ten vaults are empty now, and a recent attempt to prove otherwise by opening the vault for inspection was merely a face-saving device. Those gold bars were coated with an eighth of an inch of gold."

Hamilton Tells of Hard Times Ahead

The great statesman said through the vocal chords of Libby Collins that America would eventually go off the monetary system. "Green money will be called in, and you will get slightly smaller red notes equivalent in value to half your current worth. This country will soon experience a grave economic depression that will be followed by a major famine, and a political upheaval, and commune-style living for many Americans."

This was Hamilton's final statement. Libby Collins was out of her hypnotic trance unaware that the ghost of Alexander Hamilton had occupied her body for twenty minutes.

Mark Twain's Prophetic Dream

When Samuel Clemens (Mark Twain) was still a young man and working on the Mississippi river boats, he had occasion to spend some time at his sister's house in St. Louis. The visit was enjoyable, but he was disturbed by a recurring bad dream that came to him every night during his stay.

He dreamt that he saw his younger brother Henry dead and lying in a coffin. The coffin was made of metal and lying across two chairs. Henry had his hands crossed on his chest, and in them was a bouquet of delicate white flowers with a single red flower in the center.

Sam Clemens tried to put the dream out of his mind, but couldn't. He loved Henry and was proud of the fact that Henry wanted to become a steersman like himself. In fact, Sam pulled some strings to get Henry on his next trip. Sam was scheduled to take the Pennsylvania up river in a few days, and he had his brother taken on as a hand who would do the slop jobs nobody else wanted to do.

Before the boat sailed, Sam Clemens got into a heated argument with the pilot, a man named Brown. The argument developed into a knock-down-drag-out fistfight, and when it was over, Brown said he would not pilot a boat on which Clemens was the steersman. To placate Brown, the skipper asked Sam Clemens to take a later boat. Sam did, but before the Pennsylvania sailed, he warned his younger brother to be very careful. He then watched his brother sail away on the boat with a great deal of misgivings, for he remembered that frightful dream.

Several days later, Clemens got the sad news. The Pennsylvania had blown up. His brother was seriously injured. A boiler had ruptured, scalding as many as forty crew members. A large meeting hall was turned into a make-shift hospital to accommodate the injured. Sam hurried to the area, where he spent a week in a non-stop vigil at young Henry's side. At the end of that period Henry Clemens died.

Sam went to a friend's home in Memphis, Tennessee. He was physically and emotionally drained. So much so that he collapsed and had to be carried to bed.

The next day, sufficiently rested, he went to pay his last respects to Henry. When he entered the room he realized that what he saw now was exactly what he had seen in his dream. The coffin was metal. It rested on two chairs. Henry's hands were folded across his chest, and in them was a bouquet of white flowers. In the center was a red flower.

Until his own death in 1910 at the age of 75, Mark Twain was never able to explain the uncanny premonition.

Prime Minister Winston Churchill Had ESP

The great World War II leader had a sixth sense which not only saved his life twice, but was also responsible for saving the lives of others.

He had an astonishing ability to see danger in the future. One incident occurred when he got into the back seat of his limousine. Usually, he sat directly behind the driver, but on this occasion he heard a voice say, "Stop, go around to the other side and get in there."

Winston Churchill got out of the car and walked around to the other side. He sat down. Seconds later a bomb went off directly under his seat. Fortunately, his weight was squarely over the blast and it muffled the bomb's force. He wasn't hurt. His driver also escaped injury.

At another time he was supposed to attend an air show put on by the military. The date was April 13, 1942. Again, some inner voice or some feeling of dread told him not to go.

Churchill canceled the trip. One of his aides went instead.

When the air show opened, a fighter pilot made a dreadful mistake. He was supposed to sweep low and open fire on a row of dummy soldiers and military vehicles. Instead, he fired on the reviewing stand! Churchill's aide and 26 men were killed by gunfire.

There were many instances in which the great Prime Minister used his power of ESP to good advantage, but the event that occurred in October 1940 was truly uncanny.

At that time the Nazi Luftwaffe was bombing London to her knees. Churchill, not one to run and hide, stayed at his Downing Street home through the fearful times. One night he was about to sit down to dinner when he suddenly felt strange. He had a premonition that a bomb was going to damage the kitchen area.

Outside, warning sirens wailed. The Nazi bombers were coming. Churchill hurried into the kitchen and told his servants to bring his food into the dining room and then get to an air-raid shelter.

The bombers arrived. Churchill sat drinking his wine and eating while explosions rocked the city. Then a bomb hit the famous building at 10 Downing Street. The kitchen and the pantry were utterly destroyed, as well as other parts of the structure. If the famed PM hadn't warned his servants, they would have died in the explosion.

Two Presidents Predict a Revolution in the United States

Most of us are aware of President Eisenhower's warning about the dangers inherent in the military-industrial alliance that has been created in this country. He saw it coming long before anyone else. He was also aware of the wealthy's immoral greed for money.

In a book titled *The Hundredth Monkey*, author Ken Keyes stated that while Eisenhower was in his second term in office he said: "I like to believe that people in the long run are going to do more to promote peace than are governments. Indeed, I think that people want peace so much that one of these days government had better get out of their way and let them have it."

Obviously, President Eisenhower was right. The peace movement today is stronger than it has ever been. Witness the hundreds of thousands who have marched for peace in the various world capitals. The President also foresaw the weariness most of us are suffering because of the threat of nuclear disaster. Undoubtedly, he saw a revolution in the making—a revolution of the people who are sick and tired of living under the threat of annihilation.

Abraham Lincoln also predicted a revolution in this country, but for different reasons. In August 1861 he was in the Oval Office with a man named Father Chiniquy. He told the holy man that he was cognizant of the financial and religious interests in this country who were dedicated to the overthrow of democracy. Lincoln said that if the people ever awoke to the evil of these subversive interests the revulsion would be comparable to that which swept France in the middle 1700s.

Maybe it's about time our leaders in Washington listened more closely to the people…perhaps a lot of the "trouble" ahead could then be avoided!

Chapter Twelve: Space Visitors Watch Over America

Within recent times within the hushed halls of Congress, retired Admiral Hyman Rickover made a startling statement. "We can go to church every Sunday and pray," noted the gutsy Navy man, "but the Lord has many demands made on Him from many other worlds, and in the eyes of the Lord we are not the most important thing in the universe."

Admiral Rickover made this pungent comment during the course of airing his views on nuclear proliferation, which he feels is getting dreadfully out of hand as more and more nations hop on the atomic bandwagon. Obviously, the hero of many a battle at sea let it be known that he felt certain that we are not the only "civilized" form of life in the cosmos. No doubt, this observation was based on the fact that he knows better because in Viet Nam where he was in charge of our sea to land efforts, UFOs were seen flying overhead as a matter of course.

Every president in office since the end of World War II has realized the significance of our aerial visitors who have streaked across our nation's sky like they have carte blanche to come and go as they so please. Recently, under the Freedom of Information Act, it was discovered that all the branches of the government from the CIA, to the FBI, to the State Department, have at one time or another been confronted by this intriguing puzzle that remains in the eyes of many completely unsolved. Frequent

sightings have been made by highly technical equipment and by trained personnel directly over our top-secret missile silos and near our most classified military bases. It is furthermore an established historical fact that for several weeks in July and August of 1952 UFOs played a cat and mouse game over Washington, D.C., out-maneuvering our fastest military planes which were sent into the sky to chase the unknowns from their perch over the White House and Capitol Building.

Jimmy Carter Sees A UFO

Before Jimmy Carter became president, he promised to unlock the secret files of the Pentagon and release all the information in the government's possession on UFOS. He went back on his word some time after being elected. Nobody knows the reasons for sure why he did a double-take, but as might be expected, theories abound concerning what has become known in certain circles as the "Cosmic Watergate."

"I don't laugh at people anymore when they say they've seen UFOS, because I've seen one myself."

President Jimmy Carter made that statement on September 14, 1973 while at a speaking engagement in Dublin, Georgia. Reporters immediately pressed him to elaborate, which he did. He said that when he was campaigning for governor in the small southern Georgia town of Leary, he was standing outside the hall where he was to make a speech to members of the local Lions Club and saw a blue disc-shaped object in the sky.

Several members of the organization were with the president when the object appeared. Carter ran for a tape recorder so that his description of what he saw would be accurately recorded.

He told the newsmen, "It was about 30 degrees above the horizon and looked about as large as the moon. It got smaller and changed to a reddish color and then got larger again."

Newsmen asked him for an explanation. He said: "It was a very sober occasion. It was obviously there and obviously unidentified."

Carter was quite emphatic about what he saw. His press secretary, Jody Powell, told reporters: "I remember Jimmy saying that he did in fact see a strange light, or object, at night in the sky which did not appear to be a star or a plane, or anything he could explain. If that's your definition of an unidentified flying object, then I suppose that's correct."

Powell added: "I don't think it's had any great impact on him one way or the other. I would venture to say that he probably has seen stranger and more unexplainable things than that during his time in government."

Indeed, this is a curious statement Jody Powell has made, for we do know that Jimmy must have thought the sighting important enough as he took the time and trouble to fill out a detailed three page sighting report form and turn it over to a private UFO group which investigated his account. Furthermore, exactly what did Powell have in mind when he said that Carter had "probably seen stranger and more unexplainable things" during his time in office? Could it be, that the president has personally experienced something along the lines of a close encounter? Or perhaps he had even been taken to see the actual remains of a crashed UFO and its occupants which the government has said to be in possession of since the late 1940s?

We can openly speculate upon the various possibilities for hours, but it probably won't do us very much good for, as we have seen many times, Uncle Sam isn't about to come clean and let us have the inside scoop which would once and for all clear up the mystery of the UFOs and show that we are on the verge of some startling cosmic changes which will affect each and everyone of us alive today.

President Eisenhower Meets With Aliens

This story would be hard to believe except for the fact that it has been confirmed by many unimpeachable sources. One of those sources, the Earl of Clancarty, who is a member of the British Parliament, stated that President Dwight D. Eisenhower met with beings from outer space in 1954, and world famous language expert, Charles Berlitz, confirms the story.

The date was February 20, 1954. Eisenhower was vacationing

TIMOTHY GREEN BECKLEY & ARTHUR CROCKETT

FEBRUARY 1977

Robert Sheaffer
9305 McVilliam Avenue
Silver Spring, MD 20910

UFO INVESTIGATOR

NICAP

NATIONAL INVESTIGATIONS COMMITTEE ON AERIAL PHENOMENA

NICAP • 3535 UNIVERSITY BLVD. WEST, SUITE 23 • KENSINGTON MARYLAND 20795 • (301) 949-1267 • FOUNDED IN 1956

JIMMY CARTER'S 1973 UFO REPORT

During the autumn of 1973 hundreds of people throughout the United States reported UFOs to NICAP. Among those reports were two made by state governors. During the recent presidential campaign, Jimmy Carter was quoted by the National Enquirer as stating, "If I become President, I'll make every piece of information that this country has about UFO sightings available to the public. I am convinced that UFOs exist because I have seen one."

President Carter's conviction in UFOs is understandable since he not only saw one but also was one of the two governors who reported a UFO to NICAP in 1973.

On October 12, 1973, then-Governor Carter responded to NICAP's inquiries about his sighting with a letter and a report form. NICAP's Regional Investigator, Harry Lederman, handled the investigation.

President Carter's UFO sighting has been briefly reported by the news media, sometimes accurately, sometimes inaccurately. Since Jimmy Carter is the first U.S. President to speak publicly about a personal experience, NICAP believes that its members should have the complete report as it was submitted. President Carter's handwritten report has been typed for clarity.

NATIONAL INVESTIGATIONS COMMITTEE ON AERIAL PHENOMENA (NICAP)®
3535 University Blvd. West
301-949-1267   Kensington, Maryland 20795

REPORT ON UNIDENTIFIED FLYING OBJECT(S)

This form includes questions asked by the United States Air Force and by other Armed Forces' investigating agencies, and additional questions to which answers are needed for full evaluation by NICAP.

After all the information has been fully studied, the conclusion of our Evaluation Panel will be published by NICAP in its regularly issued magazine or in another publication. Please try to answer as many questions as possible. Should you need additional room, please use another sheet of paper. Please print or typewrite. Your assistance is of great value and is genuinely appreciated. Thank you.

1. Name Jimmy Carter   Place of Employment
   Address State Capitol Atlanta   Occupation   Governor
                                    Date of birth
                                    Education
                                    Special Training   Graduate
   Telephone (404) 656-1776   Military Service   Nuclear Physics
                                                       U.S. Navy
2. Date of Observation October 1969   Time   AM   PM   Time Zone
                                                         7:15   EST
3. Locality of Observation Leary, Georgia
4. How long did you see the object? Hours____ 10-12 Minutes____ Seconds____
5. Please describe weather conditions and the type of sky; i.e., bright daylight, nighttime, dusk, etc. Shortly after dark.
6. Position of the Sun or Moon in relation to the object and to you. Not in sight.
7. If seen at night, twilight, or dawn, were the stars or moon visible? Stars.
8. Were there more than one object? No.   If so, please tell how many, and draw a sketch of what you saw, indicating direction of movement, if any.

PROPHECIES OF THE PRESIDENTS

UFO INVESTIGATOR / FEBRUARY 1977

9. Please describe the object(s) in detail. For instance, did it (they) appear solid, or only as a source of light; was it revolving, etc.? Please use additional sheets of paper, if necessary.

10. Was the object(s) brighter than the background of the sky? **Yes.**

11. If so, compare the brightness with the Sun, Moon, headlights, etc. **At one time, as bright as the moon.**

12. Did the object(s) – (Please elaborate, if you can give details.)

    a. Appear to stand still at any time? **yes**
    b. Suddenly speed up and rush away at any time?
    c. Break up into parts or explode?
    d. Give off smoke?
    e. Leave any visible trail?
    f. Drop anything?
    g. Change brightness? **yes**
    h. Change shape? **size**
    i. Change color? **yes**

Seemed to move toward us from a distance, stopped-moved partially away—returned, then departed. Bluish at first, then reddish, luminous, not solid.

13. Did object(s) at any time pass in front of, or behind of, anything? If so, please elaborate giving distance, size, etc, if possible. **no.**

14. Was there any wind? **no.** If so, please give direction and speed.

15. Did you observe the object(s) through an optical instrument or other aid, windshield, windowpane, storm window, screening, etc? What? **no.**

16. Did the object(s) have any sound? **no** What kind? How loud?

17. Please tell if the object(s) was (were) –

    a. Fuzzy or blurred. b. Like a bright star. c. Sharply outlined. **X**

18. Was the object – a. Self-luminous? **X** b. Dull finish? c. Reflecting? d. Transparent?

19. Did the object(s) rise or fall while in motion? **Came close, moved away-came close then moved away.**

20. Tell the apparent size of the object(s) when compared with the following held at arm's length:

    a. Pinhead c. Dime e. Half dollar g. Orange i. Large
    b. Pea d. Nickel f. Silver dollar h. Grapefruit

Or, if easier, give apparent size in inches on a ruler held at arm's length. **About the same as moon, maybe a little smaller. Varied from brighter/larger than planet to apparent size of moon.**

21. How did you happen to notice the object(s)? **10-12 men all watched it. Brightness attracted us.**

22. Where were you and what were you doing at the time? **Outdoors waiting for a meeting to begin at 7:30pm**

23. How did the object(s) disappear from view? **Moved to distance then disappeared**

24. Compare the speed of the object(s) with a piston or jet aircraft at the same apparent altitude. **Not pertinent**

25. Were there any conventional aircraft in the location at the time or immediately afterwards? If so, please elaborate. **no.**

26. Please estimate the distance of the object(s). **Difficult. Maybe 300-1000 yards.**

27. What was the elevation of the object(s) in the sky? Please mark on this hemisphere sketch. **About 30° above horizon.**

28. Names and addresses of other witnesses, if any.

Ten members of Leary Georgia Lions Club

29. What do you think you saw?

    a. Extraterrestrial device?
    b. UFO?
    c. Planet or star?
    d. Aircraft?
    e. Satellite?
    f. Moon?
    g. Other? (Please specify).

INVESTIGATOR / FEBRUARY 1977

30. Please describe your feelings and reactions during the sighting. Were you calm, nervous, frightened, apprehensive, awed, etc.? If you wish your answer to this question to remain confidential, please indicate with a check mark. (Use a separate sheet if necessary)

31. Please draw a map of the locality of the observation showing North; your position; the direction from which the object(s) appeared and disappeared from view; the direction of its course over the area; roads, towns, villages, railroads, and other landmarks within a mile.

    Appeared from West--About 30° up.

32. Is there an airport, military, governmental, or research installation in the area? No

33. Have you seen other objects of an unidentified nature? If so, please describe these observations, using a separate sheet of paper. No

34. Please enclose photographs, motion pictures, news clippings, notes of radio or television programs (include time, station and date, if possible) regarding this or similar observations, or any other background material. We will return the material to you if requested. None.

35. Were you interrogated by Air Force investigators? By any other federal, state, county, or local officials? If so, please state the name and rank or title of the agent, his office, and details as to where and when the questioning took place.

    Were you asked or told not to reveal or discuss the incident? If so, were any reasons or official orders mentioned? Please elaborate carefully. No.

36. We should like permission to quote your name in connection with this report. This action will encourage other reasonable citizens to report similar observations to NICAP. However, if you prefer, we will keep your name confidential. Please note your choice by checking the proper statement below. In any case, please fill in all parts of the form, for our own confidential files. Thank you for your cooperation.

    You may use my name. (x)   Please keep my name confidential. ( )

37. Date of filling out this report   Signature:
    9-18-73   Jimmy Carter

at Palm Springs when he was summoned to Muroc Airfield by high military officials. Muroc is now known as Edwards Air Force Base, recently popularized as the landing field for the space shuttle.

The President had a press conference scheduled for that day but never showed up for it. There were rumors that he was ill. The official explanation was that he went to a dentist. Newsmen, however, were never able to learn which dentist treated him.

Actually, Eisenhower was driven to the California air base to meet with space aliens. According to Lord Clancarty, the incident was reported to him by a former top U.S. test pilot. Says the Earl: "The pilot was one of six people at Eisenhower's meeting with the beings. He had been called in as a technical adviser because of his reputation and abilities as a test pilot."

What Eisenhower and the Six Witnesses Saw

The test pilot told Lord Clancarty: "Five different alien craft landed at the base. Three were saucer-shaped and two were cigar-shaped ...and as Eisenhower and his small group watched, the aliens disembarked and approached them.

"They looked something like humans, but not exactly."

The test pilot described the beings as having human-like features, but that by our standards they were misshapen. They were the same height and weight as the average man and were able to breathe air without the use of a helmet or mask.

The test pilot reported that the aliens spoke English and wanted Eisenhower to start an education program for the people of the United States, and eventually the earth.

Eisenhower allegedly replied that he didn't think the world was ready for that. The president said that his concern was that a world-wide announcement that aliens had landed would likely cause panic.

The aliens agreed with that opinion, saying that they would continue to contact isolated individuals until the people of the earth got used to the idea of their presence.

The President Watches An Incredible Demonstration

According to the test pilot: "They demonstrated their spacecraft for the president. They showed him their ability to make themselves invisible.

"This really caused the president a lot of discomfort because none of us could see them even though we knew they were still there. The aliens then boarded their ships and departed." The pilot told Lord Clancarty that he never told another soul about this unique meeting, and that now all the others involved in the encounter are dead.

Additional Verification

A recent report in the *National Enquirer* regarding the Eisenhower incident adds a quote from UFO researcher Gabriel Green who testifies that he once held a conversation with a gunnery sergeant who had been stationed at Edwards during this period. The sergeant said he and his team were using live ammo and were ordered by a general to fire at the alien spacecraft. Their attack was futile, however, as none of the shells could penetrate the tough metal hull of the craft and eventually the men watched in amazement as the ships proceeded to land near one of the large hangars.

Additional confirmation comes from Charles Berlitz who reports in the book, *The Roswell Incident* that a man named Gerald Light was still another witness to the astonishing encounter. Light wrote a letter dated April 16, 1954 to UFO writer Meade Layne acting director of the Borderland Sciences Research Foundation. In this communication he stated that he saw the five UFOs land at the base. "I had the distinct feeling," he commented, "that the world as I knew it had come to an end. It has finally happened—we have seen and met aliens from another world!"

An Astronaut Becomes Involved in UFO Landing

Though it was some years later, it is hard to believe that this second landing of a UFO at Edwards Air Force Base doesn't somehow confirm the episode involving President Eisenhower. In this later incident—which took place either in 1957 or 1958 Gordon Cooper (a man with the "right stuff" who was to take a ride into space) saw photographic evidence of an actual UFO touching down upon the earth.

In a taped interview with NBC newsman Lee Spiegel, Cooper disclosed that after lunch this particular day, several men under his direct command who had been assigned to photograph an area of the vast dry lake beds near Edwards, came racing into his office very excited about something they had witnessed.

"While the crew was out there, they spotted a strange looking craft above the lake bed, and they began taking films of it.'

Cooper says the object was very definitely "hovering above the ground. And then it slowly came down and sat on the lake bed for a few minutes." All during this time the motion picture cameras were filming away.

"There were varied estimates by the cameramen on what the actual size of the object was," Cooper confesses, "but they all agreed that it was at least the size of a vehicle that would carry normal-sized people in it."

Cooper, then a colonel in the Air Force, was not fortunate enough to be outdoors at the time of this incredible encounter, but he did see the films as soon as they were rushed through the development process.

"It was a typical circular-shaped UFO," he recollects. "Not too many people saw it, because it took off at quite a sharp angle and just climbed straight on out of sight."

In addition, Cooper says that he didn't take any kind of poll to determine who had seen the craft, "because there were always strange things flying around in the air over Edwards." This is a statement newsman Spiegel was able to verify through his own research efforts, having obtained closely guarded tapes of conversations between military pilots circling the base and their commanding officers in the flight tower, tracking the presence of unidentified objects.

"People just didn't ask a lot of questions about things they saw and couldn't understand," noted Cooper, who adds that it was a lot simpler to just look the other way, shrug one's shoulders, and chalk up what had been seen to "just another experimental aircraft that must have been developed at another area of the air base."

But what about the photographic proof—the motion picture footage—that was taken? "I think it was definitely a UFO," Cooper states, and he makes no bones about it. "However, where it (the object) came from and who was in it is hard to determine, because it didn't stay around long enough to discuss the matter there wasn't even time to send out a welcoming committee!"

After he had reviewed the film at least a dozen times, the footage was quickly forwarded to Washington. Cooper no doubt expected to give a reply in a few weeks time as to what his men had seen and photographed, but there was no word, and the movie vanished without a trace—never to surface again!

Eisenhower's Warning

The report by Cooper, which was confirmed to me in a direct phone call to the astronaut several years ago, adds considerable substance to the accounts which say that President Eisenhower experienced a close encounter of his very own. Though he might have wanted to tell the world about what he had seen, the president kept quiet, no doubt told by his advisors that such a disclosure might cause panic in the streets. Around this same period we know for a fact that both the military and the CIA were concerned that civilization might come to an abrupt halt as we've come to know it—should word leak out that an advanced race of beings were coming to earth and had offered to exchange data with us all.

Before his death, it might be that Eisenhower had realized the error of his way and that he had taken bad advice, for he warned that the big threat to our freedom would not likely emerge from some outside source, but from the military-industrial complex which he saw as working in cahoots to enslave society. It is pretty obvious, that this unholy alliance has continued to cement itself and is responsible for the state of affairs we find ourselves in today.

Starting Revelations From a Man of God

Dr. Frank E. Stranges has had a long career in the religious sciences. Born and raised in Brooklyn, New York, he entered seminary school at an early age eager to learn all he could about God and the kingdom of Heaven. Today, Dr. Stranges is president of the International Evangelism Crusades as well as the International Theological Seminary. In addition, he holds many other honors and degrees, but most important of all perhaps is his firm commitment that UFOs play an important role in the ways of the Lord.

While he was in college he discovered that many learned men such as military personnel, as well as pilots and police officers, had been engaged by these whirling, twirling discs that have been seen overhead since the late 1940s.

In December, 1959, an event took place which was to change Dr. Stranges' life forever. Through what he says were "a series of strange and unusual circumstances," he was invited to speak with a man from another world inside the Pentagon. The meeting took place during an evangelistic crusade which he was conducting in Washington. "The invitation was given to me by a person who, for obvious reasons, cannot be named in writing. However, suffice it to say that person is a born-again Christian with a sound mind and a good position at the Pentagon building."

Dr. Stranges' meeting with Val Thor is a matter of record, as written up by Dr. Stranges in two books, *My Friend From Beyond Earth* and *Stranger At The Pentagon*. After the conference, Frank left the government building feeling totally elated; so emotionally uplifted was he by his visit with a man of supreme intelligence whose only thoughts were for the betterment of mankind. Since that day many years ago, Dr. Stranges has had further "eye opening" meetings with this man who looks as human as any of us, but who has a love of the Creator and of life that cannot be found that readily on our own planet. According to Stranges, Val Thor and other aliens are here—and have been here since Biblical times—to help with our spiritual progression.

Presidential Encounters

Recently, I had the opportunity to visit with Dr. Stranges at the church he presides over which is located at 7970 Woodman Avenue, Van Nuys, Calif. The subject from the pulpit for the evening was UFOs and the Bible, and during the course of the discussion, I was even invited up to the rostrum to say a few words. Later, after a brief recess, Dr. Stranges decided to fill his congregation in on some highly confidential information. Dr. Stranges, through his relationship with Val Thor and the Space Brothers, and his high level government contacts, had decided to reveal a series of revolutionary disclosures pertaining to extraterrestrials and how they have influenced many of our presidents from George Washington on down to the most current Chief of State. The following is a transcript of what Dr. Stranges had to say to his church followers:

• "George Washington had a spiritual experience at Valley Forge. According to the records, he experienced a space visitation regarding his own destiny as the father of our country. He didn't discuss it with his troops. He discussed it with his chaplain, with his wife, and with close friends, who were also high in military power.

• "Abraham Lincoln in the period from 1861 to 1865 was contacted by who the press of that time called, "space people, who accompanied him in his darkest time during the Civil War." He was also warned in a dream by a space entity or an angelic being, not to go to Fords' theatre. But he felt obligated to those who made plans, and he went to Fords' Theatre, and lost his life.

• "In 1941 Franklin Roosevelt had his first encounter on the third of December. He was warned about United States involvement in a European war. He did not heed the warning. He was afraid of upsetting those around him. He shot himself in 1943. Not even individuals in the U.S. high command knew what happened that day. To this day, scholars are still confused. They never saw the open coffin.

• "Harry S. Truman, the 33rd President, had his close

encounter on July 4th of 1945, just prior to August 6th of 1945, when the bomb was dropped on Hiroshima. He visually witnessed more than twelve UFO sightings during his term of office. According to two retired Secret Service agents, he met with space people on several occasions and did not deem it expedient to relate his conversation, because he did not want to rub anyone in the National Security Council.

• "In 1953 Dwight Eisenhower was the 34th president of the United States. In 1955 he was flown to Palm Springs where he dropped his wife off. His press secretary told the world he was on a golf vacation. Instead, he was flown by helicopter to Edwards Air Force Base. The truth is that three UFOs landed on the runway at Edwards Air Force Base. The pilot from the first UFO got into the second UFO. Then UFO number two and number three left, leaving one saucer-shaped craft on the runway.

"Military individuals dragged the UFO into the hangar and placed a heavy curtain of security over the whole place." It has been one of the closest kept secrets in history. The President was brought in, along with several members of the Joint Chiefs of Staff, several members of the National Security Council, and a representative from Rockefellers' office, and a representative from the Rothchilds. Why were these key people invited to see a UFO that landed at Edwards?

"When President Eisenhower viewed the UFO two individuals were able to tip it upside down. The UFO was about thirty feet in diameter. Everyone stood back and the strangest phenomenon on record at the base occurred. The UFO dematerialized right in front of their eyes. I understand they have pictures of this, moving pictures. Then it materialized again. They say that it was the direct cause of Mr. Eisenhower's first heart attack.

"To this day, that UFO has remained at Edwards'. It's still there. They have brought in scientists from all over the world to try to figure out how to crack into that UFO. They gave it every test that they gave Valient Thors' garment, including the acid test and the laser. The laser was put on that ship and it didn't even warm up the surface. It's defying the best scientific minds in the world. To this day, they are still playing with it.

"Mr. Eisenhower had to clue Mr. Nixon in on this. All he could say was, "My God, my God, my God." At first Mr. Nixon had doubts. It was disclosed that his reason for doubting was that he had not seen it himself. But Richard Nixon also flew to that place and saw it for himself. Every president since Eisenhower has been to that sight and seen that ship.

"Other countries have pleaded to be allowed to take it to their country for tests, including West Germany. But so far no good."

Great Social Change Avoided

"John F. Kennedy, the 35th president, had met many opportunities to help change the course of the United States. During the last three months of his life, in 1963, he produced a list of changes that he was about to introduce to the Congress. The list was shared with L.B. Johnson, Bobby Kennedy, and the man whose name sprung up 22 times in the recently released CIA records, Henry Kissinger. From that day to this the list has disappeared, just as mysteriously as Mr. Kennedy's brain disappeared. When they performed the autopsy, they couldn't find his brain. The intelligence report says that his brain is in the Soviet Union.

"Jimmy Carter was very fearful of intelligence forces in Washington, D.C. He was also fearful of certain foreign powers, who had a powerful influence in the American government. Following news reports about his UFO sighting, the White House was deluged with letters and phone calls from so many people, that he absolutely refused to discuss his UFO sighting any further.

"Every president, for the past ten presidents, has promised that as soon as they become president, all UFO information would be freely given to the public.

Ronald Reagan—Mystery Man

"Ronald Reagan is a puzzle. He holds membership card number one to our organization, The National Investigation Committee on UFOS. He has had opportunities to meet with people from other worlds, who are far more advanced than we are. Because of his idea, similar to Nixon's, 'I must do it myself or if I depart from the normal way of doing things, I may incur the wrath of some of my biggest supporters. He did not keep his promise.

"When he was running for governor of the State of California, Mr. Reagan promised that if he became governor he would start a state investigations office. This was during the last five days of the filming of my documentary Phenomenon 777. He was making commercials for the Boraxal company at the time. Fifteen days after he became governor, I wrote to him and he didn't know me from Adam's housecat. He didn't want to know me either, when it came to UFOS. He said, 'There are certain things that we can't get into right now. Wait until next year.'

"Next year became four years later and there was nothing. Then he became President of the United States and still there was nothing. He agreed to do something, then he disagreed. At one time he wanted to start the most powerful non-governmental UFO investigative body in the United States. Seven days later, nothing.

"President Reagan's life was spared recently by a certain Secret Service man who, to this day, cannot be located. During the attempted assassination, one Secret Service agent was so excited that he aimed his gun right at the president. Another Secret Service agent grabbed his wrist and pushed it up. That Secret Service man is gone. They have no Secret Service man that fits that description that was on the scene at that time.

"Not long before that, Mr. Ford was in a certain city in the State of California and someone aimed a gun at him. An invisible hand clamped down on that gun and caused it to misfire. I don't believe in accidents. I believe that all things are under divine control and everything is under divine power.

"There is still hope that President Reagan will condescend to meet with Val Thor or anyone else to help this nation find a proper balance. We need to pray for the leaders of our nation. We need to encourage as many clear thinking people as possible to investigate, to prove all things. We must determine in our hearts to separate fact from fiction and hold fast to that which is true.

We are living in a generation when anything good for the human family could happen."

Robert Kennedy's Devotion To The Cause Of The Space Brothers

Even though he never got to be president, Robert Kennedy had great leadership qualities. Sometime before he was shot down in a Los Angeles hotel, Bobby expressed a definite belief in UFOs. In a personal letter to publisher Gray Barker, Kennedy noted that he was a card-carrying member of the Amalgamated Flying Saucers Clubs of America (directed by Gabriel Green, a Yucca Valley, Calif. contactee) and indicated that he accepted the stories of those who said they had encountered aliens from other planets.

Kennedy wrote: "Like many other people in our country, I am interested in the UFO phenomenon. I watch with great interest all reports of Unidentified Flying Objects, and I hope some day we will know more about this intriguing subject. Dr. Harlow Shapely, the prominent astronomer, has stated that there is a probability that there is life in the universe. I favor more research regarding this matter, and I hope that once and for all we can determine the true facts about flying saucers."

While it is certainly difficult to prove, there are those who theorize that Robert Kennedy might have been killed because he was too "New Age," and because he had expressed an intense interest, not only in UFOS, but in many matters that would bring about great social change on our planet. As a footnote, it should be brought out that Kennedy's assassin had ample knowledge of the negative aspects of psychic patterns, and later, while in jail, he stated that he did not remember shooting Kennedy: but that he might have been hypnotized by someone into committing such a foul deed.

Doesn't it always seem like those who wish to bring about important social change usually meet with an untimely death? Maybe Robert Kennedy rubbed someone the wrong way—and perhaps that someone was a member of a group that has long tried to halt America's spiritual growth and keep this country and the rest of the world in virtual enslavement.

Furthermore, on the subject of Robert Kennedy, we have Dr. Stranges' solemn word that Bobby met toward his final days with the Space Brother known as Val Thor. According to Stranges' testimony, Kennedy once showed up at his Van Nuys home shortly after the dinner hour insisting upon having Stranges set up a conference between him and Val Thor.

"I told Kennedy I could not do that, that Val met with only those he wished to meet with. But I did recommend that Kennedy go into the next room and type out any questions he might have of Val Thor and promised that I would personally deliver Kennedy's message to my alien friend. Later, Val stated that he had gotten together with Mr. Kennedy and that Robert had wanted to know what his chances were of becoming president. To this question Val replied, 'Mr. Kennedy, four years from now you would stand an excellent chance of winning. But, I beg you to remain far away from the political race this year.'" History tells us that Kennedy did not heed Val Thor's advice and ended up perishing at the hands of a mad man whose devotion was to the "dark side" of the "force."

Suppression of the Truth

Messages received through telepathy from highly advanced space people who have been watching over the United States since the days of the Revolution have indicated that many of our founding fathers received inspiration from "higher sources," though it was always left to their free will to take the right course.

During one recent transmission received from extraterrestrial sources the following was stated: "The foundation of your country was originally laid on our guidance. We find it disheartening that your government officials would so easily turn from the light that has been given so freely to them. This transmission, broadcast via telepathy to a New York City businessman who has been experiencing such mental encounters for several years, included this information about the suppression of beneficial discoveries by those in power who would not care to see a change in the status quo:

"There are many on your planet now who have had at their disposal much knowledge. Yet, your governments and your scientists refuse to acknowledge their great discoveries. Many times, these individuals have come forward and tried to release their discoveries, that which they have locked onto, only to find that society is not willing to accept what they are willing to freely give out. Such an attitude in medicine, in the sciences, and in other fields, has prevented your earth from developing faster than it has." Could it be that there are those that conspire to hold mankind back in the "dark ages?" It may well be that a New Age of light, beauty, and truth could exist around the next corner if mankind were permitted to develop along the path to spiritual perfection, without being thrown off course by those who find it to their advantage to hold us back.

There are those in "high places," in "positions of power" who make great financial gain every time a new nuclear power plant is constructed, who profit from every stream that is polluted, and get fatter every time either the U.S. or Russia announce that they are going to strengthen their defenses with more missiles and atomic warheads. These powerful men are not anxious to hear what the space people have to say regarding any new form of technology that might put them "out of business," or a plan that would satisfy all political factors and allow humankind to live in total peace forever. There is no money to be made off of peace and tranquility, but vast fortunes to be reaped from turmoil and confusion in a world whose leaders have seemingly gone crazy.

As General Omar Bradley so eloquently stated before his death: "We have grasped the mystery of the atom and rejected the Sermon on the Mount. The world has achieved brilliance without wisdom, power without conscience. Ours is a world of nuclear giants and ethical infants. We know more about killing than we do about living. This is our twentieth century's claim to distinction and progress."

PROPHECIES OF THE PRESIDENTS

United States Senate
WASHINGTON, D.C.

May 9, 1968

Mr. Gray Barker
Publisher, Saucer News
Box 2228
Clarksburg, West Virginia 26301

Dear Readers:

As you may know, I am a card carrying member of the Amalgamated Flying Saucers Association. Therefore, like many other people in our country I am interested in the phenomenon of flying saucers.

It is a fascinating subject that has initiated both scientific fiction fantasies and serious scientific research.

I watch with great interest all reports of unidentified flying objects, and I hope that some day we will know more about this intriguing subject.

Dr. Harlow Shapley, the prominent astronomer, has stated that there is a probability that there is other life in the universe.

I favor more research regarding this matter, and I hope that once and for all we can determine the true facts about flying saucers. Your magazine can stimulate much of the investigation and inquiry into this phenomenon through the publication of news and discussion material. This can be of great help in paving the way to a knowledge of one of the fascinating subjects of our contemporary world.

Sincerely,

Robert F. Kennedy

United States Senate
COMMITTEE ON COMMERCE, SCIENCE, AND TRANSPORTATION
WASHINGTON, D.C. 20510

April 11, 1979

Mr. Lee M. Graham
526 West Maple
Monrovia, California 91016

Dear Mr. Graham:

It is true I was denied access to a facility at Wright-Patterson. Because I never got in, I can't tell you what was inside. We both know about the rumors.

Apart from that, let me make my position clear: I do not believe that we are the only planet, and of some two billion that exist, that has life on it. I have never seen what I would call a UFO, but I have intelligent friends who have, so I can sort of argue either way.

Sincerely,

Barry Goldwater

Chapter Thirteen: The Secret Government— Whose Really In Control?

Even though we have our President and other elected officials are these politicians really those who are in control? Or is it possible that some other group of individuals "pull the strings" behind the scenes?

There is a growing—almost nagging—feeling among many

William Cooper blows the whistle on secret government activities in regard to the UFO mystery.

that those in the White House, Senate and Congress are merely "puppet"—having their strings pulled by a "higher" source who are secretly trying to sway the destiny of the U.S. in the wrong—a much more sinister—way.

Is the battle between good and evil about to come to a head? Many "Last Days" watchers believe that a secret treaty has been rendered between certain branches of the military-industrial complex and a group of aliens who are abducting humans and planting monitoring devices inside their brains to control our actions and movements. They say that these aliens—often referred to as the "Grays"—are in league with certain "secret societies" often referred to as the Illuminati, the Jason Society and the Skull and Bones to bring about a one government world power structure which is being pushed off on us as something called the New World Order.

The late scientist Wilbur Smith knew of this grave danger for potential world control in the early 1960s. Smith, a Canadian engineer who was consulted regarding the wreckage of alien spacecraft found outside the town of Roswell, New Mexico, fully realized that there were many covert operations taking place behind our backs and that this group was behind the wall of UFO silence that prevented the public from learning the true nature of our visitors from space.

Smith spoke quite candidly when he stated:

" I propose to give a warning of a grave danger which we are all, consciously or unconsciously, facing in a world in which two great forces are striving to gain control of man's mind. This struggle has been going on from time immemorial, but never in the world's history has the conflict been more intense than it is in this present era of confusion and unrest. In the old days, mankind was often made to suffer physically, unspeakable things in the name of power, but today, with man's mind more developed and better educated, he is now facing the prospect of a refinement of even greater mental and spiritual cruelty—unless he is prepared to protect himself with right thinking.

"The two great forces involved in trying to influence man's thinking may be described as *positive*, i.e., thoughts in harmony with the concept of a love of God and the brotherhood of man, and *negative*, those encompassing anti-Christ motives designed to gain control over man for the purpose of power. This battle for Man's mind is being waged on two fronts, the physical and the metaphysical, and the object of the fight is to bring about either the spiritual salvation or destruction of homo sapiens.

"To deal first with the physical aspects, no matter how hard we may all strive to be strong-minded and individualistic, we are all subtly influenced by the spoken and written word and other forms of thought communication, particularly through the medium of books, newspapers, radio and television. In the latter field, as the sponsors know only too well, even the 'commercials' play an important role in making up our minds to purchase certain products. In our business and social lives, we are often swayed by the thoughts of others and some people too apathetic to form opinions themselves, are willing to accept the views of others more articulate, as their own. In all our daily contacts, a little of the good, bad or indifferent, as the case may be, is rubbing off on us and influencing our thinking.

"In the field of politics, often an area of great misrepresentation in order to gain votes, even greater pressures are brought to bear and we are often influenced by the seemingly convincing rhetoric of clever politicians. But it is in the area of international politics that the gravest dangers lie, for here the stakes are high and the lust for power the greatest. Because of this, many of us have been through the horrors of at least one World War, if not two. But let us first analyze how these two wars came about in the first place. In each case, a few men in power, with great personal magnetism, were able to influence and organize the minds of the common people to such a degree of mass-hypnotism, that the entire nation believed it had a true cause to fight for. Many of us watched and history books have recorded, the militarist building-up of Fascism and Nazi-ism and, because of the evil it spawned which the Free World had to fight against, we eventually witnessed the final downfall and disaster brought to these misguided people who allowed their minds to be warped by avaricious despots seeking only greater power. Unity in a country is a fine thing when it is directed into channels for the good of its people, but when it seeks to persecute others in order to gain its ends, it becomes a thing of evil and a triumph for the negative forces."

From these statements, its quite obvious that Smith realized that we were being "manipulated," that all isn't always what it seems.

William Cooper's Alien/CIA Connection

In recent times one individual has been at the forefront of trying to expose the existence of the Secret Government.

In a relatively brief period, William Cooper has surfaced as one of the all-time controversial figures in UFO research. Cooper is, however, the first to point out that he is not primarily a UFOlogist, but a government "whistleblower," whose purpose it is—he feels—to bring the truth to the public about not only any possible alien intervention in our society, but the very existence of the so-called "Secret Government" that is behind everything from the Kennedy Assassination, to international drug trafficking, MJ-12, Armageddon, the Men-in-Black, and a variety of other conspiracies that all tie in with a continuing disinformation program that molds our thinking on just about every subject.

A former U.S. Naval Intelligence Briefing Team member, Cooper was serving on the USS *Tiru* when he experienced, with four other crewmen, a dramatic sighting of a huge UFO that came up out of the water and disappeared over the horizon at fantastic speed. During his term of duty under Admiral Clarey (Commander in Chief of the U.S. Pacific Fleet), Cooper says he had the opportunity to review certain highly classified documents pertaining to an agreement that had been made between the U.S. military and a specific group of extraterrestrials who have come here to abduct humans, perform genetic experiments and implant monitoring devices inside our brain.

The following material is excerpted from Bill Cooper's copyrighted paper, *The Secret Government—The Origin, Identity and Purpose of MJ-12*, and is but an example of the type of controversial material he has been discussing in appropriate forums in recent years.

The Landing

In 1954, a race of large-nosed aliens known as the "Greys," which had been orbiting the Earth, landed at Holloman Air Force Base. A basic agreement was reached. This race identified themselves as originating from a planet around a red star in the Constellation of Orion which we called Betelgeuse. They stated that their planet was dying and that at some unknown future time they would no longer be able to survive there. This led to a second landing at Edwards Air Force Base. The historical event had been planned in advance and details of the treaty had been agreed upon. President Eisenhower arranged to be in Palm Springs on vacation. On the appointed day the President was spirited away to the base and the excuse was given to the press that he was visiting a dentist.

President Eisenhower met with the aliens and a formal treaty between the Alien Nation and the United States of America was signed. We then received our first Alien Ambassador from outer space. His name and title was His "Omnipotent Highness Krill," pronounced *Krill*. You should know that the Alien flag is known as the "Trilateral Insignia." It is displayed on their craft and worn on their uniforms. Both of these landings and the second meeting were filmed. The films exist today.

The treaty stated: The aliens would not interfere in our affairs and we would not interfere in theirs. We would keep their presence on earth a secret. They would furnish us with advanced technology and would help us in our technological development. They would not make any treaty with any other earth nation. They could abduct humans on a limited and periodic basis for the purpose of medical examination and monitoring of our development with the stipulation that the humans would not be harmed, would be returned to their point of abduction, that the humans would have no memory of the event, and that the Alien Nation would furnish MJ-12 with a list of all human contacts and abductees on a regularly scheduled basis. It was agreed that each nation would receive the Ambassador of the other for as long as the treaty remained in force. It was further agreed that the Alien Nation and the United States would exchange 16 personnel each to the other with the purpose of learning, each of the other.

The Alien "Guests" would remain on earth and the human "Guests" would travel to the Alien point of origin for a specified period of time, then return, at which point a reverse exchange would be made. It was also agreed that bases would be constructed underground for the use of the Alien Nation and that two bases would be constructed for the joint use of the Alien Nation and the United States Government. Exchange of technology would take place In the Jointly occupied bases. These Allen bases would be constructed under Indian reservations in the four corners of Utah, Colorado, New Mexico, Arizona, and one would be constructed in Nevada in the area known as S-4, located approximately seven miles south of the western border of Area 51, known as Dreamland. All alien areas are under complete control of the Naval Department and all personnel who work in these complexes receive their checks from the Navy. Construction of the bases began immediately, but progress was slow until large amounts of money were made available in 1957. Work continued on the "Yellow Book."

Redlight/Snowbird

Project REDLIGHT was formed and experimentation in test flying alien craft was begun in earnest. A super TOP SECRET facility was built at Groom Lake in Nevada in the midst of the weapons test range. It was code named DREAMLAND. The installation was placed under the Department of the Navy and clearance of all personnel required "Q" clearance as well as Executive (Presidential) approval. This is ironic due to the fact that the President of the United States does not have clearance to visit the site. The alien base and exchange of technology actually took place in an Area known as S-4. Area S-4 was code named "The Dark Side of the Moon."

The Army was asked to form a super secret organization to furnish security for all alien tasked projects. This organization became the National Reconnaissance Organization based at Fort Carson, Colorado. The specific teams trained to secure the projects were called Delta.

A second project, code named SNOWBIRD was promulgated to explain away any sightings of the REDLIGHT crafts as being Air Force experiments. The SNOWBIRD crafts were manufactured using conventional technology and were flown for the press on several occasions. Project SNOWBIRD was also used to debunk legitimate public sightings of alien craft (UFOs). Project SNOWBIRD was very successful and reports from the public declined steadily until recent years.

Secret Fund

A multimillion-dollar SECRET fund was organized and kept by the Military Office of the White House. This fund was used to build over 75 deep underground facilities. Presidents who asked were told the fund was used to build Deep Underground Shelters for the President in case of war. Only a few were built for the President. Millions of dollars were funnelled through this office to MJ-12 and then out to the contractors and was used to build TOP SECRET alien bases as well as TOP SECRET DUMB (Deep Underground Military Bases), and the facilities promulgated by "Alternative Two," throughout the nation. President Johnson used this fund to build a movie theater and pave the road on his ranch. He had no idea of its true purpose.

The secret White House underground construction fund was set up in 1957 by President Eisenhower. The funding was obtained from Congress under the guise of "construction and maintenance of secret sites where the President could be taken in case of military attack: Presidential Emergency Sites." The sites are literally holes in the ground, deep enough to withstand a nuclear blast and are outfitted with state-of-the-art communications equipment. To date there are more than 75 sites spread around the country which were build using money from this fund.

The Atomic Energy Commission has built at least an additional 22 underground sites.

Secret Alien Study

A major finding of the government's secret alien study was that the public could not be told, as it was believed that this would most certainly lead to economic collapse, collapse of the religious structure, and national panic, which could lead into anarchy. Secrecy thus continued. An offshoot of this finding was that if the public could not be told, then the Congress could not be told, thus funding for the projects and research would have to come from outside the government. In the meantime money was to be obtained from the military budget and from CIA confidential non-appropriated funds.

Another major finding was the aliens were using humans and animals for a source of glandular secretions, enzymes, hormonal secretions, blood and in horrible genetic experiments. The aliens explained these actions as necessary to their survival. They state that their genetic structure had deteriorated and that they were no longer able to reproduce. They stated that if they were unable to improve their genetic structure their race would soon cease to exist. We looked upon their explanations with extreme suspicion. Since our weapons were literally useless against the aliens, MJ-12 decided to continue friendly diplomatic relations with them until such time as we were able to develop a technology which would then enable us to challenge them on a military basis. Overtures would have to be made to the Soviet Union, and other nations, to join forces for the survival of humanity. In the meantime, plans were developed to research and construct two weapons systems using conventional and nuclear technology, which would hopefully bring us to parity.

The results of the research were Projects Joshua and Excalibur. Joshua was a weapon captured from the Germans, which at that time was capable of shattering four inch thick armor plate at a range of two miles, using low-aimed, low-frequency sound waves, and it was believed that this weapon would be effective against the alien craft and beam weapons. Excalibur was a weapon carried by missile, not to exceed 30,000 feet AGL, not to deviate from designated target more than 50 meters, would penetrate 1,000 meters of tufa hard packed soil, such as that found in New Mexico, would carry a one megaton warhead, and was intended for use in destroying the aliens in their underground bases. Joshua was developed successfully, but never used to my knowledge. Excalibur was not pushed until recent years, and now there is an unprecedented effort to develop this weapon.

Fatima/Christ

The events at Fatima in the early part of the century were scrutinized. On suspicion that it was alien manipulation, an intelligence operation was put into motion to penetrate the secrecy surrounding the event. The United States utilized its Vatican moles that had been recruited and nurtured during World War ll, and soon obtained the entire Vatican study which included the prophecy. This prophecy stated that if man did not turn from evil and place himself at the feet of Christ, the planet would self destruct and the events described in the book of Revelations would indeed come to pass. It stated that a child would be born who would unite the world with a plan for world peace and a false religion beginning in 1992. By 1995 the people would discern that he was evil and was indeed the Anti-Christ. World War III would begin in the Middle East in 1995 with an invasion of Israel by a United Arab nation using conventional weapons, which would culminate in a nuclear holocaust in the year 1999. Between 1999 and 2003 most of the life on this planet would suffer horribly and die as a result. The return of Christ would occur in the year 2011.

When the aliens were confronted with this finding, they confirmed that it was true. The aliens explained that they had created us through hybridization and had manipulated the human race through religion, satanism, witchcraft, magic, and the occult. They further explained that they were capable of time travel and the events would indeed come to pass. Later exploitation of alien technology by the United States and the Soviet Union utilizing time travel confirmed the prophecy. The aliens showed a hologram which they claimed was the actual Crucifixion of Christ which the Government filmed. We did not know whether to believe them or not. Were they using our GENUINE religions to manipulate us? Or, were they indeed the source of our religions with which they had been manipulating us all along? Or, was this the beginning scenario of the genuine END TIMES and the RETURN OF CHRIST, which had been predicted in the Bible? No one knew the answer.

A Symposium was held in 1957, which was attended by some of the great scientific minds then living. They reached the conclusion that by or shortly after the year 2,000 the planet WOULD self destruct due to increased population and man's exploitation of the environment WITHOUT ANY HELP FROM GOD OR THE ALIENS.

Alternative Three

By secret Executive Order of President Eisenhower, the Jason Scholars were ordered to study this scenario and make recommendations from their findings. The Jason Society CONFIRMED the finding of the scientists and made three recommendations called "Alternatives One, Two, and Three." "Alternative One" was to use nuclear devices to blast holes In the Stratosphere from which the heat and pollution could escape into space. Change the human cultures from that of exploitation into cultures of environmental protection. Of the three this was decided to be the least likely to succeed due to the inherent nature of man and the additional damage the Nuclear explosions would themselves create. "Alternative Two" was to build a vast network of underground cities and tunnels in which a select representation of all cultures and occupations would survive and carry on the human race. The rest of humanity would be left to fend for themselves on the surface of the planet. "Alternative Three" was to exploit the alien and conventional technology in order for a select few to leave the earth and establish colonies in outer space.

I am not able to either confirm or deny the existence of "Batch Consignments" of human slaves, which would be used for the manual labor in the effort as a part of the plan. The Moon, code named "Adam," would be the object of primary interest followed by the planet Mars, code named "Eve." As a delaying action, ALL THREE ALTERNATIVES included birth control, sterilization, and the introduction of deadly microbes to control or slow the growth of the Earth's population. AIDS is only ONE result of these plans. There are others. It was decided, since the population must be reduced and controlled, that it would be in the best interest of the human race to rid ourselves of the undesirable elements of our society. The joint U.S. and Soviet leadership dismissed "Alternative One," but ordered work to begin on Alternative Two and Three virtually at the same time.

In 1959, the Rand Corporation hosted a Deep Underground Construction Symposium. In the Symposium report, machines are pictured and described which could bore a tunnel 45 feet in diameter at the rate of five feet per hour. It also displays pictures of huge tunnels and underground vaults containing what appear to be complex facilities and possibly even cities. It appears that the previous five years of all-out underground construction had made significant progress by that time.

Kennedy Assassination

The "Official" Space Program was boosted by President Kennedy in his inaugural address, when he mandated that the United States put a man on the Moon before the end of the decade. Although innocent in its conception, this mandate enabled those in charge to funnel vast amounts of money into black projects and conceal the REAL space program from the American people. A similar program in the Soviet Union served the same purpose. In fact, a joint alien, United States, and Soviet Union base already existed on the Moon at the very moment Kennedy spoke the words. On May 22, 1962, a space probe landed on Mars and confirmed the existence of an environment which could support life. Not long afterward, the construction of a colony on the planet Mars began in earnest. Today cities exist on Mars populated by specially-selected people from different cultures and occupations, taken from all over the Earth. A public charade of antagonism between the Soviet Union and the United States has been maintained over all these years in order to fund projects in the name of National defense, when in fact we are the closest allies.

At some point President Kennedy discovered portions of the truth concerning the drugs and the aliens. He issued an ultimatum in 1963 to MJ-12. President Kennedy assured them that if they did not clean up the drug problem he would. He informed MJ-12 that he intended to reveal the presence of aliens to the American people within the following year and ordered a plan developed to implement his decision. President Kennedy was not a member of the Council On Foreign Relations and knew nothing of "Alternative Two" or "Alternative Three." Internationally, the Operations were supervised by an Executive Committee known as the "Policy Committee." In the United States they were supervised by MJ-12 and in the Soviet Union by its sister organization. President Kennedy's decision struck fear into the hearts of those in charge. His assassination was ordered by the Policy Committee and the order was carried out by agents of MJ-12 in Dallas.

Moon Bases

During the era of the United States initial Space exploration and the Moon landings, every launch was accompanied by alien craft. A Moon Base dubbed Luna was sighted and filmed by the Apollo Astronauts. Domes, spires, tall round structures which look like silos, huge "T"-shaped mining vehicles, which left stitchlike tracks in the Lunar surface, and extremely large as well as small alien craft appear in the photographs. It is a joint United States, Russian, and Alien base. The Space Program is a farce and an unbelievable waste of money. Alternative Three is a reality and is not at all science fiction. Most of the Apollo Astronauts were severely shaken by this experience and their lives and subsequent statements reflect the depth of the revelation and the effect of the muzzle order which followed. They were ordered to remain silent or suffer the extreme penalty, death, which was termed an "expediency." One astronaut actually did talk to the British products of the TV expose "Alternative Three," confirming many of the allegations.

Psychic Predictions for the Future of the United States

John Culbertson, who says that he is not a doomsday prophet, has made available information that he says was given to him by his spirit teachers, animal spirits, and angel guides. Culbertson stresses that these predictions don't necessarily have to come true. We all have free will and can make choices to avert what may occur.

If nothing is done, here is what may happen.

- Citizens of the U.S. are in the process of losing and totally destroying the country which your forefathers worked so hard to discover and build for you. Freedom and rights, which you were always taught that you had, are in a slow process of being taken away. The U.S. is going from a democracy, to a tyranny.

- If something doesn't change soon, our country, the United States, will crumble far worse than it already has. The U.S. will be shunned by the world far worse than what it already is, and it will be involved in wars which cannot be won.

- The United States economy is going to crumble again, this time worse than what it had originally. People of this day and age say it can't get any worse, those people did not live through the great stock market crash and depression of the late 1910s through the early 1960s. Especially, the worst times of the late 1920s to the late 1930s. It can get worse. If something doesn't change, it will get worse.

- The people of the U.S. have and continue to elect leaders who not only don't know what they are doing, but worse still, are following a personal agenda. A personal agenda which is jeopardizing not just some, but the whole of the United States.

- There is the strong potential for there to be much life lost through new and useless wars. Wars which, as previously mentioned, are motivated through a personalized agenda.

- There will be new bills and legislation which the government claims is for the protection of the people and yet in the course of trying to protect the people, the government will be making the people of its own country far more vulnerable to losing their own basic essential rights as Americans.

- If nothing changes, the United States boarders will be closed off at some point in the next 5-6 years. Flying to and from the United States will be impossible.

- If nothing changes, you can easily expect gas prices at around $6.75 to $7.25 a gallon before the end of 2015.

- If the government does not change, the United States can expect a rebellion and revolution once again within the country, a possible second Civil War.

- If you, the people and your government, change nothing, U.S. citizens will be held against their will in concentration like camps. This is currently anticipated to happen by 2018.

- Tolerance must be learned by the people of the world, but especially the United States citizens. If this does not occur a variety of different social groups, cultures, ethnic groups, and sub cultures, will be at literal war with each other....

- If nothing changes, united we stand will no longer be a motto, rather the United States will fall because of the division amongst each other, much of which will be fueled by the government and media.

- Suicide rates will continue to grow and be at a all time highs – most people seeing no way out of the hellish torment of everyday living.

- Various religious organizations will far apart completely. People no longer trusting in religion or God. Many will claim to be servants of a higher power, yet use their claims to control and manipulate others.

- The United States Military will decline due to many reasons, including loss of lives. As wars continue both in and outside the country more and more men and women die. Another draft is instituted to keep up with these losses.

- Great catastrophic natural events will occur more frequently. This includes earthquakes around Missouri, Maine, and California. Additionally, flooding in various parts (Midwest, North East, South East, West Coast) of the U.S. will occur. Tornadoes will be especially numerous and violent.

- Cures for various terminal illness are discovered, yet the secrets of their discovery hidden away from the people.

- Around the year 2033, if nothing changes, there will be one power…one group… attempting to control the world. At the time it looks to be warmly welcomed, especially among the U.S., due to the conditions of the country that has fallen from a 1st world country to, in some places, almost 3rd world poverty. Long term effects, however, will be undesirable.

http://www.mysticjohnculbertson.com/psychic/psychic-predictions/psychic-predictions-for-the-future-of-the-united-states/

Obama Presidency Predicted in 1926 Novel

In 1926, a Brazilian writer named Monteiro Lobato wrote a book called ***The Black President***, subtitled ***The American Roman***. The book was published in Brazil, but never in the United States.

The fictional book details a future election in the U.S. where a character named Jane looks into a machine called a "futuroscope." With this device, she sees into the future where an African-American man has been elected President. According to the book, two Democrats, a black man and a white woman, will be running for election against a white Republican man. The final winner is the "Black President." The book isn't precisely accurate, but the number of right predictions is pretty impressive.

The Black President: 1926 Novel Versus 2008 Facts

Population
1926 Novel: 314 million people in the US
2008 reality: about 304 million people in the US

Democrats
1926 Novel: Black man against white woman
2008 reality: Black man (Obama) against white woman (Clinton)

Republican
1926 Novel: White man, trying for reelection
2008 reality: White man (McCain), Republican, while current President is a Republican

Year
1926 Novel: 2228
2008 reality: 2008

Election
1926 Novel: From 88th to 89th
2008 reality: From 43th (Bush) to 44th (half of 88)

Winner
1926 Novel: The Black President
2008 reality: Barack Obama

Hopi Indians: The USA will be Destroyed!

According to Hopi Prophecy, the United States will be destroyed, land and people, by atomic bombs and radioactivity. Only the Hopis and their homeland will be preserved as an oasis to which refugees will flee.

Bomb shelters are a fallacy. "It is only materialistic people who seek to make shelters. Those who are at peace in their hearts already are in the great shelter of life. There is no shelter for evil. Those who take no part in the making of world division by ideology are ready to resume life in another world, be they Black, White, Red, or Yellow race. They are all one, brothers."

Hopi prophecy states that World War III will be started by the people who first received the Light: China, Russia, Palestine, India and Africa. When the war comes, the United States will be destroyed by "gourds of ashes" which will fall to the ground, boiling the rivers and burning the earth, where no grass will grow for many years, and causing a disease that no medicine can cure.

This can only mean nuclear or atomic bombs; no other weapon causes such effects. Bomb shelters will be useless, for "Those who are at peace in their hearts already are in the Great Shelter of Life.

There is no shelter for evil. When the Saquahuh (blue Star) Kachina dances in the plaza and removes his mask, the time of the great trial will be here." The Hopi believe that only they will be saved.

Henry Gruver: USA Invasion Prophecy

On December 14, 1986 Henry Gruver had a Vision: "I Saw Submarines Attack America!"

"I was in Wales in 1986, I went up on top of the Eagle Tower in the Caernarvon Castle. All of a sudden I was up above the earth looking down upon the earth like a globe. As I looked down on the earth, I saw massive amount of all kinds of ships and airplanes. They were coming from up above Norway, out of this inlet. They headed down between the United States and Europe. They covered the Atlantic between the U.S. and Europe. Then I wanted to see what was happening to the United States. I looked over on the globe at the United States. I saw coming out of the United States these radio communication towers. I saw the jagged lines like they draw to show that communications are coming out. They were in our territorial waters! Then I saw missiles come out of them! They hit eastern and western coastal cities of the United States."

Gail Smith: Earthquakes and USA Invasion

Shortly after a second, devastating earthquake, the United States will be attacked by invading forces. Russia will invade the East coast and China the West coast. The invasion will include missile attacks.

She was shown that the invasion would occur when people were eating and drinking which Gail believes to be Thanksgiving, but possibly Christmas. There will be nuclear attacks on both coasts, Las Vegas, and perhaps in Utah.

A long-lasting quake and a major quake will break many dams. She saw the invasion taking place near or shortly after the second quake. 3 1/2 years after the first two quakes, two more mega-quakes will hit that will shake the entire planet and will kill millions and literally cause whole mountain ranges to rise and fall.

PROPHECIES OF THE PRESIDENTS

A Prophecy Written in the Year of Washington's Birth
By Manly P. Hall

Sir William Hope noted the birth overseas of an infant starred by fate to rule both freemen and slaves, and named the year of the American Declaration of Independence forty-four years before it was signed. He gave in Cabalistic form the patriot leader's name, and the years of his lifetime span.

...The prophecy also singled out Abraham Lincoln, designated the term of Benjamin Harrison as the one to mark the first century of the new nation's progress. ... It is a reasonable assumption that the Hope prophecy is a genuine example of fore-knowledge of the destiny of the United States.

George Washington had just been born when the governor of Edinburg Castle wrote a prophecy that this infant born overseas was starred by fate to lead the colonies to freedom; this prediction also named, four decades in advance, the year of the Declaration of Independence.

In the Congressional Library at Washington, D.C., is a curious little book entitled, Vindication of the True Art of Self Defense. It is a work on fencing and dueling, published in 1724 by Sir William Hope, Bart., a deputy governor of Edinburg Castle. In this copy and facing the title page an engraving has been inserted of the badge of the Royal Society of Swordsmen; underneath it is written, "Private Library of Sir William Hope." The Library of Congress has had this book since 1879.

The text of this curious little book is of no special interest, but on the blank flyleaves is written in the hand of Sir William Hope an extraordinary prediction concerning the destiny of the United States of America. It was written, signed and dated forty-four years before the beginning of the Revolutionary War.

PROPHECIES OF THE PRESIDENTS

At the time the thirteen American colonies seemingly had no dream of independence. George Washington had just been born, in Virginia. Twenty of the fifty-six men who were to sign the Declaration of Independence were then small boys, and eighteen others were yet unborn.

Little information is available concerning Sir William Hope; but from the text of his prediction it appears that he was devoted to the study of astrology, and based his strange prophetic poem upon an interpretation of the starry influences. There is also a hint of the Cabala in the manner used by Hope to indicate the men referred to in his prediction.

The prophecy of Sir William Hope begins with these lines:

'Tis Chaldee says his fate is great
Whose stars do bear him fortunate.
Of thy near fate, Amerika,
I read in stars a prophecy:

Fourteen divided, twelve the same,
Sixteen in halfs--each holds a name;
Four, eight, seven, six--added ten--
The life line's mark of Four gt. men.

From the text, the prophecy covers the period from 1732 to 1901. From the history of our country during this period of time, Hope selected four men, and the numbers which he used to indicate them are shown as the prophecy unfolds. He summarizes the lives of these four men by totaling the number of years that each lived. He does this in the line, Four, eight, seven, six--added ten--" Four plus eight, plus seven, plus six, equal 25, the added ten is the cipher making a total of 250. At the time of his death George Washington was 68, Abraham Lincoln 56, Benjamin Harrison 68, and William McKinley 58. The total of these years is 250.

The next twelve lines are devoted to a description of George Washington and the struggle of the American colonies for independence.

This day is cradled, far beyond the sea,

PROPHECIES OF THE PRESIDENTS

> One starred by fate to rule both
> bond and free.

The prophecy is dated 1732, and in that year George Washington was born beyond the sea, in Virginia. The reference to bond and free is believed to indicate that slavery would exist during Washington's time in the colony of Virginia.

> Add double four, thus fix the destined day
> When servile knees unbend 'neath
> freedom's sway.

By double four we can read 44, which if added to the date, 1732, gives 1776, the year of the American Declaration of Independence.

> Place six 'fore ten, then read the patriot's name
> Whose deeds shall link him to a deathless fame.
> Add double four, thus fix the destined day

There are six letters in the name George, and ten in Washington, and this Cabala when added to the previous and subsequent descriptions, can leave no doubt as to the man intended in the prophecy.

> Whose growing love and ceaseless trust wrong none
> And catch truth's colors from its glowing sun !
> Death's door shall clang while yet his century waits,
> His planets point the way to other's pending fates.

These lines contain not only a glowing tribute but an exact bit of prophesy. Washington died on December 14, 1799, just 17 days before his century passed into history.

> Till all the names on freedom's scroll shall fade,
> Two tombs be built, his lofty cenotaph be made--

Freedom's scroll is the Declaration of Independence, which is now carefully preserved under yellow cellophane because the signatures have begun to fade.

PROPHECIES OF THE PRESIDENTS

The body of George Washington has rested in two tombs; and his lofty cenotaph, the Washington Monument, is 555 feet high, the tallest memorial ever constructed to the memory of a man.

> Full six times ten the years must onward glide,
> Nature their potent help, a constant, prudent guide.

If six times ten years, or sixty years, be added to the date of the death of Washington the result is 1859, when John Brown raided Harper's Ferry and was hanged for attempting to incite a slave revolt, a circumstance leading directly to the United States of America engaging in the great Civil War to preserve the freedom of all of its people.

> Then fateful seven 'fore seven shall sign heroic son
> Whom Mars and Jupiter strike down before his work is done.
> When cruel fate shall pierce, though artless of its sword;
> Who leaves life's gloomy stage without one farewell word.
> A softly beaming star, half veiled by Mars' red cloud
> Virtue, his noblest cloak, shall form a fitting shroud.

There are seven letters in Abraham, and seven letters in Lincoln. He is the "heroic son" elected to the Presidency in 1860, re-elected in 1864, and assassinated April 14, 1865. He was indeed struck down before his work was done, for slavery was not abolished by constitutional amendment until the end of that year, and the Civil War was not proclaimed to be at an end until August 20, 1866.

The reference to life's gloomy stage is the more extraordinary because Lincoln was assassinated at Ford's Theater while watching a play; and he never spoke again after the assassin's bullet struck him although he lived for several hours.

References to President Benjamin Harrison are contained in the two following lines:

> Then eight 'fore eight a later generation rules,

PROPHECIES OF THE PRESIDENTS

With light undimmed and shed in progress' school.

There are eight letters in Benjamin, and eight in Harrison. He ruled in a later generation, 1889 to 1893. His administration was justly climaxed by the great Columbian Exposition at Chicago in 1893. Here, invention, transportation, industry, art, science, and agriculture exhibited the progress which they had made in the first century of American national existence. This is probably the 'progress school' referred to in the prediction. Harrison's administration was not dimmed by war or by any scandals in high office.

Then six again, with added six shall rise,
Resplendent ruler – good, and great – and wise.
Four sixes hold a glittering star that on his way shall shine;
And twice four sixes mark his years from birth to manhood's prime.

While the verses accurately describe President McKinley, this is the only instance in which the numbers do not appear to fit the name. Research, however, indicates that the original form of the family name would permit it to be divided, thus, Will-Mc Kinley, which means, Will, the son of Kinley. In this form, each of the combinations would contain six letters. Four sixes, or 24, agrees with President McKinley being the 24th man to hold the presidential office. And twice four sixes, or 48, was the age of McKinley at the time he was elected Governor of his native state, which might be said to be his 'manhood's prime'. There is no reference to McKinley's second term or his assassination. But the prophecy definitely states that it goes no farther than the end of the 79th Century. It does indicate earlier however, that McKinley's life was to be 58 years, which was correct.

The prophecy ends with four more lines:

These truths prophetic shall completion see
Ere time's deep grave receives the Nineteenth Century !
All planets, stars, twelve signs and horoscope
Attest these certain truths foretold by William Hope.

Following this, is the statement that the prophecy was 'Writ at Cornhill, London, 1732.' At the bottom of the page are four other lines written by some later member of the Hope family as a tribute to the memory of Sir William Hope:

The learned hand that writ these lines
no more shall pen for me,
Yet voice shall speak and pulses beat for long posterity.
This soul refined through love of kind bewailed life's labors spent,
Then found this truth, his search from youth, Greatness is God's accident.-

James Hope

As is usual with material of this kind, efforts have been made to prove the Hope Prophecy to be a forgery; but up to the present time no tangible evidence has been advanced to disprove the prediction. Always in these matters, the critic takes the attitude that such predictions cannot be made, and if a writing appears to be authentic then it must be imposture. The book has been in the Library of Congress for more than 60 years. The prediction about both Harrison and McKinley relate to incidents taking place after the book was placed in the Congressional Library.

In facsimile, one of the two pages of the original prophecy is illustrated here; both have every appearance of being genuine and authentic.

It is most reasonable to assume that the Hope prophecy is a genuine example of foreknowledge concerning the future of the United States of America.

ABOUT THE AUTHORS

Timothy Green Beckley

He calls himself "Mr. UFO." Timothy Green Beckley is a UFO & paranormal pioneer. Since an early age his life has more or less revolved around the paranormal. The house he was raised in was thought to be haunted, he underwent out of body experiences at age six, and saw his first of three UFOs when he was ten. Over the years he has written over 50 books on everything from rock music to the secret MJ12 papers. Beckley has made available a total of approximately 250 titles by other authors, such as T. Lobsang Rampa, Brad Steiger, Tim R. Swartz, Sean Casteel, and Maria D' Andrea. Today he is the president of Inner Light/Global Communications and editor of the Conspiracy Journal and Bizarre Bazaar.

America's Strange and Supernatural History

Tim R. Swartz

Tim R. Swartz is an Indiana native and Emmy-Award winning television producer/videographer, and is the author of a number of popular books including *The Lost Journals of Nikola Tesla, Secret Black Projects, Evil Agenda of the Secret Government, Time Travel: A How-To-Guide, Richard Shaver-Reality of the Inner Earth, Admiral Byrd's Secret Journey Beyond the Poles*, and is a contributing writer for the books, *Sir Arthur Conan Doyle: The First Ghostbuster, Brad Steiger's Real Monsters, Gruesome Critters, and Beasts from the Darkside, and Real Ghosts, Restless Spirits and Haunted Places*.

As a photojournalist, Tim Swartz has traveled extensively and investigated paranormal phenomena and other unusual mysteries from all over the world. He has also appeared on the program "Ancient Aliens" and the History Channel Latin America series "Contacto Extraterrestre."

His articles have been published in magazines such as Mysteries, FATE, Strange, Atlantis Rising, UFO Universe, Flying Saucer Review, Renaissance, and Unsolved UFO Reports.

As well, Tim Swartz is the writer and editor of the online newsletter Conspiracy Journal; a free, weekly e-mail newsletter, considered essential reading by paranormal researchers worldwide. www.conspiracyjournal.com

Sean Casteel

Sean Casteel is a freelance journalist who has written about UFOs, alien abduction and related subjects since 1989. His articles have been featured in "UFO Magazine," "FATE Magazine," "UFO Universe Magazine," and "Open Minds Magazine," among many other paranormal-themed newsstand publications.

Casteel has also written several books for Global Communications, to include "The Heretic's UFO Guidebook" and "UFOs, Prophecy and the End of Time." In addition, he has co-authored or contributed to numerous other Global Communications books, such as "Disclosure: Breaking Through the Barrier of Global UFO Secrecy" and "The Ark of the Covenant and Other Secret Weapons of the Ancients." He is a frequent contributor to the paranormal website "UFO Digest," as well as the online magazine "Phenomena."

Wm. Michael Mott

Wm. Michael Mott is a writer, artist and educator who has six books and many magazine features in print or electronic book form. He's written about paranormal phenomena; comparative myth, religion and folklore; UFOs; cryptozoology; pulp, adventure, science fiction and fantasy fiction; and art and education topics. He's been a guest on in excess of 40 national and internationally-syndicated radio programs, and currently he's one of the co-hosts at THE OUTER EDGE, a weekly program at www.theouteredgeradio.com. Recently he was also a guest on the 7th season of the television show Ancient Aliens.

He's also been Creative Director for a national toy and manufacturing company, a software company, the Art Director for a city newspaper, has worked as an artist/designer for Fortune 500 companies, an NSF Engineering Research Center, and for a variety of clients such as book and magazine publishers. He's also a freelance artist and writer, and writes both fiction and non-fiction. His work has appeared or been featured in many publications, such as Computer Graphics World Magazine, Computer Artist, IEEE Computer, IEEE Computer Graphics and Applications, Syllabus Magazine, PHOTO-Electronic Imaging, DRAGON Magazine, FATE, NEXUS, World Explorer, and others. He's also won several design awards, from Addy and other awards, to awards for web site graphics and design.

Mike's personal web site is mottimorphic.com/blog/, where info about his writing and a gallery of his artwork can be found.

Olav Phillips

Olav Phillips is a regular writer for Paranoia Magazine and ConspiracyHQ. He also wrote and consulted for Mysteries Magazine and served as Executive Producer and Principle Researcher for Ground Zero Radio with Clyde Lewis (Nationally Syndicated by Premiere Radio Networks). He is also author of the books *The Secret Space Age: Secret Space Programs, Breakaway Civilizations, Nazi UFOs, SDI and Alternative Three*, and *Tales of a Heretic: The Collected Writings of a Heretic Conspiracy Researcher*.

With 24 years of experience in UFO and Conspiracy research and study, Olav's self-proclaimed passion is serving as archivist for the UFO and paranormal community and is the owner of The Anomalies Channel, a online video channel with over 18,000 subscribers and hundreds of videos available to ROKU players all over the world. His area of interest is the Secret Space Program/Breakaway civilization and is considered an international expert on "Alternative Three."

He has appeared on many popular radio shows as well as television presentations including: Shadows In the Dark Radio, Coast to Coast AM, Voyager (RAI Due), as well as being a long time contributor to Ground Zero Radio's investigations including the famous Tracy, CA UFO Crash case featured on UFO Hunters.

Write us to request our free catalog of books, DVDs, audio CD's and other items of extreme interest.

Global Communications
P.O. Box 753
New Brunswick, NJ 08903

mrufo8@hotmail.com

www.conspiracyjournal.com

TOUR GUIDE TO THE SPOOKIEST PLACES ON EARTH
JOIN A JOURNEY TO A LAND OF MYSTERY AND MYSTICISM ON THE EDGE OF REALITY
HERE ARE STRANGE TALES OF WITCHCRAFT, SPIRITUALISM, LOST RACES AND RELIGIOUS MIRACLES

South American folklore has its share of unique and fantastic myths and legends. There are incredible tales of magicians and their weird magical arts, strange creatures, ghosts and other unexplained mysteries. The first explorers that entered Latin America were dazzled by the endless tropical rainforests, the strange and diverse wildlife, and the indigenous peoples and their mysterious ways. Even today, South America, offers unique perspectives and influences on the paranormal that can not be found anywhere else on the planet.

Editor, writer, researcher, travel specialist and producer, John Wilcock has circled the world in search of the strange and unusual. He has also been editor of the Witches Almanac and is the co-founder of the Village Voice and Andy Warhol's Interview.

Wilcock states: — "The people of South America live in a world steeped in ancient traditions that enhance their lives with a rich taperstry of mystical beliefs. In modern Latin America, Catholicism is the predominate religion. However, especially in Brazil, Spiritism has become extremely prevalent, believing in the survival of the human personality and the possibility of communication with the spirit world."

This Guide includes sections on ...—**The Dead Are Alive — **Spiritism In Brazil — ** Demons And Sinister Spirits — **Creatures From Out of This World —**Living Dinosaurs — **Here There Be Giants, etc.

Nearly 250 Large Format Pages – Send $20+ $5 S/H for AN OCCULT GUIDE TO SOUTH AMERICA.

THESE 'SPOOKY' TRAVEL GUIDES ALSO AVAILABLE

( ) SECRETS OF DEATH VALLEY – MYSTERIES AND HAUNTS OF THE MOJAVE DESERT – Includes the full text of George Van Tassel's *I Rode In A Flying Saucer*. Tales of Abandoned Mines, Mysterious Creatures, Deranged Killers, Spook Lights, Albino Bigfoot, Haunted Opera House. — $22.00

( ) LOST WORLDS AND UNDERGROUND MYSTERIES OF THE FAR EAST – Lost Cities and Civilizations. The Serpent Race. Shape Shifters of the Jungle. Forbidden Magick of Ancient Secret Societies. — $22.00

( ) The Magick And Mysteries Of Mexico: Arcane Secrets and Occult Lore of the Ancient Mexicans and Maya – Authored by Lewis Spence and Dragonstar. All that is known regarding the arcane knowledge and occult lore of the ancient Mexican peoples and their neighbors, the Maya of Central America and the Yucatan. It is the product of more than 35 years of research into the Pure Magic, Astrology, Witchcraft, Demonology and Symbolism practiced south of the border. — $20.00

( ) Kahuna Power: Authentic Chants, Prayers and Legends of the Mystical Hawaiians. Explore with Tim Beckley the most sacred knowledge of the Islanders, including a way to raise the dead. - $22.00

( ) SUPER SPECIAL – ALL FIVE "TOUR GUIDE BOOKS" AS LISTED JUST $75.00 + 8 S/H
From – TIMOTHY BECKLEY · BOX 753 · NEW BRUNSWICK, NJ 08903

GET READY FOR A BIG CHANGE IN YOUR LIFE THROUGH OCCULT MEANS!

This Book Contains Secret Occult Strategies Enabling You To Become All You Were Meant To Be! Here Are Dozens Of Spells And Rituals That Will Bestow Upon You The Mental And Psychic Powers Of A Super-Being!

Are you troubled? Worried? Anxious? Can't sleep? Have you come to the realization that there is a lot more to life than you are currently experiencing? Do you see other people living in what appears to be the lap of luxury while you can hardly cope with "simple," everyday situations? Do you feel you have been "blocked" by outside forces content to see you shuffle through each day at a snail's pace without anywhere to turn?

Dragonstar knows how to direct the "cosmic winds." He is the head of an occult lodge that dates back to the time of Atlantis. He is considered by many who have studied with him to be a master alchemist and metaphysician who is on a high spiritual path. And he is willing to share his knowledge with a trusted few.

Unlike most sages who speak of lofty ideals, Dragonstar here offers principles that can put you into the "driver's seat" and improve your life in matters of money, romance and personal growth.

Utilizing a variety of occult tools, you will be able in no time to perform these – as well as dozens of other easy to learn spells and rituals to:

* Encourage Love, Affection and Romance. * Increase Your Income * Improve Sexual Performance * Rid Yourself Of Unwanted Relationships * Become Highly Successful In Business * Promote Clairvoyance, Inspiration, Astral Energy And Intuition * Rid The Physical Body Of Emotional Pain And Suffering And Enjoy Good Health * Win In All Legal Matters

REMEMBER . ...AS YOU WEAVE AND SPIN YOUR SPELL THREEFOLD RETURN THE TALE WILL TELL

Send $20.00 + $5.00 S/H for your personal copy of BECOME A SUPER-BEING by Dragonstar.

WISH TO LEARN MUCH MORE?
3 Disc Dragonstar "Miracle" DVD Set

Dragonstar is one of the master metaphysicians practicing today. He is the author of New Magick Handbook and How To Develop Your Paranormal Powers. Trained in an ancient secret lodge with its lineage in Atlantis and MU, this living avatar brings the air of spellcasting alive on your tv set. These DVDs contains subliminal magical commands that will charge your super-conscious with magical vibrations, capable of making a reality of your heart's desires. By watching these DVDs, you become an active participant in their magical evoking energies that can be applied to matters needing metaphysical solutions.

Send $20 for your DRAGONSTAR PSYCHIC DVD SET which includes the following three DVDs:
   ( ) Attract Good Luck - Banish Bad Luck: Dragonstar's Mental Magick DVD
   ( ) Attract Money and Prosperity: Command The Mystical And Secret Powers of the Universe
   ( ) Rituals and Spells To Attract A Lover Or Soulmate: Dragonstar's Mental Magick DVD

Timothy Beckley · Box 753 · New Brunswick, NJ 08903

www.ingramcontent.com/pod-product-compliance
Lightning Source LLC
Chambersburg PA
CBHW081914170426
43200CB00014B/2727